ANTI-GAY RIGHTS

Assessing Voter Initiatives

EDITED BY
Stephanie L. Witt
and
Suzanne McCorkle

PRAEGER

Westport, Connecticut
London

Library of Congress Cataloging-in-Publication Data

Anti-gay rights : assessing voter initiatives / edited by Stephanie L.
  Witt and Suzanne McCorkle.
    p. cm.
    Includes bibliographical references and index.
    ISBN 0–275–95461–7 (alk. paper)
    1. Gay rights—United States.   2. Referendum—United States.
 I. Witt, Stephanie L.   II. McCorkle, Suzanne.
   HQ76.8.U5A67   1997
   305.9'0664'0973—dc21   96–53619

British Library Cataloguing in Publication Data is available.

Library of Congress Catalog Card Number: 96–53619
ISBN: 0–275–95461–7

First published in 1997

Praeger Publishers, 88 Post Road West, Westport, CT 06881
An imprint of Greenwood Publishing Group, Inc.

Printed in the United States of America

The paper used in this book complies with the
Permanent Paper Standard issued by the National
Information Standards Organization (Z39.48–1984).

10 9 8 7 6 5 4 3 2 1

Contents

Acknowledgments   vii

1.   Introduction   1

2.   No Longer a Sleeping Giant: The Re-Awakening of
Religious Conservatives in American Politics   7
Steven Shaw

3.   Taking the Initiative: Anti-Homosexual Propaganda of the
Oregon Citizen's Alliance   17
David Douglass

4.   The Constitution as Rhetorical Symbol in Western
Anti-Gay Rights Initiatives: The Case of Idaho   33
Daniel Levin

5.   The Idaho Anti-Gay Initiative: A Chronology of Events   51
Suzanne McCorkle and Marshall G. Most

6.   Fear and Loathing on the Editorial Page: An Analysis of
Idaho's Anti-Gay Initiative   63
Suzanne McCorkle and Marshall G. Most

7.   In Their Own Words: Conversations with Campaign
Leaders   77
Harvey Pitman

8.   Secular Anti-Gay Advocacy in the Springfield, Missouri, Bias Crime Ordinance Debate   95
Ralph R. Smith

9.   Direct Democracy and Minority Rights: Opinions on Anti-Gay and Lesbian Ballot Initiatives   107
Todd Donovan and Shaun Bowler

10.   The Correlates of Tolerance: Analyzing the Statewide Votes on Anti-Gay Initiatives   127
Stephanie L. Witt and Leslie R. Alm

11.   *Romer v. Evans*: The Centerpiece of the American Gay-Rights Debate   133
Sean Patrick O'Rourke and Laura K. Lee Dellinger

Appendix A: Tables   141

Appendix B: Text of Anti-Gay Initiatives   163

Bibliography   169

Index   193

About the Editors and Contributors   199

Acknowledgments

We would like to thank the contributors to this volume for their hard work and patience. We would also like to thank the activists on both sides of the initiative campaigns who shared their perspectives and experiences with us. We gratefully acknowledge the editorial assistance of Sandy McConnell and Tricia Trofast in the preparation of this manuscript. Portions of the research reported in this book were funded by the Boise State University Faculty Research Grant Program.

Introduction

"The only good queer is a dead queer." "Idaho is too great for hate." "No special rights." "No on Proposition One." These were the slogans held up on banners by two groups of deeply divided Idahoans in June of 1994. Separated by the width of a street in front of their Capitol and a difference of opinion larger than the highest western peak, these Idaho citizens were replicating a battle over values fought in Colorado, Oregon, Maine, Missouri, Ohio, and many other places throughout the country where citizens grappled with the issue of initiatives aimed at homosexuals. It is significant that the confrontation described above took place *on the steps* of the capitol building rather than *inside*. The struggles to define, defend, and attack the rights of gays and lesbians described in this book take place in that indistinct battleground of public opinion where voter initiatives are decided. Stripped of traditional cues like party labels, voters confronting complicated, legally worded initiatives are fair game for interest groups trying to pass or defeat an initiative. If they had been asked, the vast majority of Idahoans would probably have felt little urge to join the protesters on either side of the street that June day. However, forcing citizens to choose between two fixed sides, yes or no, is the essence of initiative politics. All deliberative process must take place under the glare of media coverage and advertising blitzes.

The chapters in this volume explore the implications of making decisions over our most deeply held values through the initiative process. What led to the use of the anti-gay initiatives by conservative Christian interest groups? How do citizens sort out constitutional questions about initiatives aimed at homosexuals? What argumentation strategies do interest groups and citizens on both sides of the initiative use to pass or defeat anti-gay measures? How did people actually vote on the anti-gay initiatives? Finally, how did the U.S. Supreme Court reason in its decision about anti-gay initiatives? Before addressing these questions, however, we will review the initiative process itself.

THE INITIATIVE PROCESS IN AMERICAN POLITICS

This section describes the types of initiatives available to voters in the United States, their prevalence, and the general background of the use of this device to pass legislation related to gays and lesbians. The anti-gay measures discussed in this book are all forms of voter initiatives. (A listing of various statewide ballot measures related to homosexuals appears in Table A.1. All tables appear in Appendix A.) The initiative is a form of direct democracy because it allows the voters to directly create and adopt legislation or constitutional amendments without going through the state legislature and governor (or the mayor and city council if it is a local initiative). When laws are made by elected representatives, on the other hand, the process is called an indirect democracy (or republican form of government). The indirect democracy established in the United States (and its several states) is characterized by the many checks and balances inherent in separation of powers, which divides government into legislative, executive, and judicial branches.

The legislative process in this country is typically long and difficult. Our bicameral Congress and state legislatures (with the exception of Nebraska) provide the opportunity for one house to check the activity of the other. To successfully pass a law, it is usually necessary for legislators to compromise and seek consensus on difficult issues (Magleby, 1995). The requirement of a presidential or gubenatorial signature on legislation provides a further check on the legislative process. If the legislators do not compromise to suit a governor's or president's preferences, they face the risk of an executive veto. In contrast, the initiative process requires none of the compromise and negotiation of our regular law-making process. Advocates place their proposition, worded exactly the way they wish, directly on the ballot. There is no possibility of compromise since initiatives cannot be edited once titled, and there are no checks and balances except the knowledge of the voters.

The initiative process differs from state to state but usually requires the collection of varying numbers of signatures of registered voters in order to qualify an initiative for the ballot. It is similar to the other related direct democracy devices utilized in the United States: the referendum and the recall.[1] All three direct democracy devices were popularized during the Progressive Reform era of the late 1800s and early 1900s (Magleby, 1995). The Progressive Reformers were concerned about wresting power away from corrupt political parties that controlled many state legislatures and city councils

(Kehler & Stern, 1994). The initiative provided a way for citizens to bypass the special-interest controlled legislators. The irony is that the modern initiative process—with its high-priced consultants, paid signature gatherers, sophisticated media campaigns, and single-issue focus—is now frequently a tool of the special interests the Progressives wanted to avoid.

Twenty-four states and the District of Columbia allow the use of statewide initiatives (Kehler & Stern, 1994). There are two types of initiatives: constitutional and statutory. Constitutional initiatives allow voters to place changes to the state constitution on the ballot, and statutory initiatives allow the creation of new state laws. Several states allow only statutory initiatives, while some states allow either a constitutional amendment or statutory initiative procedure (see Table A.2). Statutory initiatives may be considered the "weaker" of the two types since state legislatures may later enact laws that diffuse or abolish the voter-adopted initiative (Magleby, 1995). Of the four statewide anti-gay initiatives discussed in this book, the Oregon and Colorado measures were constitutional initiatives while the Idaho and Maine measures were statutory initiatives.[2]

The initiative process is also available to voters at the local governmental level in many states. In several jurisdictions, voters have used the initiative as a "referendum" to repeal ordinances prohibiting discrimination against gays and lesbians passed by city councils.[3] This is the process described in the Springfield, Missouri, case covered in Chapter 8. It should be noted that, as a preemptive move, anti-gay activists have placed local initiatives on the ballot to prevent the future passage of gay-rights laws by local governments[4] (Galvin, 1993).

A key difference among states that allow initiatives is the number of signatures required to place an initiative on the ballot. The more stringent the signature requirement, the fewer initiatives qualify for the ballot (Magleby, 1995). Table A.2 displays the states with initiatives by the stringency of their signature requirement. Most states tie the required number of signatures to a percentage of the vote for the governor or some other statewide elected official in the last election (see Table A.2 for a listing of these percentages). There may also be requirements that signatures come from a certain number of counties or regions within the state (Kehler & Stern, 1994). The geographical signature requirements used by the states with initiatives appear in the notes to Table A.2. There may also be limitations on the time allowed to collect signatures (Kehler & Stern, 1994). Each requirement makes it more difficult to qualify an initiative for the ballot.

The gathering of signatures to qualify an initiative for the ballot has become an industry unto itself (Magleby, 1995). A 1988 U.S. Supreme Court ruling prevents states from limiting the paying of petition signature gatherers (*Meyer v. Grant*, 1988). There are now consultants and corporations that virtually guarantee, for a price, that they can get your initiative on the ballot. The price tag for the initiative process has grown rapidly. Magleby (1995) estimates that in 1992 $117.3 million was spent on ballot initiatives in twenty-one states. This price would reflect the cost of the media campaigns in addition to the signature gathering. Kehler and Stern (1994) report that in 1988 more money was spent on initiative campaigns in California than was spent on lobbying the legislature. States are not permitted to limit expenditures on initiatives. Several United States Supreme Court cases have reaffirmed that limitations on contributions to initiative campaigns are unconstitutional (see *Citizens Against Rent Control v. Berkeley*, 1981; *First National Bank of Boston v. Bellotti*, 1978). The need for ever-increasing amounts of money is mentioned frequently in the interviews with initiative activists in Chapter 7.

The experts for hire and the presence of relatively low signature thresholds in most states have contributed to the explosion in the number of initiatives put before voters in recent elections. Magleby (1995) projects that over 350 initiatives will appear on ballots in the United States in the 1990s. The increasing number of initiatives puts a burden on the voter. The California voter's pamphlet in 1990 was 224 pages long (Magleby, 1995). Only the most dedicated voters attempt to wade through this much material. The long and technically worded initiatives confuse many voters. Both sides in the 1994 Idaho anti-gay initiative battle conceded that many voters did not know which way to vote to match their stance on the issue (see Chapter 7). Magleby (1995) notes that a study of a 1980 California vote on an initiative to create rent control revealed that 75 percent of the voters did not match their views on rent control with their vote on the rent control measure.

When reaching for an understanding of the initiative process, however, knowledge of the technical legal requirements or voting patterns is not enough. By definition, a voter initiative moves the law-making enterprise from the realms of lawyers and legislators to the doorsteps of ordinary citizens. No longer do legal argument and legislative debate dominate the reasoning that spurs law making. By rule, legislatures examine prospective legislation in committees and through debate, a format that encourages negotiation. Legislators are keenly aware that judges who examine the legality of enacted laws must only accept arguments based on the highest standards of evidence. The legislative process, while not always totally rational, was designed to promote slow, cautious, and reasonable action.

The initiative process simply bypasses the requirements for in-depth examination of the issues, rational argument, and sometimes a refined sense of constitutionality. The realm of popular discourse is governed by its own rules, where value arguments carry more or as much weight as reasoned argument and what serves as evidence seems almost a matter of personal taste.

To understand the initiative process fully, it is necessary to explore how the public perceives and shapes its knowledge of the issues raised in initiatives, to understand how initiative advocates and opponents strategically manipulate argumentation, and, in anti-gay initiative attempts, to understand how citizens weigh value conflicts against pragmatic economic and legal reasoning. A full understanding of the initiative process requires a combination of political and rhetorical analysis.

The use of the initiative process to pass anti-gay measures presents a fundamental difficulty: how to balance the right of the majority to pass laws with the rights of numerical minorities. Both Chapters 4 and 9 address some of these constitutional concerns as they relate to anti-gay initiatives. James Madison defended the use of a republican form of government in the United States (1949, p. 10), a form of government that is guaranteed to every state in Article Four of the United States Constitution. Magleby quotes Madison in his discussion of the initiative's potential threat to representative democracy:

> Madison's alternative [to direct democracy] would be a republican form of government, which he believed would "refine and enlarge the public views, by passing them through the medium of a chosen body of citizens, whose wisdom may best discern the true interest of the country, and whose patriotism and love of justice, will be least likely to sacrifice it to temporary or partial considerations." The very nature of the initiative is to ask voters to make "temporary" and "partial" considerations. (Magleby, 1995, p. 20)

The United States Supreme Court has already decided that the anti-gay measure in Colorado is an unreasonable limitation on the rights of homosexuals to seek redress from their government (see Chapter 11).

It is unlikely that the decision in *Romer v. Evans* (1996) will put a halt to anti-gay activity. The politics surrounding an equally divisive social issue, abortion, are instructive. In spite of the fact that the United States Supreme Court legalized abortion with the landmark case *Roe v. Wade* in 1973, mobilizations and countermobilizations of both pro-choice and pro-life groups continue to this day, and over fifty abortion cases have been decided by the Supreme Court (Goggin, 1993). Goggin correctly applies the framework of Schattschneider's 1960 concept of the "scope of conflict" to abortion politics, noting: "It is to the advantage of the one who is losing a contest to 'expand the scope of the conflict' " until the balance of power changes and he or she can win (1993, p. 9). Expanding the scope of the conflict is done by drawing "spectators," or those who normally watch politics rather than actively participate, into the fight on your side. Goggin writes, "One tactic used by the faction that is not getting its way is to involve more and more people by making the issue more visible—by provoking those people who are sitting on the sidelines to take a stand on the issue" (1993, p. 9). There are few better tools to give your issue increased visibility and media coverage than a divisive initiative. Moving the location of decision making on policies about gays from the legislature to the initiative process expands the scope of the conflict. Research by Haider-Markel and Meier (1996) confirms that once the scope of the conflict has been expanded to the initiative process, the politics of anti-gay initiatives resembles that of other "morality politics" issues, such as abortion. Morality politics tend to be "partisan, seek nonincremental solutions, focus on deeply held values, and flourish in areas with competitive political parties" (Haider-Markel & Meier, 1996, p. 334).

Even an initiative doomed to failure at the ballot box or in the courts can generate a wealth of media attention and serve to mobilize supporters. The initiative itself may turn out to be a secondary goal for an interest group. As Kelly Walton, head of the Idaho Citizens Alliance (proponents of the anti-gay initiative), remarked in his interview for this volume, "one of the main results [of the initiative effort] is we were able to rob left-wing candidates of precious campaign money that was devoted to this initiative, and the election night results of the candidates clearly shows that to be true" (Chapter 7).[5] A further example of the initiative itself becoming secondary to another goal is occurring in California, where gubernatorial candidates have begun backing initiative campaigns tailored to further policies complementing their run for office (Magleby, 1995). As long as the signature thresholds used to qualify initiatives remain low and easily attainable through paid signature gatherers, limits to spending on initiative campaigns remain unconstitutional, and single-interest groups want to keep attention on their issue, the initiative will remain a popular tool for interest groups in this country.

NOTES

1. A referendum is a vote on a law that has been referred by the legislature to the voters for approval (Schacter, 1995). A recall is a way to remove elected officials from office.

2. A distinction can be made between direct initiatives, in which the measure is placed on the ballot for voter consideration after the requisite number of signatures are collected, and an indirect initiative, which requires that the initiative be submitted to the legislature after enough signatures have been collected to place it on the ballot (Kehler & Stern, 1994).

3. There are approximately seventy-five cities and countries in the United States that have passed ordinances preventing discrimination based on sexual orientation (Galvin, 1993). Cities that have had initiatives to consider repeal of these ordinances include Cincinnati, Ohio; Lewiston, Maine; Portsmouth, Ohio; and Springfield, Oregon.

4. This is, of course, also the strategy utilized by the statewide anti-gay initiatives, which would (in part) prevent the future passage of gay-rights ordinances by any local governments in the state.

5. Mr. Walton was correct in his assessment of the 1994 Idaho election to the extent that Idahoans elected the most Republican legislature in the country, elected only one Democrat to a statewide office, and sent an all-Republican delegation to Congress. Whether or not these victories are the result of less money being available to Democratic candidates is persuasive, but speculative.

2

No Longer a Sleeping Giant:
The Re-Awakening of Religious
Conservatives in American Politics

Steven Shaw

BACKGROUND: THE OLD RELIGIOUS RIGHT

In 1965, a relatively obscure independent Baptist minister delivered a sermon entitled "Ministers and Marchers." In it, he clearly and forcefully advocated a doctrine of separation concerning the church's relationship with the world of politics:

As far as the relationship of the church to the world, it can be expressed as simply as the three words which Paul gave to Timothy—"Preach the Word." We have a message of redeeming grace through a crucified and risen Lord. This message is designed to go to the heart of man and there meet his deep spiritual need. Nowhere are we commissioned to reform the externals. We are not told to wage war against bootleggers, liquor stores, gamblers, murderers, prostitutes, racketeers, prejudiced persons, or institutions, or any other evil as such. . . . We pay our taxes, cast our votes as a responsibility of citizenship, obey the laws of the land, and other things demanded of us by the society in which we live. . . . Believing the Bible as I do, I would find it impossible to stop preaching the pure saving gospel of Jesus Christ and begin doing anything else—including fighting Communism, or participating in civil-rights reforms. (Fitzgerald, 1981, pp. 62–63)

The minister concluded by proclaiming, "Preachers are not called to be politicians, but soulwinners" (D'Souza, 1984, p. 81).

The separationist doctrine expressed in the sermon given by Reverend Jerry Falwell reflected the conventional wisdom in conservative Protestant churches a generation ago with respect to the necessary and proper relationship between pew and precinct. For more than five decades in the twentieth century, following the failed crusade of Prohibition and the Pyrrhic victory at the Scopes trial in 1925, the overwhelming majority of American evangelicals and fundamentalists worked to put politics, like Satan, behind them. They were energized over evangelism, not electioneering; they pursued piety and personal salvation rather than politics and power. In effect, conservative Protestants, particularly fundamentalists, went into self-imposed political (and often social and cultural) exile, where they would remain clear of the contaminating contents of an increasingly secular, modernist, and animus-ridden culture.

Things began to change, however, in the 1970s. While at the beginning of the decade evangelical and especially fundamentalist Protestants largely ignored social and political efforts for reform, near the end of the decade several organizations, such as Christian Voice, Religious Roundtable, and, most notably, Moral Majority (founded by Jerry Falwell), were created that would largely constitute what soon would be most popularly known as the New Religious Right (see Fowler & Hertzke, 1995; Lienesch, 1993; Moen, 1992a; Wald, 1992; Zwier, 1982). At the end of the decade, on October 3, 1980, Reverend Falwell, speaking at the annual convention of the National Religious Broadcasters held in Lynchburg, Virginia, home to Falwell's Thomas Road Baptist Church, confessed that his 1965 separationist sermon, in which he attacked the involvement of clergy in civil rights protests, entailed "false prophecy" (Fitzgerald, 1981, p. 63).

This self-critique of Falwell's *also* expressed what was slowly yet surely becoming the new conventional wisdom concerning politics and religion in the United States among conservative evangelical and fundamentalist Protestants. *Christianity Today*, perhaps *the* leading evangelical periodical, editorialized in 1980 that "as good disciples we must take seriously the lordship of Jesus Christ over every aspect of human thought and life, including man's political life, and we must function as Christian citizens of the State" ("Getting God's," 1980, p. 11). In the words of one observer, the "Revolt of the Evangelicals" was under way (J. Reichley, 1985, p. 311; see A. J. Mayer, 1980; Zwier, 1982).

According to Kenneth Wald, "Of all the shifts and surprises in contemporary political life, perhaps none was so wholly unexpected as the political resurgence of evangelical Protestantism in the 1970s" (Wald, 1992, p. 223). The fact that scholars and others, including and perhaps especially the media, were virtually wholly unprepared for such an event should not be seen as a surprise. In writing about the involvement of conservative evangelical and fundamentalist Protestants in American politics, Garry Wills argues, "It seems careless for scholars to keep misplacing such a large body of people. Nonetheless, every time religiosity captures the attention of intellectuals, it is as if a shooting star had appeared in the sky" (Wills, 1990, p. 15). Reminding us that "the Christian Right has a long legacy in American politics," Michael Lienesch observes that in this century "the Christian Right has followed a fairly predictable pattern of activism followed by relative quietude." He concludes, "[T]he Christian Right is less like a meteor or a fixed star than a comet that appears and retreats along a more-or-less regular path, attracting our attention periodically and then seeming to disappear, retreating but always returning" (Lienesch, 1993, pp. 4, 248). Thus, the reemergence, Lazarus-like, of what became known as the New Christian Right must be put in its necessary and proper historical context.

The old Christian Right (see Ribuffo, 1985) was supposed to have disappeared following the battle over evolution and the Scopes trial in 1925. However, the 1920s witnessed the first of "three waves" of political activism on the part of religious conservatives (Hunter, 1987, pp. 116–154). During this decade, liquor and evolution were identified as the central cultural contaminants, assisted by Bolshevism, socialism, Catholicism, immigrants, the social gospel, and sexual permissiveness (see Diamond, 1995; Jorstad, 1981; Marsden, 1980; Wilcox, 1992). With Billy Sunday as their frenetic national spokesman, "groups such as the Flying Fundamentalists lobbied state legislatures to ban the teaching of evolution and eventually agitated against communism" (Wilcox, 1995, p. 23).

In the 1950s, in the context of the Cold War, "the second wave crested with the campaign against international communism led by prominent preachers such as Carl McIntire, Billy James Hargis, and Edgar C. Bundy" (Lienesch, 1993, p. 5). This second fundamentalist crusade featured such organizational organs as the Christian Crusade, headed by Hargis; the Church League of America, led by Bundy; and, most prominently, the American Council of Christian Churches, formed in 1941 by fundamentalist ministers and spearheaded by McIntire (see Diamond, 1995; Wilcox, 1992). According to Jerome Himmelstein, "The important fact about this Old Religious Right, in comparison to the New Religious Right, was that it consisted of narrowly sectarian groups with limited political appeal" (Himmelstein, 1983, p. 114; see Wilcox, 1992).

THE 1980s: THE "THIRD COMING OF THE FUNDAMENTALIST RIGHT"

The 1980s ushered in "the third coming of the fundamentalist right" (Wilcox, 1992, p. 10), whose "distinctive emphasis was a moral traditionalism characteristic of evangelicals and fundamentalists since the early twentieth century" (Himmelstein, 1990, p. 97). This third wave of political activism by the religious right possessed similarities to the first two, but it also entailed some significant differences (see Liebman, 1983a, 1983b; Moen, 1992a; Wald, 1992). Each of the three movements was "a crusade in defense of traditional Christian values and institutions" (Wald, 1992, p. 229), yet this third wave of the 1980s "did not merely enlarge the battle for single issues. It embarked on a war of ideologies" (Liebman, 1983a, pp. 229–230). According to Robert Liebman, "The New Christian Right had little in common with its predecessors. What was new about the movement was its scope, its scale, and its size. In all three of its features, the New Christian Right represented a significant departure from the traditions of evangelical involvement in politics. . . . What was new about the New Christian Right was its insistence on joining a variety of issues into a broad sociomoral program" (Liebman, 1983a, p. 229).

According to Wald, "The return of evangelicals to organized political action . . . was facilitated by a number of local movements that developed during the social ferment and upheaval of the 1970s" (Wald, 1992, p. 228). Scholars, along with operatives of the Religious Right, have cited numerous factors that contributed to the resurrection of the New Christian Right in the late 1970s and early 1980s. Crawford, for instance, in 1980 identified abortion, school busing, gay rights, and the content of school textbooks as principal items on the political agenda of the New Christian Right (Crawford, 1980). Jorstad cited concerns over pornography in 1981 (Jorstad, 1981), as did Hunter in 1983 (Hunter, 1983b). In 1982, Zwier listed as "trigger events" the *Roe v. Wade* abortion decision, the gay-rights movement, battles with the Internal Revenue Service over the tax-exempt status of private religious schools, and the contest over the proposed Equal Rights Amendment (Zwier, 1982). Moen adds to this list the debate concerning tuition tax credits (Moen, 1992a).

Activists in the movement also had their list of key events or issues that precipitated this third wave of political activism by religious conservatives. In January 1980, Jerry Falwell argued that the feminist and gay-rights movements had eroded the "moral fiber" of the country (Ogintz, 1980, p. 5). Later that year he identified the *Roe* decision, pornography, the Internal Revenue Service (IRS) battle, and the application by the Federal Communications Commission of the "fairness doctrine" to remarks by teleevangelists such as Reverend James Robison about homosexuals (Fitzgerald, 1981, pp. 120–122). In 1981, he added the United States Supreme Court decisions in *Engel v. Vitale* and *Abington v. Schempp* to the list and deleted the fairness doctrine controversy (Fitzgerald, 1981, p. 122).

Specifically, the IRS battle concerning the tax-exempt status of private religious schools is cited by both scholars and activists. According to Moen, this issue that flared in the late 1970s "was probably the single issue among all others that directly spurred many fundamentalists into politics" (Moen, 1989, p. 27; see Lienesch, 1982, p. 409). According to one movement participant, the announcement by the commissioner of the IRS in August 1978 to strip private schools of their tax-exempt status "kicked the sleeping dog" (Von Drehle & Edsall, 1994, p. 7). In the words of Ralph Reed, Jr., executive director of the Christian Coalition, "More than any other single episode, the IRS move against Christian schools sparked the explosion of the movement that would become known as the religious right" (Reed, 1996, p. 105).

One can, and should, cite all these factors for the role they played, singularly and collectively, in sowing the seed for the rebirth of the New Christian Right. Moen argues, however, "Perhaps the single most important factor motivating Christian-Right leaders, though, was the decline of traditional values and morality that occurred in the 1960s and early 1970s. Believing the nation was in the throes of moral decline, they sought to redeem it" (Moen, 1992a, p. 119). Moen quotes one person who was involved with the movement from the beginning: "What began the movement was concern among many of us involved about the slippage of morality that had occurred in our country. It was a series of Supreme Court decisions, especially on abortion, when coupled with the gay-rights movement and the attempt to legitimize homosexuality, that got us started" (Moen, 1992a, p. 119).

What was occurring, in the opinion of Nathan Glazer, was "a defensive offensive" (Glazer, 1987, p. 251) in defense of traditional morality. The "revolt of the evangelicals" was a revolt not against the loss of status but the loss of culture (see Bruce, 1988). From their vantage point, the forces of modernity and secularism, especially secular humanism, were destroying the country from within (see Falwell, 1980; LaHaye, 1982; Lienesch, 1993). In the words of two movement insiders, "The perceived threat of secularism became the catalyst that bound together religiously and politically conservative people. . . . Like the fundamentalists of the early twentieth century who forged a coalition against theological liberalism, the New Right forged a coalition against political liberalism" (Dobson & Hindson, 1988, p. 36). Thus, a God-fearing country had become or at least was on the verge of becoming a godless country. "There is," one scholar wrote, "the conviction that restoring America to its former state of moral propriety and therefore national resilience must be actively pursued" (Hunter, 1983a, p. 113; see Lienesch, 1993, pp. 139–194). According to Jorstad, "The theme brought home in every speech, every sermon, every pamphlet, every request for funds was that of saving America by a return to what the leaders called its traditional morality" (Jorstad, 1981).

Consequently, political activism, eschewed for the most part in the past, was now virtually unavoidable, for these ambivalent activists "perceived themselves as having a special message to bring to the American people" (Wuthnow, 1983, p. 177). Writing in 1982, Zwier concluded, "The New Christian Right wants to turn the United States around. It wants to restore this nation to the biblical morality that it claims was the guiding light for our founding fathers" (1982, p. 37). This effort was conducted by "troubled patriots" who practiced "a prophetic brand of politics," in which "they see themselves as modern versions of the ancient prophets who denounced their country's decline, exhorted the people to repent of their sins and reform their unrighteous ways, and promised either deliverance or destruction" (Lienesch, 1993, pp. 155, 157; see Bellah, 1975).

This third wave of political activism by religious conservatives was most closely associated with Reverend Jerry Falwell's Moral Majority. When Falwell announced in 1989, ironically in Las Vegas, that the Moral Majority was closing its doors, the New Christian Right was declared dead (see Bruce, 1988; D'Antonio, 1989). However, the demise of the movement was exaggerated, and soon observers would depict the New Christian Right as "a movement with real clout" (Guth, Green, Kellstedt, & Smidt, 1993, p. 175). "Indeed," according to one analyst, "few political movements have generated so much overwrought commentary" (Persinos, 1994, p. 21).

THE NEW CHRISTIAN RIGHT TODAY

Today we are witnesses to the fourth wave of twentieth-century political activism by religious conservatives as the New Christian Right "has entered a new phase of political sophistication, on the airwaves, in the lobbies of Congress, at precinct meetings" (Von Drehle & Edsall, 1994, p. 6). In the 1990s, in spite of earlier observations that little if any activity was occurring within the movement at the time (Wilcox, 1992), the New Christian Right "has emerged as a leaner, more experienced, more locally based movement that is a force to be reckoned with in U.S. politics" (Fowler & Hertzke, 1995, p. 142).

According to Moen, the New Christian Right "is a very different movement than it was a decade ago" (1992a, p. 95). Contrary to what was declared at the outset of the decade, the New Christian Right is no longer the stealth movement of American politics (see Blumenthal, 1994, Conason, 1992, DeParle, 1996; Green, 1995a; Lawson, 1992a, 1992b; Wilcox, 1992). Ralph Reed of the Christian Coalition, which is considered by most observers to be the political heart of the contemporary Religious Right, claims "The religious conservative community is one of the best-organized and most effective constituencies in American politics today" (Reed, 1996, p. 70). Given the role of the New Christian Right in the 1994 midterm congressional elections and the 1996 presidential race, especially the battle for the Republican party presidential nomination, in which the Christian Coalition exercised a virtual veto power during the primary season, few today question the accuracy of Reed's statement (see Birnbaum, 1995; Wilcox, 1996).

The New Christian Right of the 1990s bears more than a passing resemblance to its earlier twentieth-century predecessors, particularly with respect to its animus toward what Reed calls "a polluted culture" (1996, p. 75). Reed would have "It's the culture, stupid!" replace the 1992 refrain, "It's the economy, stupid!" preferred by the presidential campaign staff of then-Governor Bill Clinton. Reed contends that "the most important issue in the nation" for religious and political conservatives is "the culture, the family, a loss of values, a decline in civility, and the destruction of our children" (Reed, 1996, p. 5). For Reed, "To look at America today is to witness a nation struggling against forces as dangerous as any military foe it has ever faced. The threats, however, come not from without but from within" (1996, p. 9).

The object of the animosity and activism of Reed and others in the New Christian Right, in general, is liberalism and its apparent cultural hegemony. In 1994, Reed asserted, "Policy failures and cultural excesses since the 1960s must be redressed if we are to move forward. The seeds of cultural and moral decay have now flowered to full bloom" (1994a, p. 39). In 1996, he declared, "Our message is simple. For thirty years the left has had its chance to social-engineer, to try liberal experiments, to tinker and toy with the government. They have failed. Now it is our turn" (1996, p. 195). In such a hostile, oppressive climate, one that, according to Reed, "treats faith as a form of pathology" (1994a, p. 49), political activism is necessary in order to mount a counteroffensive on behalf of traditional morality. "Our political agenda," Reed writes, "is based on the need to affirm the basic social and religious values upon which the nation was built. Ours is largely a defensive movement. We are not revolutionaries but counter-revolutionaries, seeking to resist the left's agenda and to keep them from imposing their values on our homes, churches and families" (1996, p. 195).

THE NEW CHRISTIAN RIGHT AND THE TRADITIONAL FAMILY

Central to the social regeneration project of the New Christian Right, and therefore central to the movement's political agenda, is a spirited, serious defense of the traditional family. In the words of Reed, "We must never retreat from our principled defense of the traditional, marriage-based family as the foundation of our society" (1996, p. 264). The family is *the* one institution that, according to Reed and others, such as James Dobson of Focus on the Family, Gary Bauer of the Family Research Council (the political arm of Focus on the Family), and Louis Sheldon of the Traditional Values Coalition, has been most heavily and directly assailed by an antagonistic culture over the past generation. Today, virtually all Christian Right leaders refer to their movement or their respective groups as pro-family (see Wilcox, 1996). In 1994, Reed, for example, stated that the most accurate depiction of the movement of the 1990s is that it is a pro-family movement, one composed of "pro-family conservatives" (1994b, p. 2). Fittingly, the principal political document of the best-known organization in the movement, the Christian Coalition, is the coalition's Contract with the American Family, modeled on the Republican party's Contract with America, released to the public with great publicity in May 1995. According to the document's main author, "[R]eligious conservatives are poised to enter an era of American life in which moral issues, and the pro-family agenda, will predominate" (Reed, 1996, p. 10).

In the early 1980s, Donald Heinz predicted that the family "may be the issue on which the New Christian Right can ride to power" (Heinz, 1983, p. 141). In their effort aimed at stopping what they perceive to be the delegitimation of the traditional family (see Reed, 1993, 1994a), Heinz argued that the movement "finds in the family a means to recover a lost meaning as well as a lost past" (Heinz, 1983, p. 142). In the words of Lienesch, religious conservatives "have embraced the family as a focus of public policy taking positions on the most intense and intimate of 'hearth and home' issues, including abortion, homosexuality, and sex education. Considering themselves to be defenders of a besieged Christian culture, they describe the family as a fortress" (1993, p. 52).

Indeed, "the family is considered by religious conservatives to be the most important of social institutions" (Lienesch, 1993, p. 52). Jerry Falwell wrote that the family's "continued health is a prerequisite for a healthy and prosperous nation" (1980, p. 205). Others in the movement today, such as James Dobson and Gary Bauer, make similar assertions (see Lienesch, 1993; Wilcox, 1996). With the family as the "decisive battleground" in this Kulturkampf, "the contest is over what constitutes the family in the first place" (Hunter, 1991, pp. 176–177). Hunter observes, "The contest over the family, in fact, reflects fundamental differences in the assumptions and world views of the antagonists. . . . If the symbolic significance of the family is that it is a microcosm of the larger society, . . . then the task of defining what the American family is becomes integral to the very task of defining America itself" (1991, p. 177). While religious conservatives in fact struggle over the specific details of what actually constitutes the "traditional" family form, of one thing they are abundantly certain: it is a two-parent, heterosexual unit (see Lienesch, 1993, pp. 52–93). In the words of Reed, the movement seeks "to restore the centrality of the two-parent, intact family as the foundation of our democratic society" (1994a, p. 39). Speaking to the Detroit Economic Club in January, 1995, Reed outlined four priorities for the newly elected, 104th Congress, the first of which is that "the government should promote and defend rather than undermine the institution of the family" (Christian Coalition, 1995, p. 138).

The New Christian Right, in sum, sees itself as *the* cultural defender of the 1990s, committed to, among other things, "protecting the family from any number of insidious enemies" (Lienesch, 1993, p. 82). These enemies abound in today's culture, such as the public schools and sex education courses. Other such foes exist, too: the Internal Revenue Service, the tax code, abortion, pornography, and the entertainment industry. "Of all social specters, however, the most terrifying to the Christian conservatives is homosexuality" (Lienesch, 1993, p. 84).

THE NEW CHRISTIAN RIGHT AND
HOMOSEXUALITY

In the words of James Davison Hunter, "Perhaps with the exception of abortion, few issues in the contemporary culture can generate more raw emotion than the issue of homosexuality. The reason is plain: few other issues challenge the traditional assumptions of what nature will allow, the boundaries of the moral order, and finally the ideals of middle-class family life more radically" (1991, p. 189). In the late 1970s and early 1980s, as the pro-life movement attempted to make the symbolic and substantive transition to a pro-family movement, opposition to civil liberties for homosexuals became more visible and pronounced. "Not until the late 1980s and 1990s, however, would the Christian Right make the prevention and reversal of gay rights initiatives a centerpiece of its activist program" (Diamond, 1995, p. 171). However, as the movement has tried to become more mainstream and less extreme, at least as in the case of the Christian Coalition, vitriol against gays and lesbians has lessened in some quarters. Reed has argued, for instance, for "casting a wider net" beyond the issues of abortion and homosexuality, and in the coalition's Contract with the American Family, discussion of homosexuality as a threat to the family is prominent by its absence (1993, 1996). Nonetheless, homosexuality is definitely not a part of what Reed has called the Christian Coalition's "family-friendly agenda" (Von Drehle & Edsall, 1994, p. 6).

Ted Jelen (1991) has suggested that mobilization by and support for the Christian Right ebbs and flows in a cyclical fashion. He argues that normally religious belief stays privatized but that it encroaches into politics when social groups disliked by most orthodox Christians, such as gays and lesbians, become too vocal and visible. Contemporary conflicts seem to support Jelen's thesis. Also, if his thesis is correct, the Christian Right has a long future ahead of it. Whether it's a successful one is much less certain (see Fowler & Hertzke, 1995).

Part of the strategy of the Christian Coalition, for instance, has been a concentrated focus on grassroots politics and local organizing throughout the country (see Conason, 1992; DeParle, 1996). In the words of Ralph Reed, "Our goal was to transform the religious conservative community from a political pressure group to a broad social reform movement based in local communities. . . . States and localities would become the 'laboratories' for testing our policy ideas, and for building a 'farm system' of future candidates . . ." (Reed, 1996, p. 157). In discussing the future of the Christian Right, Wilcox concludes that it has "its greatest potential in mobilizing diverse constituencies in support of local (and occasionally national) moral crusades" (Wilcox, 1995, p. 37). Fowler and Hertzke concur. They argue that the emphasis on local politics is "a declaration of hope. It follows from the fact that many of the moral issues in conflict—educational issues, pornography, the rights of gays—are fought out in local settings . . ." (Fowler & Hertzke, 1995, p. 149). In fact, as most scholars recognize, the greatest impact of the New Christian Right on public policy has come at the state and local level (see Moen, 1992a; Wald, 1992; Wilcox, 1996). Given the organizationally decentralized, locally focused nature of the New Christian Right, along with the emergence on homosexual civil rights as a salient political issue, the use of referenda and initiatives in states, counties, and cities was actively pursued by this movement in a number of states and localities (see Diamond, 1995; Wald, 1992; and Zwier, 1982).

In the 1980s, gay civil rights activism, in the absence of protective federal legislation, "began to focus on the drafting of local ordinances and state initiatives to eliminate anti-gay discrimination in employment, housing, and access to public facilities" (Diamond, 1995, p. 25). Not unexpectedly, these efforts were strongly opposed by the New Christian Right, on whose "pro-family" agenda any laws favorable to gays and lesbians were decidedly unwelcome.

One analysis of the New Christian Right concludes that the movement was most effective when it focused on clearly defined issues and specifically attainable goals (Dobson & Hindson, 1988). In its opposition to homosexual civil rights and its aggressive (and often successful) use of the "no special rights" theme, the New Christian Right "found an issue that appealed to large numbers of voters beyond the movement's own cadre" (Diamond, 1995, p. 302). As Wald notes, "Religion can become the foundation for public policy in several ways. When laws are decided through public referenda, religious groups may simply vote their preferences into law" (Wald, 1992, pp. 191–192).

CONCLUSION

In sum, the initiative route is an appealing, convenient one to travel, especially for those individuals and groups within a movement who find themselves frustrated with "politics as usual" and who perceive an unsympathetic and hostile political elite. These "ambivalent activists" often chafe at the relative glacial pace of political and social change. Consequently, direct political action in the form of referenda and initiatives offers itself as a necessary and proper political option. The reliance on such efforts aimed at saving or recovering a lost society and corrupt culture allowed the New Christian Right to bypass the political elite, most of whom were seen as foes in the movement's culture war.

3

Taking the Initiative: Anti-Homosexual Propaganda of the Oregon Citizen's Alliance

David Douglass

INTRODUCTION

In a recent letter to *The Oregonian*, a reader describing himself as "a relatively conservative Republican and not an ardent diversity proponent" wondered "why homosexuals in Oregon are such a problem that we [Oregonians] have to vote over and over again on ballot measures [dealing with homosexuality]" (Springer, 1994, p. C8). One need not look far for the cause of his complaint: During a three-year period from 1991–1994, Oregon voters considered state and local ballot measures dealing with homosexuality on thirty separate occasions.

Oregon might seem an unlikely context for political division over homosexuality. The state's long tradition of liberal social policy, coupled with the fact that gay and lesbian communities in Oregon maintain a much lower and less militant profile than counterparts in neighboring states of California and Washington would suggest little reason for controversy. Moreover, the sponsor of virtually all of the anti-homosexuality legislation in the state, the Oregon Citizen's Alliance, or OCA, has consistently received strongly negative assessments in polls of voters around the state (Rubenstein, 1992). According to the president of one small Oregon community's chamber of commerce, homosexuality "wasn't an issue" before OCA legislation; further, he reported that many in his community "wish it would go away" (Rubenstein, 1993c, p. D2).

Contrary to what might be surmised from this context, the OCA has met with surprising success, passing virtually all of its local ballot initiatives and narrowly failing to achieve majorities with two statewide measures. This success has been achieved in the face of unified, high-profile opposition and sharply disproportionate funding. The OCA has been outspent, outnumbered, and seemingly overmatched from the onset of its first campaign. Moreover, close examination of statewide discourse constituting homosexuality as a political issue reveals that, in traditional argumentative terms, the OCA has advanced an inadequate rationale in support of its legislative agendas. An inordinate preponderance of credible endorsement, expert testimony, scientific data, and media resources have all favored the opposition. However, more often than not, majorities of voters have failed to take this disparity as sufficient reason to vote down OCA-sponsored initiatives.

Although the OCA cannot be held entirely responsible for its legislative successes—some measure is clearly due to pre-existing voter beliefs regarding homosexuality—its achievements do draw attention to the propaganda campaign waged in support of OCA legislation. The object of this essay is to characterize the rhetorical significance of OCA anti-homosexual propaganda as a strikingly distinctive and pragmatic campaign that has made use of narrative rather than objective appeals. I hope to show that the OCA has offered an audience of Oregon voters what opposition forces largely failed to provide, a unified source of understanding and invitation to community. Ironically, this invitation to rhetorical community has functioned at the expense of sharp divisions among citizens of the state, and privileged particular elements of the American myth to the exclusion of others. In spite of these moral shortfalls, or because of them, the OCA's propaganda campaign serves as a valuable artifact for understanding the process by which audiences construct social reality.

CONTEXT

For Oregon voters, the battle over homosexuality began in earnest in 1991 with the introduction of Measure 9. Sponsored by the Oregon's Citizens Alliance, the measure stood to amend the Oregon Constitution to define homosexuality as "abnormal, wrong, unnatural, and perverse" (see Appendix B for full text of the measure). The initiative also included provisions to prohibit state and local government agencies from encouraging homosexual behavior and from extending civil rights legislation to gays and lesbians as a group. Finally, the measure would have required the State Department of Education to set a standard for youth that discouraged the practice of homosexuality.

The campaigns for and against the measure deployed sharply contrasting tactics. Opposition forces leaned heavily on what *The Oregonian* ("For the Record," 1992) referred to as "a parade of public denunciations" (p. B5) from diverse groups such as the Ecumenical Ministries of Oregon, the Oregon AFL-CIO, the Oregon Educational Association, the Oregon Medical Association, the Oregon Psychiatric Association, and Associated Oregon Industries. Hundreds of community leaders and influential citizens of bipartisan affiliation declared their opposition, including the current governor and four past governors, the Republican and Democratic party leaders, the attorney general, senators, congressmen, and associations of Catholic, Jewish, Lutheran, and Presbyterian clerics. Nor was opposition limited to residents of the state. National figures such as Jesse Jackson, William F. Buckley, and David Dinkins also denounced the initiative. Virtually all of the major media in the state editorialized against the measure, and none supported it.

For their part, supporters of the measure generally avoided traditional media in favor of a grassroots "No Special Rights" campaign utilizing flyers, speeches, video-taped presentations, and mass mailings. Typical of the handful of organizations that publicly supported the measure were Tiny's Towing and Mechanical Service in Medford, Sid's Little Copy Connection in Roseburg, and All Occasion Insurance in Springfield ("OCA Family Business Listing," 1992). Few lists of citizens in support of the measure were advertised, and still fewer religious, educational, or medical organizations declared open support ("For the Record," 1992). This lack of high-profile support made fund-raising difficult, and resulted in disproportionate spending by opponents of Measure 9. The twenty-two committees created to oppose the initiative spent a total of $2.2 million, nearly quadruple the $582,000 spent by the single "No Special Rights" committee in favor of the measure ("Foes Outspend," 1992). Still, according to OCA leader Lon Mabon (as cited in "OCA Banking," 1992), the organization had "enough money to do what we want to do" (p. D4).

In fact, assuming that what Mabon and the OCA wanted to do was win, he was very nearly correct. Although the measure was defeated by a fifty-seven-to-forty-three ratio on November 3, 1992, more than half a million votes were cast in favor of the measure, and it passed in twenty counties around the state. An exit poll conducted by Voter Research and Surveys (as cited in "Measure 9," 1992), an association of ABC, CBS, NBC, and CNN, showed that support was especially high among certain demographic groups, particularly rural dwellers, Christians, parents, Republicans, and youth. In a statewide mock election, 38,000 high-school students passed the measure by a seven percent margin ("Students Pass," 1992). Altogether, according to political analyst and pollster Tom Hibbits (as cited in "Measure 9," 1992), the results of the election suggested that a measure "drawn less restrictively and with less inflammatory language might do significantly better or even pass" (p. A1).

Appearing to take this advice to heart, OCA Chairman Lon Mabon promised the day after the election to put a refined version of Measure 9 on the 1994 ballot (Meehan, 1992). Debate renewed almost immediately as the OCA began a series of city and countywide campaigns in support of the new version of the measure. In rapid succession, the initiative was passed in Cornelius, Canby, Junction City, and in Douglas, Josephine, Klamath, and Linn counties. This process of what Mabon called "field testing" the measure gave promising results, as the measure generally achieved greater margins of approval than had the previous statewide ballot Measure 9 (Rubenstein, 1993b, p. D1).

Events took a twist when in July of 1993, the Oregon Legislature passed House Bill 3500 prohibiting local governments from enacting or enforcing laws that single out groups or individuals on the basis of sexual orientation, effectively nullifying OCA victories around the state. The OCA responded by challenging the constitutionality of the bill, and by launching recall efforts against fourteen of the thirty-eight Oregon House members—seven Democrats and seven Republicans—who had voted for the measure. Local voting on OCA-sponsored initiatives continued in Creswell, Estacada, Lebanon, Medford, Molalla, Sweet Home, and Jackson County, but enforcement of the initiatives was held in abeyance by HB 3500 (Rubenstein, 1993a).

The new statewide ballot measure, Measure 13, was unveiled in December 1993, titled by the OCA as the "Minority Status and Child Protection Act" (see Appendix B for full text of the initiative). Like its predecessor, Measure 9, Measure 13 was aimed at amending the Oregon Constitution. It sought to prohibit governments from approving or creating classifications based on homosexuality. It also contained provisions to bar expenditure of public money in a manner deemed to express approval of homosexuality. However, Measure 13 differed from its predecessor in that it did not seek to introduce strong moral denouncement of homosexuality into the state Constitution. In addition, a previously volatile debate over censorship in public libraries was "spiked" with a clause explicitly allowing books dealing with homosexuality for adult use only.

The propaganda campaigns waged for and against the measure set standards of dramatic enactment more usually associated with burlesque. In one case, a legislative advocate bared a handgun at an opponent and later characterized his act as a "preventative measure" (Tims, 1994). In another instance, an opponent of an antihomosexual initiative was challenged to take a polygraph test to prove his heterosexuality (Tims, 1994). More conventional political strategies on the part of the OCA included continued recall efforts against state and local legislators, and continued dissemination of many of the same broadsheets and videotapes used previously in support of Measure 9 and various local ballot measures (Paulson, 1993).

When the general election was held in November of 1994, Measure 13 was defeated, but by a closer margin than Measure 9 had been—51.5 percent to 48.5 percent. The measure lost in Portland by 70,000 votes, or more than a two-to-one ratio, but it passed in the rest of the state by a margin of 30,000 votes (Sarasohn, 1994). Far from disappointed at the second statewide defeat of his measure, Lon Mabon reported being "highly encouraged" by the results and speculated that with another revision of the language of the ballot measure, together with additional campaign funds, success would be achieved (Suo, 1994, p. A1). At the time of this writing, two OCA-sponsored ballot initiatives opposing homosexuality have been filed for the 1996 statewide elections. (Editor's note: both of the 1996 OCA initiatives failed to secure the required number of signatures to qualify for the ballot.)

THE OCA AND NARRATIVE RATIONALITY

It is difficult to construe an effective argument out of much of the OCA's propaganda campaign against homosexuality. This is true whether we define argument in a narrow sense, as "a line of reasoning, with evidence, in support of a conclusion" (Eisenberg & Ilardo, 1980, p. 2) or in broader terms as "a process by which people reason their way from one set of problematic ideas to the choice of another" (Brockriede, 1990, p. 4). These definitions, which may be taken to represent opposite ends of a definitional spectrum, share a reference to reason, and imply that argument possesses an essentially rational identity. However, many of the strategies enacted by the OCA seem strongly irrational. For example, a wide variety of media sources around the state editorialized in opposition to the initiative. Rather than ignoring, downplaying, or constructing a reasoned defense against these attacks, the OCA seemed to revel in them, even going so far as to reprint particularly excoriating excerpts in the group's in-house periodical, *The Oregon Alliance*. An article entitled "Media Explodes in Anti-OCA Hysteria" (1991) dominated the front page of the June/July 1991 issue and contained, among other samples, *The Oregonian*'s denunciation of the initiative as "bigotry" and an "abomination," the *Scappoose Spotlight*'s characterization of it as "hatred and discrimination, pure and simple," the *Medford Mail-Tribune*'s judgments of "homophobic" and "draconian," and the *East Oregonian*'s description of the whole idea as "bizarre, demeaning," "hateful and poisonous" (p. 1).

Many of the reprinted excerpts target the OCA itself. For example, the *Daily Astorian* ("Media Explodes," 1991, p. 1) called the organization "Oregon's linear descendant of the Ku Klux Klan." Other media characterizations include "the bedroom police," "peeping toms," "redneck jingoists," "gay bashers," "fascists," and "the kind of people who are the underbelly of the worst that is in America" (pp. 1, 3). The OCA's course of action was predicted to set off a "pogrom," a "climate of hate," and result in "the worst witch-hunt and bigotry the state has experienced this century" (p. 3).

Given this extended survey of negative media coverage and reprint of substantive attack, the OCA expended disproportionately little energy refuting the charges or constructing a defense, other than to assert on page three of the same issue of *The Oregon Alliance* that mainstream media "reflected the official party line of the homosexual movement" ("Media Explodes," 1991, p. 3). In light of the scope of attack, this response seems exceedingly weak, and appears to constitute a clear failure to defend either the initiative or its sponsor.

In other cases, OCA propaganda seems merely ineffective or amateurish. For example, consider *No Special Rights* (1992), a typical issue in a series of video-taped messages released by the OCA in support of various local and statewide ballot initiatives. The twenty-eight-minute tape begins with a brief overview by Lon Mabon, the leader of the OCA. In spite of poor lighting, the scene is slightly overexposed and yellowish. Mabon appears seated behind a desk, dressed in a coat and tie, and delivers the following introduction:

The film you are about to see is graphic and frightening. Frightening because these events are actually occurring in our nation. The footage you are about to see represents events that occurred in 1991 in a gay and lesbian pride day march in San Francisco. Also footage taken from the 1987 march on Washington, DC. These events need to be resisted because this could be a glimpse into Oregon's future. The homosexual movement is starting to put forth ordinances in Corvallis and Portland, and they have plans for the whole state. As you view this footage, realize that this could happen in your community. This could be your state.

Mabon appears to be speaking extemporaneously and to be slightly ill at ease. He commits several small verbal errors and demonstrates little non-verbal enthusiasm for his subject. This portion of the film lasts less than a minute. The body of the presentation is, as Mabon indicated, footage taken from two gay- and lesbian-rights demonstrations. This material is not narrated other than by occasional subtitles referencing the scenes depicted visually, such as "This is what gay-rights means," or "A depiction of Jesus Christ as a transvestite." The quality of the footage is poor, rather like that of home movies. The frame jumps unexpectedly, and shifts quickly from subject to subject. Splices are abrupt, with no visual or audio transitions. Ten minutes into the film, parade footage gives way to brief interviews with individuals who presumably took part in the demonstrations. These interviews focus primarily on the practice of sadomasochism and pedophilia. Several short statements are made by opponents of gay rights, including Congressman William Dannemeyer and "Sean," an acquired immune deficiency syndrome (AIDS) patient. More footage of the demonstration fills in much of the remainder of the film. The conclusion contains a brief segment of a counterdemonstration and another extemporaneous statement by Lon Mabon in which he indicates that "these events are the things that we are trying to stop with the initiative."

As rational argument, *No Special Rights* leaves much to be desired. The bulk of the film is simply spliced parade footage, set off by the briefest of introductions and conclusions. Little effort is made to interpret the demonstration footage or otherwise indicate its significance. No attention is given to how OCA legislation would affect events of the type depicted in the footage, nor is the connection between demonstrations in San Francisco and Washington, DC, and the affairs of Oregon made explicit. In short, very little about the film seems reasoned or rational, and the whole artifact has a shoddy, homemade aura about it.

It is difficult to explain the effectiveness of the OCA's print or video-taped campaign from within the rational-world paradigm, in which public moral decision making is a logical, thoughtful process (Fisher, 1987). At its best, this process should resemble a mathematical or philosophical equation that proceeds by isolation of propositions or facts, evaluation of those facts by experts, and subsequent policy decision based on the application of particular ethical codes. This model is characterized by sharp divisions among information, auditors, and audience. Experts are distinct from the general public by virtue of esoteric, context-specific knowledge. The realm of fact is strictly separate from that of value, which is subsequently imposed as order on objective reality. Judgments are the final step in a chronological equation, each stage of which occurs in order. Lay persons are removed from the active process of investigation and assessment, and serve instead as auditors of the process that is conducted before them.

However, increasing evidence suggests that humans may find stories and story-like qualities of language more compelling than formal grounds of argument (Fisher, 1987). This narrative paradigm defines humans as essentially storytelling beings whose paradigmatic mode of decision making is the use of "good reasons," which are contingent on frame and context. Rationality is a product of humans' inherent sense of narrative probability, which is a story's level of internal coherence and narrative fidelity, which is the degree to which a story fits with other stories we know. All told, our world is "a set of stories that must be chosen among in order for us to live life in a process of continual recreation" (Fisher, 1987, p. 65).

The assumption of the narrative paradigm gives us a very different understanding of public moral argument. Rather than spectators or auditors of argument, audience members are active, even "irrepressible" participants in the creation of meaning by way of narrative logic (Fisher, 1987, p. 72). This logic is not irrational in the traditional sense, but it is a distinctively narrative rationality. Central to this narrative rationality is the quality of coherence, by which we may understand disparate events, opinions, and facts. We seek out coherence in the stories told by various public interest groups and politicians; indeed, we require a "plot" in order to make sense of facts at all.

These assumptions direct attention to alternative features of OCA propaganda. Characteristics that might otherwise have been considered cues indicating low credibility or factual error may not be isolated as cues at all, depending on the story in which they are framed. In effective public moral discourse, we should expect to encounter not complete analysis and full-fledged argument to be audited, but well-developed narrative themes that enable audience members to actively resolve uncertainty. "In place of presenting open and flexible analyses of situations," Bennett and Edelman (1985) write, such discourse offers "formulaic stories that dissolve ambiguity and resolve possible points of new understanding into black and white replays" of the same thematic narrative (p. 158).

From within the narrative paradigm, the extended negative press coverage of the OCA and its various ballot measures may take on quite different significance than otherwise would be the case. Rather than undermining support, unified, credible public denunciation of the initiative may be read as a "David and Goliath" story in which the OCA heroically battled impossible odds in the name of righteousness or as a conspiracy on the part of public officials, media, and the homosexual lobby opposed only by the OCA and its backers. Given either plot, the OCA's focus on negative media coverage makes perfect sense according to the local narrative logic of the story. By demonstrating the unity of opposition and strength of denunciation, the OCA provided itself with its *raison d'être* and inspired followers to greater cohesion.

Similarly, various OCA videotapes featuring gay and lesbian demonstrations are a sort of story told, one that is "true" in the sense that it represents a historically verifiable event, and it is further a story about a subject that many auditors find disturbing. It does not matter a whit that most gays and lesbians may not be like those featured in the footage, or even that such demonstrations may not pose a threat to others' liberties. The decision that proceeds from the story is not a linear, logical event. Rather, a vote for OCA initiatives can be seen as one in accord with a disturbed reaction to the extreme behaviors witnessed in the video. In a like manner, the degree to which OCA propaganda at large dwells on themes of gay sexuality and unconventional modes of dress or behavior makes no sense in rational-paradigm terms. The material depicted constitutes at most a tenuous threat to convention in any reasoned sense; however, reason is not the operative mode or the dominant appeal. Visceral disapproval, grounded in difference, is perfectly adequate grounds for a yes vote in narrative terms.

STORIES OF THE OCA AND THE CONSTRUCTION OF SOCIAL REALITY

Without doubt, narrative elements are strongly present in OCA discourse. For example, the first of two campaign flyers widely distributed throughout Oregon contains the text of Measure 9 ("Vote Yes on Measure 9," 1992), subcaptioned "read the exact wording of Measure 9 for yourself. What does it say? What does it mean?" Somewhat surprisingly, given this captioned frame, the text is surrounded by boxes that "gloss" various clauses of the measure. Each of the boxes contains an anecdote relating to a particular portion of the initiative or to anticipated results. In reference to the ballot title, "AMENDS CONSTITUTION: GOVERNMENT CANNOT FA-

CILITATE, MUST DISCOURAGE HOMOSEXUALITY, OTHER BE-
HAVIORS," the boxed gloss describes how in December of 1991, the
Oregon Supreme Court "illegally rewrote" the original title, leading to a
"blistering dissent by the minority." Regarding the second clause of the
measure involving the use of state properties and monies, the boxed caption
details how "multiple thousands of tax dollars are currently being used to
promote the homosexual agenda in Oregon." The third clause of the initiative, dealing with educational policy, is glossed by a description of Project
10, a California educational program. Each of these boxes is entitled, "Van
Hoomissen's Dissent," "Misuse of Public Funds," and "Protecting Our
Children from an Unhealthy Lifestyle," and so forth. The effect of the titles
and stories is to replace "rational" consideration of the ballot measure itself
with a series of local anecdotes. Thus, the esoteric language of the initiative
that states "the State Department of Higher Education and the public
schools, shall assist in setting a standard for Oregon's youth . . ." becomes,
by way of the gloss, associated with a narrative about protecting children
from health risks, especially important now "in light of the AIDS crisis." In
each of the cases that the gloss is used, arcane legal language is translated
into one of a few dominant narrative themes. The initiative as a legal document is subsumed into these themes, recreated in a narrative image by
voters who understand first and foremost in narrative terms.

This textual gloss is especially useful to the voting public, as well as the
student of narrative argument, because it sums up in short order the primary
narrative themes that the OCA considers implicit in the initiative. On a
single page, we find the four stories that effectively bind the campaign for
Measure 9 together. The first of these, "Van Hoomissen's Dissent," is a
story of conspiracy in government. Justices and other governmental officials
entrusted with overseeing fair use of public resources have betrayed that
trust. The second story, "No Special Rights for Private Behavior," identifies
homosexuals as "a well housed and well employed" class that uses private
behaviors to constitute its identity, and which is especially prone to use the
media to "manipulate public opinion" in its favor. The third story, "Misuse
of Public Funds," tells how homosexuals are spending our tax dollars in their
own special, illegitimate interest. The fourth story is about our desire to
protect our children from health risks of AIDS, as well as other risks associated with the homosexual lifestyle. These narratives are neither entirely
discreet nor mutually exclusive, but overlap and serve to cross-reference each
other, thus making the narrative resources of one available to all.

These stories are heuristic in the sense that they instruct audience members how to interpret new information and facts. For example, the opposition
coalition's heavy reliance on public denunciation of OCA legislation by ostensibly credible opinion leaders fits the first story line of conspiracy. The
story line asserts betrayal by many of those in authority. Far from impeach-
ing the strength of the narrative, mounting attacks by public figures against

OCA measures confirms the accuracy of the plot. Media editorializing against the initiative is likewise interpreted as evidence of the homosexual lobby's manipulation of the press. The meanings of various attacks on the measures are not taken at face value, but translated by narrative logic so as to cohere with the larger narrative theme.

In addition to this heuristic function, these narratives are also generative. New information not contained in any particular version of the narrative may be inferred from the plot, extrapolated, as it were, by narrative logic from what we know of the story and its characters. For example, OCA campaign propaganda was ostensibly aimed at motivating voters to approve its ballot measures. However, virtually all of its narrative themes emphasize the deceitful, grasping, and immoral nature of homosexuals. This emphasis strongly implies a variety of courses of action surpassing support for ballot initiatives. Failing to hire a homosexual, or refusing to grant homosexuals access to housing, for instance, are actions justified by OCA narratives, even though these actions are never explicitly recommended in OCA propaganda. Explicit reference is unnecessary at the level of discourse given the generative capacity of the plot.

I have suggested that the OCA made use of relatively few narrative plots, and that these plots were represented in the boxed explanations of the text of the initiative found in their campaign flyers. However, these short anecdotes in the gloss do not exhaust the narrative potential of the stories, nor do they "contain" the plots. Rather, narratives are comprised of two primary levels: the story, or what is told, such as events and descriptions of people and objects; and discourse, or the means by which the story is told, including the words, images, and sounds that constitute the telling of the story (Chatman, 1979). In simplest terms, the story is what is told and discourse is how it is told. Any story may thus be considered a thing apart from any particular telling, no matter how seemingly complete or eloquent, or how terse and cryptic. In this sense, the events and objects that make up a story are never synonymous with the words that are used to refer to them in the telling.

Plots connect story and discourse. They are the "thread of design" that we as listeners identify among events and objects described in discourse. Plots may be indicated in discourse, but they also transcend discourse, ordering and making comprehensible all the narrative events and descriptions that are depicted. It is in this manner that our reading of plot enables us to construct the story out of discourse (Brooks, 1984). From this we may say that any story is both more and less than its material manifestation. More, in the sense that we must infer the design of plot and interpret the events and descriptions represented so as to arrive at the story. Less, in the sense that any discourse contains filler, unimportant details mandated by convention or grammar that play no essential role in the story at hand. These elements are necessary for discourse, but unnecessary for the story; hence, they do not "mean" anything within the narrative frame.

Just as it is not necessary to completely retell a story in order to invoke it as an interpretive frame, any given discourse need not refer to all the important events and descriptions that a story might be thought to contain, even at the level of discourse. Rather, it may be enough to index one or more significant cues relating to the narrative theme whereby readers may find direction and resolve moral uncertainty. Political propaganda may be fruitfully considered as a great number of renditions, more and less complete, of far fewer discrete narrative themes. I suggest that the four themes of political conspiracy, homosexuals as behavioral interest group, misuse of tax public resources, and threat to children function as archetypal themes in the OCA's campaign for both its statewide and local ballot initiatives. The reader exposed to OCA propaganda very quickly learns to catalogue the primary narratives and begins to assimilate details thereafter according to their plots. Put another way, various facts are defined, sources evaluated, and moral valences assigned in accordance with this handful of stories. Evidence that does not seem salient to these plots is simply unimportant, ancillary filler in the discourse.

The process of telling these stories is quintessentially a community-building endeavor. The construction of narratives enthymematically relies upon the participation of the audience. That is, stories invariably draw from their audiences the raw materials of narrative—values, contexts, emotions, presuppositions, and the like. The presentation of consistent narrative themes provides an invitation to listeners to collaborate in the creation of community and a shared social reality. This invitation at the level of narrative form was amplified in OCA propaganda by the substance of the narratives, each of which casts homosexuality as a threat to the larger rhetorical community shaped by the narrative. Manipulation of the media and public officials, misappropriation of public funds, moral depravity, and corruption of youth, all represent a threat to the established orthodoxy and to the common good.

These considerations cast new light on our reading of much OCA propaganda. For example, the video-taped presentation, *No Special Rights*, takes on entirely different significance. Elements that could, under the rational paradigm, be taken to detract from ethos, such as the poor technical merit of the film or Lon Mabon's lackluster introduction and conclusion, are now taken as mere elements of performance, or discourse, inessential to the story being told. At worst, the viewer familiar with the OCA's narrative themes might respond that this is a poor rendition of the story; however, poor telling need not detract from the story itself. More likely, the viewer ignores these meaningless details in favor of the cues that index particular narrative themes. Less important than production details are the scenes of naked, gyrating participants in the gay-rights parade. The extended footage of these scenes reinforces the narrative theme that homosexuality is comprised of behaviors that exist in the realm of choice rather than that of biology.

Freeze-frame shots of children in the parade evoke the narrative theme of threat to our children in the form of health risk and pedophilia. These and other such details index appropriate stories for viewers familiar with OCA propaganda, enabling the construction of a coherent plot, and thus transforming what in argumentative terms is a poorly produced, loosely organized, and largely incoherent artifact, into a rich and meaningful text.

These narrative considerations have rhetorical implications that might profitably be made more explicit. First, the notion that "every acceptance of a narrative involves a rejection of others" (Bennett & Edelman, 1985, p. 160) may shed light on the seeming invincibility of OCA propaganda to reasoned argument. To the degree that narrative themes privilege a certain reading of propaganda, they cast shadows on other, competing narratives and the alternative readings of facts that could be made. Thus, in some sense stories provide for their own defense, not by actively negating other narratives, but by constituting the world in such a way that other stories cannot be heard. Second, narrative structure hides the articulation of value that it contains. Stories, as much as arguments, are statements of value; however, the fashion in which stories are constructed lends them an especially potent rhetorical force. Rather than presenting value propositions, stories instantiate or demonstrate value enthymematically by drawing on the audience's experiences to complete the story line. Both of these rhetorical operations can be illustrated by a reading of a brief narrative that appeared in the second flyer in the OCA's series of publications.

The theme of the OCA's second flyer in support of statewide legislation was "Homosexuality, the Classroom, and Your Children" (1992). Most of the material in the publication dealt with gay youth culture, such as "homosexual terms toward youth," and recent political events such as California's Project 10. The one anomalous feature, entitled "Billy and Chuckie," appeared set off in a box on the front page, identified by its subtitle as a "fictional story"; indeed, the feature presents a more complete narrative at the discursive level than is generally the case in public moral argument. The discourse begins by describing a "sunny fall afternoon" in which two boys, Billy and Chuckie, walk home following school. Billy Johnson is a small, shy twelve-year-old, the son of recently divorced parents and a newcomer to the small Oregon mill town in which they live. Chuckie Bissel is slow, overweight, and "rather intimidating" to the smaller Billy. On the way home, Chuckie reminds Billy of his promise to go to the fort to "try it." Billy is reluctant to "do that kinda stuff," and thinks he wants to go watch television instead. Chuckie recounts the endorsements of the gay health teacher, the police chief, doctors, the newspapers, and "even the Governor," all of whom indicate that "it's perfectly normal." In the midst of this discussion, Chuckie tackles Billy into a pile of leaves and tickles him unmercifully, reminding him that he, Chuckie, is Billy's best friend and would never harm him. Together they conclude that "doing those things couldn't be wrong," and head "full-tilt toward the fort." The story concludes with a separate scene in which, even as Billy and Chuckie make their way to the fort, two of their schoolmates, Sara Evans and Tina Copper, discuss their approval of Ms. Ireland, the lesbian physical education (PE) coach. The story closes as the girls agree that they have changed their minds about homosexuality. Below the final line of the narrative, a stipulation to vote for OCA legislation appears in bold face.

The status of "Billy and Chuckie" as fiction may seem to constitute a special case until we recall, with Ursula Le Guin (1989), that "fiction in particular, narration in general, may be seen not as a disguise or falsification of what is given but as an active encounter with the environment by means of posing options and alternatives, and an enlargement of present reality by connecting it to the unverifiable past and the unpredictable future" (p. 5). In this sense, fiction and what poses as more truthful narrative share the service of setting forth a group of relations and possibilities. What relations and possibilities, in this case, are set forth? Drawing on our previous distinction between story and discourse, we may say that "Billy and Chuckie" is a story about how children might be influenced by adult role models to engage in homosexual behaviors. However, the narrative's rhetorical significance far exceeds this synopsis.

We might note first, in an effort to take stock of this influence, that the narrative advances a wealth of characterizations at the level of discourse. Chuckie, the child advocate of homosexuality, is described as large—"a head taller than Billy, and about fifty pounds heavier" (p. 1)—sluggish, yet dominant. Mr. Carson, the gay health teacher, is permissive, flamboyant, and personally interested in children—"he lets everybody do what they want in his class. He even gives some kids rides in his Porsche after school" (p. 4). Ms. Ireland, whose status as PE coach suggests a butch, masculine figure, is also interested in small children, although girls in this case. Other children in the narrative, Billy, Sally, and Tina, are described as "shy and self-conscious," and in diminutive terms that emphasize their innocence and naiveté, as, for example, "little Tina Copper" (p. 4).

A causal relationship is also advanced over the course of the narrative. Chuckie and Billy, Sally and Tina were all initially opposed to homosexuality—the mere thought of it made Billy nauseous—but later come to approve of gays and lesbians, or actually engage in homosexual acts themselves. This change is brought about by the influence of adult role models, both those who are homosexual, and those who advocate homosexuality as an acceptable lifestyle.

We may sum these characterizations in propositional form for clarity. Homosexuality coincides with undesirable personal traits. Homosexual adults are likely to have jobs that bring them in direct contact with children. In this capacity, they inculcate acceptance of homosexuality into children, possibly in the interest of sexual gratification and certainly in the interest of recruitment in the homosexual movement. If successful, this inculcation leads children to engage in homosexual acts with each other. This process of recruitment is aided by other adult role models who do not actively and publicly oppose homosexuality. Homosexuality itself is a matter of choice open to anyone, and engaging in homosexual acts requires overcoming an inherent repulsion.

Although this translation of the story into propositional form highlights some of the values and assumptions implicit in the narrative, it does not explain the suasory force with which they are conveyed. These values and assumptions are not present in the literal artifact of the discourse, but in the story that readers construct from the discourse. They are evoked in enthymematic fashion from readers themselves. Further, they are not isolated and evaluated as propositions, according to reason, but experienced as story, according to narrative logic. The reader does not test various propositions against standards of truth or objectivity, but, rather, weighs the story in terms of narrative fidelity and coherence. The reader does not ask, "Is homosexuality really a choice?" but, rather, "Does this story seem internally consistent?" or "Does this fit with other stories I know?"

"Proofs" of the story's internal validity include its high level of narrative competence. The narrative conforms to traditional conventions regarding pacing and exposition, structure and dialogue. It has a protagonist and antagonist, an easily extracted plot, an unresolved exigence to inspire dramatic tension, and a tragic resolution. Dialogue, including the use of popular idiomatic terms currently used by young boys, lends the work authenticity. The boys behave quite consistently within their context and characters.

Moreover, the story fits easily with a variety of other common narratives with which we are familiar. We can easily identify with Billy's loneliness and uncertainty in a new town, and we intuitively understand Chuckie's goodwilled manipulation to get what he wants. What parent or caring adult would not, upon reading the story, feel a strong desire to protect innocent children from a "tragic" resolution? As readers, we are not asked to judge homosexuality; the story makes that judgment for us. Instead, we are asked to experience the story itself by our enjoining it; this process proceeds according to quite different standards than argument by proposition.

The discrete narrative strategy of "Billy and Chuckie" was deployed by the OCA with greater frequency over time. For example, the entire first page of a widely disseminated broadsheet supporting Measure 13, entitled "Homosexuality in the Schools" (1994), is dominated by a series of stories regarding events in Oregon public schools. In one story, a Beaverton teacher is alleged to have advised his male students to "try homosexuality at least twice" (p. 1). In another, the reading list for Cottage Grove's Head Start program is described as amounting to "gay curriculum" (p. 1).

The functions described as performed by these fully developed stories also obtain in the larger, less discursively discrete narratives that appear throughout the OCA propaganda campaign. In performing these rhetorical functions, narrative themes enabled supporters of the OCA to reconstruct objective evidence and reconstitute public moral argument in good faith. Indeed, participation in campaign narratives enabled audience members to identify with entirely productive and positive roles in our society: parent, fair-minded citizen, and defender of the common good. Supporters of the OCA were not necessarily bigoted or foolish, small-minded or misled. They simply listened to a different story than did opponents of the measure, a story that was effectively wrought in OCA propaganda.

CONCLUSION

This analysis has suggested that the OCA anti-homosexual campaign has been rhetorically significant in terms of its reliance on narrative characteristics of language. Participation in OCA stories has enabled listeners to interpret complex legal language, judge esoteric disputes among experts, and resolve disturbing challenges to orthodox behavior. OCA stories have helped participants to explain the world and to reduce uncertainties as they arise. Moreover, these narratives have offered an invitation to community with others who share in the creation and maintenance of a social reality. That this invitation has been made at the expense of the larger community of the state of Oregon mars what has been, against all odds, a largely successful grassroots campaign.

Consideration of the OCA's propaganda within the narrative paradigm suggests strategies for those seeking to participate in effective public moral argument. Attacks on the OCA and its various ballot measures have largely taken the form of reasoned propositions. For example, the widely distributed "Impact Statements" (1992) generated by the opposition coalition divided the anticipated results of OCA legislation into various subtopics, such as "child custody," "state licensing," "public television and the arts," and "public libraries." Under each heading, the expected effect of the measure on a particular area was detailed according to an implicative structure. In another example of opposition propaganda, a manifesto of the People of Faith Against Bigotry (1992), opposition to the measure on religious grounds was given abstract theoretical rationale, and divided into subarguments that proceeded by way of biblical exegesis. These artifacts are typical of opposition propaganda: prototypes of the rational-world paradigm, exemplars of reasoned argument, but nearly devoid of sustained narrative themes.

Extensive division of arguments into small units of proof moves in the opposite direction from narrative, which unifies and lends coherence. The antinarrative tone of the opposition campaign does not provide undecided voters with an encompassing rationale or story by which discrete data and facts might be assessed and made meaningful. In sharp contrast, the overarching, occasionally mythic themes sounded by the OCA provided voters with effective constructs for understanding and organizing the world.

A similar tone is characteristic of the opposition campaign's explicit response to OCA propaganda. Certainly, opposition forces subjected specific elements of OCA discourse to heavy fire. For example, the opposition coalition publicized an alternative assessment of California's educational program, Project 10, and advertised the federal Lesbian and Gay Civil Rights Bill, which specifically states that homosexuals should not be the object of affirmative action ("Impact Statement," 1992). However, these salvos constituted attacks on the discursive manifestation of narrative rather than the story that organized and made meaningful this information. Responses to particular descriptions or themes in OCA narratives in some fashion missed the point or substance of the stories. The negation of a story is not no story, but another, an alternative story. It is not enough to deny that a story is true without offering an alternative account, in this case, a story that runs counter to OCA narratives. Successful public moral argument is constituted at the level of narrative. Thus, opposition forces might more effectively have constructed competing stories that implicated or construed facts in different ways. To the degree that stories compete for explanatory control, effective alternative narratives stood to undo much of the appeal of the OCA.

The effectiveness of the OCA's propaganda campaign also has implications for the initiative system in Oregon. Long considered an essential element of Oregon government, the initiative system may now face amendment. According to *The Oregonian* (1992, November 29), interviews with legislators, lobbyists, and political leaders reveal support for reform of the initiative system because of what some characterize as "a good idea gone haywire" (Meehan, 1992, p. D1). Of the twenty-three states that currently make use of the initiative process, Oregon affords about the easiest access to the ballot. For constitutional amendments like Measures 9 and 13, for example, petitioners must collect 8 percent of the vote in the last governor's election. For local initiatives, the threshold drops to 6 percent. According to proponents of change, the OCA has subverted the process with legislation that "would never have survived the give-and-take of a legislative session" (Meehan, 1992, p. D1). The OCA's success with narrative in direct appeals to voters may thus spell eventual removal of some measure of popular control over Oregon legislation.

A final implication of this study concerns civic education. As public moral argument, rhetorically effective stories are those that express a culture's most profound values. In the event that we find ourselves at the mercy of what we perceive to be unethical or divisive uses of narrative, we may do well to remember that the resources of narrative are accessible to all, and that a democratic society has the obligation to educate its citizens in the effective use and abuse of the tools of persuasive argument.

4

The Constitution as Rhetorical Symbol in Western Anti-Gay Rights Initiatives: The Case of Idaho

Daniel Levin

In 1993 and 1994, Idahoans discussed gay rights and the Constitution. The impetus for this discussion was a proposed initiative that would have prohibited civil rights laws benefiting gay men and lesbians, prohibit positive depictions of homosexuality in the public schools, and restrictions on library materials that referred to homosexuality. That measure, entitled alternatively "Stop Special Rights" and Proposition One, raised serious questions about a variety of constitutional issues: What is a constitutional right? Which groups should receive civil rights protections, whether a majority may prevent an unpopular minority from securing newly won rights, and whether the public schools and libraries may keep positive depictions of sexuality from children? These questions were debated, not only by lawyers, but by leaders of interest groups, clergy, the media, and, ultimately, the electorate.

The electorate would eventually reject Proposition One by a very narrow margin—three thousand votes or approximately 1 percent of the votes cast in the 1994 election (Pursley, 1995). However, the campaign leading up to that vote would be far more interesting than the final tally in what it revealed about Idahoans' attitudes towards homosexuality, constitutionality, and the rights of minorities. The campaign would also show interest groups carefully planning their messages around the themes of homosexuality, constitutionality, and the rights of minorities. In those campaign messages, they offered their own interpretations of the status and characteristics of minorities in a democracy, the community's power over its schools and libraries, and the power of the state to regulate morality. While these varying messages contained many subtle differences, the debate over Proposition One could be divided into two distinctive understandings of the Constitution, both of which had roots in local culture.

In the first understanding, what might be termed the "liberal" theory, the Constitution is primarily a document that creates individual rights against government regulation. The liberal theory emphasizes privacy as a constitutional right, identifies governmental regulation of morality as governmental intrusion into citizens' lives, and that institutions of cultural transmission, such as schools and libraries, are to provide a free forum for ideas. Liberals would also urge that governmental regulation should not reflect the prejudices of the majority but tolerate minorities. Finally, liberals venerate the *processes* of constitutional democracy, especially the courts, while viewing the legal process, by which they would enforce many of the rights of minorities, to be an expensive, but legitimate, way of asking constitutional questions.

The second understanding, which might be labeled "communitarian," is based on the proposition that the Constitution stands for a larger moral consensus about proper public and private behavior. In this vision, the Constitution becomes the synonym of the word "culture" and the Latin root *constitutio*, which served Cicero as "a descriptive term for the political community 'as it actually is'" returns to its original meaning (Maddox, 1989, pp. 51, 59). For the communitarian, a constitutional polity's first priority is thus the preservation of its culture, by regulating morality if necessary. Schools and libraries, as institutions of cultural transmission, are responsible for teaching clear lessons of right and wrong, while the creation of new rights for minority groups is viewed as a limitation on the community's right to make the distinctions it wishes. Finally, communitarians view democracy as a means by which to assess the prevailing morals of the time. Rather than valuing the judicial process, many communitarians, perhaps blaming the courts for a number of past losses, view it with a form of legal realism, in which many decisions are reduced to the values of the judges who make them (Oldfield, 1990; Sandel, 1984).

Both the liberal and communitarian conceptions of constitutionalism resound in the political culture of Idaho. The liberal understanding appeals to the strong libertarian strain in the culture of the American West. The liberal vision was elaborated in the claim that Proposition One was "Too much government, and not enough Idaho," which associated Idaho with individualism and portrayed Proposition One as another form of government regulation (*No on One*, 1994). The communitarian vision focused on the regulation of morality. James Dobson, president of Focus on the Family, a national Christian Right organization, combined this view with an argument for popular sovereignty when he told Idahoans in a public letter that "Idaho law currently recognizes the right of the citizens of Idaho to judge sodomy and other 'crimes against nature,' to be worthy of criminal sanctions" (Dobson, 1994). In the communitarian understanding, traditional morality merged with populist democracy to characterize homosexuals as out of touch with the character of Idaho.

The debate over the constitutionality of Proposition One was not likely to change many minds. Using survey data from a similar referendum in Houston, James Gibson and Kent Tedin argue that those persons who are least supportive of democratic processes in the abstract are also least tolerant of unpopular minorities generally, and gay men and lesbians more specifically. The second strongest indicator of hostility to gay rights was how threatened individuals felt by homosexuals and the acquired immune deficiency syndrome (AIDS). A lack of involvement in the political process was the third strongest predictor of hostility to homosexuals, and numerous other studies demonstrate that tolerance of unpopular minorities is highest among those involved in politics, who have to work with many diverse groups (Gibson & Tedin, 1988). The first and third results combine to show those hostile to the rights of lesbians and gay men to be less supportive of the political process and uninvolved. Alienation from the political system allows hostility for gay men and lesbians to become intolerance, while participation might restrict such hostility to social intolerance that does not spill over into the political arena.

In contrast to those democratic norms closely related to the liberal view which sustain the political system as a separate sphere, communitarian concern over gay rights is largely motivated by concern for preservation of the culture. Where advocates of gay rights see those rights as essentially political and legal in nature, communitarians, who in Idaho were often Christian fundamentalists, view them as rife with moral implications. If there is a an essential attribute to the Christian Right, it is a world view in which science integrates with religion and morality fuses with the political sphere (Lienesch, 1993). For communitarians, church and state may act together to enforce public morality. In the words of a manual distributed by the Idaho Citizens Alliance, "[t]he 'politically correct' version of church and state is nothing short of rank falsehood" (D. Miller, 1993). By viewing the personal behavior of homosexuals as necessarily interwoven with their political goals, communitarians equate gay rights with the practice of sodomy.

While communitarians view society as an integrated whole, liberals may separate their beliefs about moral behavior and legal behavior. Separating morality and legality allows liberals to tolerate practices, including homosexuality, of which they may not approve, and protect persons engaging in such practices from discrimination, without believing that they are thereby approving of such practices. By differentiating between the political, legal, and moral spheres, liberals may still maintain that they disapprove of homosexuality but that the polity must not discriminate against gay men and lesbians. This was the position taken by many of Idaho's conservative political elite, such as Congressman Mike Crapo, who opposed the initiative because "the initiative goes beyond permissible constitutional boundaries" while also stating that he opposed "special rights" for homosexuals as well as positive treatment of homosexuality in the schools (Prichard, 1994b, p. C1).

A SHORT HISTORY OF IDAHO'S PROPOSITION ONE

Given the history of the American West, it is ironic that western states have been at the forefront of anti-gay politics in the 1990s. In the early West, "fur trappers, who often spent months away from female companionship, considered homosexual relations perfectly normal. So did everyone else" (Gerassi, 1966, p. 131). That tradition of the old West passed with the settling of the frontier. By the 1950s, intolerance of homosexual relations had grown so that Boise experienced a short panic over revelations of a male homosexual "underground" and allegations that over one hundred teenagers were involved. At least seven men served terms in the state penitentiary as a result of the work of a private investigator and the efforts of the district attorney's office (Gerassi, 1966).

The contemporary movement in Idaho to prohibit civil rights protections on the basis of sexual orientation began in early 1993 following the defeat of a similar measure in Oregon and the passage of Amendment Two in Colorado in November 1992. Of the two 1992 measures, Oregon's was the more important influence; Idaho borders Oregon, and Idaho has close commercial and cultural connections to Oregon and Washington as part of the Pacific Northwest. More importantly, the Idaho Citizens Alliance (ICA), the organized manifestation of the anti-gay movement in Idaho, was largely modeled after the Oregon Citizen's Alliance, which had sponsored the Oregon initiatives. The language of Idaho's Proposition One followed that of Oregon's 1994 Measure 13, the "Minority Status and Child Protection Act II," which prohibited "minority status" for gay men and lesbians, restricted how homosexuality could be presented in the schools, regulated access to library books, and denied marriage or domestic partnerships to gay couples (*deParrie v. Keisling*, 1993).

The text of Idaho's Proposition One began with its primary purpose, language prohibiting the state or any instrumentality from granting "minority status" or extending affirmative action to homosexuals. It then forbade state recognition of same-sex marriages or domestic partnerships and proscribed public schools from teaching about homosexuality in a positive way. A limitation on public funding "that has the purpose or effect of promoting, making acceptable, or expressing approval of homosexuality" included restricting access to library materials "which address homosexuality" to adults, and counseling, to providing "positive guidance toward persons experiencing difficulty with sexual identity." The measure would also have allowed state agencies to consider "private sexual behaviors" as "non-job factors" in employment matters. Finally, the proposition included a severability clause which would preserve other sections of the measure if any were struck down as unconstitutional, and evinces its authors' concerns over its constitutionality (*ACLU v. EchoHawk*, 1993).

As one of the more detailed measures restricting the rights of lesbians and gay men, Idaho's Proposition One both shared features with, and differed from, initiatives considered in other states. Unlike some of the others, it contained no derogatory language stigmatizing gay men and lesbians as "unnatural" or "perverse," nor did it associate homosexuality with pedophilia, sadism, masochism, or transvestism or label it "inappropriate sexual behavior."[1] Unlike many of the others, it also lacked a long, substantive preamble which might elucidate the aims of the text. Its sometimes confusing text, filled with multiple negatives, combined many of the substantive measures of the other Pacific Northwest initiatives, including restrictions on the public school curricula, public library materials, and prohibitions on gay marriage or domestic partnerships.

Idaho's Proposition One lacked the obvious and superfluous hostility of the other Pacific Northwest measures, but its substantive provisions were among the most restrictive of the initiatives. William Adams categorizes anti-gay-rights initiatives according to the mechanism by which they limit legislation protecting individual rights on the basis of sexual orientation. Some measures, which Adams labels "stealth proposals," avoid all mention of homosexuality or sexual identity, but propose limiting civil rights protections to those classifications already recognized by the federal government and that state's legislature. Such stealth initiatives were proposed in Florida and Maine in 1994, although neither was placed on the ballot (Adams, 1994, pp. 589–590).[2] The second type of anti-gay initiative, "specifically targeted proposals," mention homosexuality or sexual orientation, but restrict their goals to the prohibition of state action to prevent discrimination against gays or lesbians; these include Colorado's 1992 Amendment Two, as well Arizona's and Missouri's proposed initiatives in 1994. The third type of anti-gay initiative, "overtly hostile proposals," both limits civil rights protections and targets positive treatment of homosexuality in public settings. This type of initiative seems particularly at home in the Pacific Northwest, and includes initiatives proposed in Oregon, Washington, Nevada, and Idaho (Adams, 1994).

The reason for such an anti-gay initiative in Idaho must be largely symbolic. Even to opponents of gay rights, the need for Proposition One would seem less necessary in Idaho than in Oregon or Colorado, where the largest cities, Portland and Denver, had adopted laws prohibiting discrimination in employment, housing, and public accommodations (Note, 1993). Unlike Colorado and Oregon, where anti-gay initiatives might be easily understood as an attempt by a largely rural electorate to slow down social change in metropolitan areas, no Idaho municipality provided civil rights based on sexual orientation when Proposition One was announced. The only municipality in Idaho with such a law, the 800-person hamlet of Troy, adopted its measure prohibiting discrimination on the basis of sexual orientation in municipal employment, only after the initiative was filed ("City Employees," 1994). Instead, the dragons of the "homosexual agenda" lay in a few scattered cities outside the state. The ICA's chairman and proposition's chief proponent, Kelly Walton, explained that, while there was no militant or organized gay-rights lobby in Idaho, there were "ominous signs" including the plans of the local chapter of the American Civil Liberties Union (ACLU) to repeal Idaho's law criminalizing "the infamous crime against nature," and a lesbian couple which addressed a local high-school class on childrearing (Miller, n.d.).

Discussion of the need for the measure and its constitutionality began as soon as the initiative's language was introduced. State Attorney General Larry Echohawk issued a legal opinion, required for all ballot initiatives, which stated that the measure was "fatally flawed," and opined that if Proposition One's proponents wanted to "Stop Special Rights," they should instead prohibit discrimination based on sexual orientation (Eckart, 1993i). In particular, the attorney general's opinion noted that the proposition selected a single group for hostile treatment and denied them equal access to the political process. It noted specific constitutional problems with the restrictions on public school curricula, counseling for both adults and public school students, and library materials, and with the measure's authorization of discrimination against lesbians and gay men in public employment. Finally, the attorney general's opinion noted that the section dealing with marriage and domestic partnership merely restated current state law (Attorney General's Office, 1993). The attorney general's opinion led the ICA to change some sections of the proposed initiatives. The particular revisions, which changed a prohibition on all positive discussion of homosexuality in the public schools to a requirement that school boards approve any material dealing with homosexuality and ensure that it be "age-appropriate," and required that libraries not only restrict access to material but also dictated that such material meet "local standards" (LaMay, 1993). The changes solved particular constitutional problems with the initiative but did not alter its meaning and implications and even made the restrictions on library materials even more burdensome by requiring that materials meet "local community standards."

The next legal battle over the initiative involved the wording that would appear on the ballot. In Idaho, an initiative must be given both long and short titles by the state attorney general before it can be placed on the ballot. Both the state ACLU and the ICA challenged the attorney general's proposed wording, and, while the State Supreme Court approved the attorney general's wording, two of the five justices used the opportunity to announce "serious questions concerning the vagueness of some of the terms of the proposed act" (*ACLU v. EchoHawk*, 1993; "High Court," 1993). These concerns likely referred to the term "minority status," which was undefined, and to the provisions dealing with schools, libraries, and public employees. This was the last legal challenge Proposition One faced as it was defeated at the polls by a small margin on November 1994 (Pursley, 1995).

Although Proposition One's defeat at the polls would seem to have ended the controversy, it began again when Alan Lance, Idaho's new attorney general, signed an *amicus curiae* brief to U.S. Supreme Court then considering the constitutionality of Colorado's Amendment Two. The brief, in support of the Colorado initiative's constitutionality, was also signed by the attorney generals of Alabama and Virginia and was written by conservative jurisprude Robert Bork. The brief argued that the Colorado Supreme Court's ruling that Amendment Two in *Evans v. Romer* unconstitutionally abridged the sovereignty of the people of Colorado, and that the Colorado Supreme Court's discovery of a "right of political participation" was improper. Bork's brief characterized the Colorado Supreme Court as creating "a constitutional right of any 'independently identifiable class of persons' to have its political agenda insulated against normal democratic processes" (Bork & Duncan, 1995, p. 9). Lance claimed that he joined Bork's brief because of the possibility that another anti-gay initiative might pass in Idaho and that defending such an initiative would cost the state a large sum. Joining Colorado's brief would provide "savings in avoiding litigation as well as the opportunity to have the underlying constitutional issues decided" (Attorney General's Office, 1995). This explanation may be treated skeptically as Lance had previously announced his intent to offer legislation that would substantially follow the language of the ICA initiative in denying gays and lesbians "minority preferences or special status" while condemning the initiative itself as unconstitutional ("AG Candidate," 1993; Wickline, 1994). He could also have joined an *amicus* brief which supported the Colorado Court's decision.

Unsurprisingly, Proposition One had a future in Idaho. On June 23, 1994, the ICA introduced a new initiative which would take its campaign to the 1996 election. The new initiative differs in several important respects from Proposition One. Because the ICA's Kelly Walton claimed that many voters had been confused over what a yes vote entailed, the initiative's language includes the word "yes" three times in the statutory language. The initiative's title was changed to the "Family and Child Protection Act," and a brief preamble states that the initiative's purpose is "prohibiting government promotion of the so-called 'homosexual rights' agenda" ("What the 'Family and Child Protection,'" 1995). One provision had changed significantly, prohibiting the state and all agents from declaring lesbians and gay men "to constitute an official sanctioned or recognized 'minority,' or otherwise establish or grant to such individual(s) any special, exclusive, or preferential status, treatment, or classification under law." Unlike the previous initiative, the measure does not use the term "sexual orientation," and thus does not forbid laws prohibiting discrimination on the basis of sexual orientation, as all current "gay rights" laws do. It also prohibits "quotas" or "special rights, privileges or benefits" for homosexuals, proscribes the expenditure of public money to promote "homosexual behavior," bans positive depictions of homosexual behavior in the public schools, and forbids the creation of "domestic partnerships" that have privileges of marriage. Two other significant changes were the removal of the provision classifying homosexuality as a non-job-related factor in public employment and the replacement of language requiring the separation of "library materials addressing homosexuality" away from minors by language requiring parental permission for children to have access to "any publication which promotes, advocates, endorses or encourages homosexual behavior" (Flagg, 1995).

Like the 1994 Proposition One, the proposed 1996 ICA initiative posed many constitutional problems. Those particular to the newer initiative include the restrictions on public school curricula and minor's access to library materials with positive approaches to homosexuality, which, because the restriction only applies to one position regarding homosexuality, would violate the First Amendment. Yet, by jettisoning the language regarding the phrase "sexual orientation," the newer initiative might, because of its lack of effect, otherwise pass constitutional measure precisely because it would make no legal difference, and would therefore be unenforceable.

The debate on the proposed 1996 ICA initiative ended when, in the aftermath of the *Romer v. Evans* decision (see Chapter 11 for a summary of the case), the ICA withdrew from its efforts to gather enough signatures to place their 1996 effort on the ballot.

THE RHETORIC OF SPECIAL RIGHTS AND MINORITY STATUS

At the heart of the rhetoric surrounding Idaho's Proposition One was the assertion that civil rights protections for lesbians and gay men were "special rights." Like anti-gay initiatives in Oregon and Colorado, Proposition One's would have forbade the state and any other agency from conferring "minority status to persons who engage in homosexual behavior, solely on the basis of such behavior" (*ACLU v. EchoHawk*, 1993). "Minority status" was not defined, and the term "minority status" is foreign to the American constitutional tradition and cannot be found in the either statutes or the Supreme Court's decisions. As Oregon's Supreme Court noted while considering the wording of 1994's Ballot Measure 13, "the concept of government granting minority status to homosexuals has no recognized meaning outside of this measure" (*Mabon v. Keisling*, 1993). In the American constitutional tradition, discrimination on the basis of a protected status, whether that status has been based in religion, race, national origin, or citizenship has been treated as a problem of "suspect classification," in which the state's adverse treatment of an individual or a group is treated to more stringent judicial scrutiny and where such scrutiny is not dependent on the disadvantaged group being a minority or the individual being a member of a minority group.[3] Indeed, women's rights prove the point that a group may be protected from hostile state action on the basis of gender, although women are not a minority and do not have minority status.

The phrase "minority status" is doubly problematic because those states that have extended civil rights protections to gay and lesbians have done so by prohibiting discrimination on the basis of sexual orientation, a phrasing that protects heterosexuals as well as gay men and lesbians. Had the authors of Proposition One in 1994 simply wished to ensure that such measures would not be enacted in Idaho, they could have used the phrase "sexual orientation," which they only used later when prohibiting the use of "special classifications such as 'sexual orientation.' " By defining the pursuit of protections by lesbians and gay men as minority status or a "special classification," the authors attempted to conflate civil rights protections with affirmative action programs which have been undertaken in redress for past discrimination against other groups, such as African-Americans and women. In Idaho, anti-gay-rights activists asserted that "[e]very time minority status is granted by law to a particular group, it leads to special job quotas, scholarships, contracts, and other preferential treatment required by law" (Thorne, 1994). Such a statement is less relevant to the history of gay rights than to White backlash against the civil rights victories of African-Americans and women in the 1960s and 1970s (Delgado & Stefancic, 1994).

This movement from minority status to affirmative action takes place in the plain language of 1994's Proposition One which first asserted that the state shall not "enact or adopt any law, rule, policy, or agreement which has the purpose or effect of granting minority status to persons who engage in homosexual behavior" and continued that "*therefore* affirmative action, quota preferences, and special classifications such as 'sexual orientation' or similar designations shall not be established on the basis of homosexuality" (*ACLU v. EchoHawk*, 1993). The rhetorical progression from equal rights for lesbians and gay men to affirmative action for sexual minorities consists of several different movements. In the first, any governmental prohibition against discrimination on the basis of sexual orientation is renamed as the pursuit of "minority status," equating sexual minorities with racial minorities. The second rhetorical move is the definition of "minority status," not as negative right against private discrimination, but in the sense of affirmative action, a positive entitlement to preferential treatment by the government or private parties.

Because of phrasing which equates civil rights with minority status, and because much of this argument has been shaped through comparisons of African-Americans and gays as disadvantaged groups, public discussion of the anti-gay initiatives has been characterized by what Jane Schacter has labeled a "discourse of equivalents," which focuses on "whether gay men and lesbians are sufficiently 'like' other protected groups, and whether sexual orientation is sufficiently 'like' race, gender, disability, religion, or national origin, to merit the legal protection of civil rights laws" (Schacter, 1994, p. 285). This discourse of equivalents poses multiple questions about the authenticity of a group's claim of minority status involving both the historical and cultural circumstances of the group and the remedial rights which the group might gain. In particular, anti-gay activists generally argue that they are opposed to racial discrimination, but that sexual orientation is different from race because (1) it is behavior and not status, and (2) unlike Blacks, gays have not been, and are not currently, disadvantaged.

To further their depiction of gay rights as "special," the Idaho Citizens Alliance went to great pains to deny that gays and lesbians were analogous to African-Americans or other minorities that had already gained legal protections. In one ICA television advertisement, a conservative African-American minister from Cincinnati declared, "I dare gays to say (the Black struggle) was *their* [emphasis added] civil rights movement," while video of Martin Luther King, Jr. and the 1963 March on Washington was shown (Flagg, 1994x, p. B1). Gay-rights supporters, while rarely comparing themselves with the African-American struggle for civil rights, often compared their opponents with the opponents of that struggle. When civil rights activist Julian Bond spoke in Boise, he made that comparison explicitly: "[t]he opposition is couching its argument in the same language, which is, 'Why should these people have special privileges?' " ("Gay Freedom," 1994). The irony only increased when the ICA's Kelly Walton criticized Bond by also invoking Martin Luther King, with whom Bond had worked: "I think Martin Luther King, if he were still alive, would severely disagree with this gentleman. Civil rights were [fought] around the immutable characteristic of race. Legitimate minorities should be alarmed at the hijacking of the civil rights movement by a behavior-based group" (Flagg, 1994a). Anti-gay activists' focus on differentiating between legitimate and illegitimate minorities demonstrates how civil rights protections are most often identified with minority groups. As a matter of democratic theory, it is presumed that the beliefs and practices of an enfranchised majority are unlikely to face discrimination by private actors or the government (Grossman & Levin, 1995). Historically, the invocation of civil rights has been associated with minority groups.

Hostility towards civil rights protections for lesbians and gay men also reflects the associations between discreet groups' interests in civil rights protections and the larger discussion of "special interests" in American politics, leading to the equation of those interests in civil rights as "special rights" (Schacter, 1994, pp. 300–306). According to Samuel Marcossan, the idea of special rights has two connotations: the first is that a right is special because it is restricted to a single group and is not shared by others, the second is that "civil rights protections are by their nature 'special rights' " and that only certain groups should qualify for such benefits (Marcossan, 1995, p. 140). The notion of special rights is given a different spin by Richard Delgado and Jean Stefancic, who argue that "imposition language" begins when the majority finds a group's demands "excessive, tiresome, or frightening, and includes the characterization of that group as demanding 'special status' " (Delgado & Stefancic, 1994, p. 1026).

Language characterizing gay rights as involving a "minority status" is thus more likely to draws a hostile reaction from the larger public, as demonstrated by an ICA poll which asked "do homosexuals qualify as a legitimate minority classification [*sic*]?" Fifteen percent of respondents responded in the affirmative, 72 percent in the negative, and the remainder undecided. A second question asked whether the respondent "believe[s] that designating homosexuals as a minority classification [*sic*] would result in hiring quotas?" Half of respondents agreed, 29 percent disagreed, while 21 percent were undecided (Woolsey, D., 1993c). The connection between civil rights and affirmative action in the American subconscious might also be seen in the comments of a candidate for the state attorney general's office, who, while announcing his opposition to Proposition One, felt the need to deny that he favored homosexuals qualifying for minority preferences in government contracts, stating that "[t]hat makes no sense to me" (Wickline, 1994).

By asserting that lesbians and gay men were claiming minority status and by distinguishing between legitimate and illegitimate minorities, anti-gay activists could denounce affirmative action and minority preferences for sexual minorities without sounding racist or exclusionary. Their position, they could claim, was to "Stop Special Rights," as stated in the title of the 1994 proposition. Indeed, supporters of Proposition One often used themes familiar from arguments against the modern civil rights movement, in particular in their rhetorical rejection of special rights, and the nightmare scenarios of lesbians and gay men being hired for jobs that are denied to heterosexuals. Moreover, by denying minority status for gay men and lesbians, they could also achieve their goal of defining homosexuality as purely behavioral by rejecting any category that accounted for sexual identity or community. ICA leader Kelly Walton thus depicted gay rights as "a desperate attempt [by gays and lesbians] to distinguish themselves as a separate group, where my view would be to look at all human beings as people" (Arbanas, 1993b).

WHAT TEACHER CAN'T TEACH, WHAT JOHNNY CAN'T READ

From a constitutional standpoint, one of the most fascinating elements of the anti-gay rights initiatives is the manner in which they symbolize citizen distrust of political elites. One of the more detailed initiatives, Proposition One, contained restrictions on state funding, the practices of public libraries, and the curriculum of public schools. While its ultimate aim was to deny civil rights protections to gays and lesbians, Proposition One would also have restricted the professional discretion of legislators and public employees, including teachers and librarians. As a statewide initiative, it would have placed limitations on the powers of all state agencies and instrumentalities, including local school boards, in how they present homosexuality. Proposition One thus reflected a populist distrust of the elites who run schools and libraries, and was motivated by the particular concern that these institutions of cultural transmission might not communicate conservatives' aversion towards homosexuality to children, and that they might teach children to be more tolerant of homosexuality, or might even teach children to become homosexuals themselves. The full range of possibilities was suggested by a minister's wife in one of the ICA's television advertisements: "[i]f homosexuals are granted minority status, they have the right to advertise their lifestyle in my children's school. Think about it" (Flagg, 1994x, October 20).

In Idaho, conflict over educational policy was at the root of the anti-gay rights initiatives. Conservative Christians had objected to education about AIDS, and teachers had been suspended for inviting a lesbian couple to speak with high-school students in a Boise suburb. In the past, the Christian Right has often organized around educational issues, including sex education as well as school prayer and "secular humanism" (Hunter, 1991). Depictions of homosexuality in the schools and the employment of gay or lesbian teachers was the subject of the first statewide anti-gay initiative, the "Briggs Amendment" in California in 1978, which would have empowered school boards to fire teachers and administrators for "soliciting, imposing, encouraging, or promoting homosexual conduct" (Schacter, 1994, p. 288). Other anti-gay initiatives, including Oregon's 1992 Measure 9, have explicitly linked homosexuality with pedophilia. The view that protecting individuals from discrimination on the basis of "sexual orientation" might also protect pedophiles has found legal expression even in states where civil rights laws otherwise provide protection on the basis of sexual orientation.[4]

Proposition One restricted academic freedom and professional discretion by requiring that "[n]o employee, representative, or agent of any public elementary or secondary school . . . promote, sanction, or endorse homosexuality as a healthy, approved or acceptable behavior." Similarly, while children would be denied positive information on homosexuality in classrooms, they would also be denied access to library materials "addressing homosexuality" as such materials would have their use restricted to adults only. The restrictions on library materials were phrased to avoid the specter of censorship, but refocused readers' attention to the segregation of materials "which address homosexuality" away from children. The restrictions on library materials had two elements in common with the restrictions on schools. The first was an emphasis on shielding children that followed from the assumptions that homosexuality is "learned" and that children are particularly susceptible to suggestion. The second was the creation of rules for governmental action closely tied to local community standards; this section of the initiative reflected a populist distrust of elites and the fear that outside values incompatible with local values might be transmitted to their children.

The focus on local oversight of professionals resulted in the requirement that "any discussion of homosexuality within such schools shall be age-appropriate as defined and authorized by the local school board of trustees" and that library material "meets local standards as established through the normal library review process." By emphasizing "local standards," the measure redefines censorship as a matter of popular conscience. One librarian spoke against the measure as "a work of mischief at best, and a totalitarian step at limitation of information at worst," while others noted that the phrase "address homosexuality" encompassed such texts as the Bible and encyclopedias (Flagg, 1994f, June 10). The cost of separating "material addressing homosexuality" into sections restricted to adult access was estimated at $26 million by the Idaho Library Association, which also opposed the measure.

Proposition One's focus on the content of library books and classroom discussions about homosexuality was clearly aimed at controlling the public image of homosexuality and sexual identity. These questions also touched on basic fault lines in the civil liberties of gays and lesbians, pitting their rights of expression in conflict with those processes of education and socialization most valued by conservatives. National surveys have shown that support for the civil liberties of gays and lesbians has increased for the last two decades. The National Opinion Research Center's General Social Survey has asked respondents whether an "admitted homosexual" should be able to teach college, whether that same individual should be able to give a speech in the respondent's community, and whether a pro-gay book by an openly gay author should be removed from the local public library. All three questions have received answers which are increasingly supportive of gay civil rights (see Table A.3).[5]

The greatest difference in public attitudes towards tolerance of homosexuality occurs between the single speech in a public forum and tolerance of a more permanent symbol of homosexuality. Thus, both the presence of gay or lesbian teachers and a library book on homosexuality were less tolerated than the speech incident by a substantial margin. While some of this margin is explicable as the result of concern that institutions of education and socialization, such as schools and libraries, might be "endorsing" or furthering homosexuality, the public function of these institutions and their dependence on public finance may also explain why more Americans believe that the community has a greater right to fire a lesbian or gay teacher or remove a book on homosexuality from the library than forbid a speaker on homosexual themes. The restrictions proposed by the Idaho Citizens Alliance reflected not only anti-gay activists' disapproval of homosexuality but also their sense of alienation from local political institutions and professional elites. Proponents' concerns were well expressed in James Dobson's pastoral letter on behalf of Idaho Family Forum, which asserted that Proposition One "protects the rights of parents to teach their children about homosexuality, factually and morally, and to elect school boards which will reflect and promote the values taught at home" (Dobson, 1994). Reiterating the populist theme that homosexuality is a threat to children, and that school boards and other educational elites must be closely watched, Dobson's idea of rights attaches to the democratic majority who would impose their own values on political institutions.

LAW MORALITY AND PUBLIC CULTURE

In a guest editorial in *The Idaho Statesman*, Boise real estate attorney Barry Peters provided two major arguments for Proposition One's constitutionality, while completely avoiding discussion of court decisions in Colorado and Cincinnati, which had declared similar initiatives unconstitutional. Peters asserted that the initiative constitutionally served the government's interest in promoting health because of studies showing that "the homosexual lifestyle is deadly" and thus "prohibiting governmental employees from advocating a lifestyle which cuts nearly in half the life span of its participants will help to keep people from harm." Peters' second argument focused on the constitutionality of Idaho's criminal sanctions against sodomy, and asserted that gay rights were incompatible with those prohibitions. Arguing that the Supreme Court's decisions have held that "public consensus regarding the immorality of sodomy provided a sufficient rational basis to uphold the [statute's] constitutionality," Peters (1994) equated gay identity with sodomy, and placed himself clearly within a communitarian tradition of enforcing community morality through the power of the state.

In communitarian rhetoric, gay and lesbian identity was equated with homosexual behavior and thus reduced to the illegal act of sodomy. The fear that any public expression of gay identity constituted a governmental endorsement of sodomy was certainly active in Idaho. Over one hundred callers phoned the mayor's office in Boise to protest that city's gay pride parade, most of the calls viewing the parade as simply the promotion of sodomy. One caller told the newspaper, "Homosexuality is something that should be in the bedroom, if that's what they believe in. I don't want my kids to go ahead and learn it from the streets" (Flagg, 1994g). Hoping to use the stereotype of gay promiscuity, ICA Chairman Kelly Walton announced the newest anti-gay initiatives in front of the bathrooms in a Boise park where, he alleged, "homosexual rendezvous have occurred" (Flagg, 1995). The other states in which the voters have considered anti-gay rights initiatives, Oregon and Colorado, both decriminalized private, consensual homosexual activity in 1971 (Hunter, Michaelson, & Stoddard, 1992, pp. 152, 168). In contrast, Idaho law prohibits commission of "the infamous crime against nature, committed with mankind or with any animal," an offence which

accrues to anal or oral sex whether performed by homosexuals or heterosexuals (married or not) (Idaho Code, Title 18, §6605).

The reasoning of anti-gay activists focused on perceived substantive harms
to the community. Anti-gay activists perceived the danger of AIDS, the criminal act of sodomy, and deviancy from dominant norms as threats to the
perpetuation of community's culture. In their Christian Right version of
constitutionalism, the preservation of traditional values was synonymous
with their own understanding of the American character, and thus the Constitution. Homosexuality, because it was incompatible with such values, could
thus be constitutionally restricted. In order to demonstrate public disapproval of homosexuality, they would enlist the state in a campaign to convince youth to avoid the "choice" of a "homosexual lifestyle" without any
requirement of neutrality. Such a position is reasonable if one accepts anti-
gay activists' view of homosexuality as a public health problem, but it becomes more problematic if one views arguments about homosexuality as
political arguments.

On the same page as Peters' editorial, the liberal position on Proposition
One's constitutionality was presented by Jack Van Valkenburgh, director of
the American Civil Liberties Union of Idaho, who argued that the central
question concerned gay and lesbian citizens' right to engage in the political
process. Without mentioning sodomy and avoiding any mention of homosexuality as a sexual practice, Van Valkenburgh relied on the Colorado and
Cincinnati court decisions overturning such initiatives for his evidence.
While Peters described his nightmare version of the moral and medical dan-
gers of homosexual practices, Van Valkenburgh depicted his own worst case
scenario of "[s]cientific study and scholarly discussion . . . cut off," "censorship—in public libraries, public universities, public television—of books,
magazines, research and the arts," and "high school students barred from
keeping up on current events." While Van Valkenburgh's editorial focused
almost entirely upon First Amendment and equal protection problems inherent in the initiative, reflecting his solid position within the liberal tradition, his final contention implied a concern that Idaho was infertile soil for
civil libertarian concerns. Having argued that other courts had struck down
similar initiatives, Van Valkenburgh asked, "Is it worth spending hundreds
of thousands of taxpayer dollars to defend Proposition One in court?" (Van
Valkenburgh, 1994).

Van Valkenburgh's question concerned one of the most interesting elements of the argument over Proposition One—that both sides had different
but equally derogatory attitudes towards the judicial system's capacity to
resolve the questions around Proposition One. Liberals believed that they
knew the result, in which the courts would declare Proposition One to be
unconstitutional, but that the process would cost the state and others too
much money in order to discover what was already known. Estimates of the
cost to defend the measure against a legal challenge ranged from a mini-

mum of $20,000 to $300,000 ("Initiative Foes," 1993). Both sides of the debate over the proposition's constitutionality often accused the other of bad faith. In an attack following the state attorney general's opinion condemning the initiative, Van Valkenburgh declared that "For the ICA to go forward now is a complete waste of money. If they don't drop it, they'll show they're only after one thing—to exploit people's fears about others" (Eckart & Arbanas, 1993, March 19). In response, the ICA declared that the ACLU should be held responsible for the legal costs of a court challenge ("ICA Initiative," 1994).

Where opponents of Proposition One equated the legal process with expense and hassle, anti-gay activists equated the legal process with politics. While legal elites generally opined that the initiative was unconstitutional, anti-gay activists discounted any legal opinion that differed from their own as politically biased, while holding out little hope that the courts would favor their own interpretation. In one instance, the ICA's chairman, Kelly Walton, referred to an attorney general's opinion on the measure's constitutionality as "the opinion of a left wing deputy attorney general exercising his political correctness" (Eckart & Arbanas, 1993, p. A4). On another occasion, Walton declared that the state Supreme Court was filled with democratic appointees, and suggested a campaign to remove the justices from the Court if they declared the initiative to be unconstitutional; his communications director suggested that Coloradans "need to get a new Supreme Court" after that Court invalidated Colorado's Amendment Two ("ICA Initiative," 1994; Richert, 1994). Walton's response to the Colorado Supreme Court's decision insisted that he had expected it "whether it came in the form of a Denver judge, an Idaho judge, or an Idaho attorney general. They're trying every anti-family trick in the book" (Eckart, 1993x). Who "they" were was left unsaid, but the larger discourse about political correctness provided Walton with a language to use in denouncing any decision.

Anti-gay activists were able to assert those who deemed the measure unconstitutional were simply biased because of their capacity to find prominent conservative attorneys who agreed with their position. Thus, in one editorial, Walton cited the authority of "[l]egal giants such as former U.S. Attorney General Edwin Meese and Judge Robert Bork" in affirming Proposition One's constitutionality and acknowledged "invaluable input" from other attorneys affiliated with the Christian Right in formulating the initiative's language (Walton, 1994). James Dobson's public letter on behalf of the Idaho Family Forum reassured readers that "the Initiative Review Committee (consisting of active members of the Idaho State Bar) has submitted [Proposition One] to thorough analysis, and determined that the provisions include in the Initiative are constitutional." In the next sentence, Dobson disclosed that this official sounding committee was "brought together by Idaho Family Forum," its local affiliate (Dobson, 1994).

The battle of the lawyers is only symptomatic of the larger conflict over the constitutionality of such anti-gay initiatives. To this date, Idaho's debate over Proposition One has raised many constitutional questions, and all of those questions remain without any absolute resolution. While the Colorado courts have struck down parts of that state's anti-gay Amendment Two, Idaho's Proposition One went beyond Amendment Two's language, which only prohibited the granting of "special rights" on the basis of homosexuality, to include the restrictions on public services and education. Those questions have been further discussed during the controversy surrounding the Idaho Citizen's Alliance's 1996 initiative. In those discussions, liberals continued to depict the Constitution as a set of procedural values that safeguard the rights of minorities, while communitarians portrayed that same document as a symbol of democratic decision making and the popular will. The two camps are likely to fail to convert any of their adversaries, as those who least value civil rights are most likely to view lesbians and gay men as a threat, while those most likely to value such rights are least likely to view gay men and lesbians as a threat. Ultimately, anti-gay initiatives demonstrate how the Constitution is an ambiguous figure which may serve to symbolize both majority values and minority rights.

NOTES

1. Oregon's 1992 Ballot Measure 9 associated homosexuality with pedophilia, sadism, and masochism, and further labeled homosexual behavior as "abnormal, wrong, unnatural, and perverse." Arizona's proposed initiative of 1994 associated homosexuality with pedophilia, and Washington's Initiative 608 associated homosexuality and bisexuality with transsexuality and transvestism. Both Nevada's proposed initiative and Washington State's proposed Initiative 610, both subtitled "The Minority Status and Child Protection Act," defined homosexuality as "inappropriate sexual behavior" (Adams, 1994, Appendix A–J).

2. Another similar proposition was successfully placed on the ballot in Maine in 1995. The results of that vote are covered in Chapter 10.

3. See, for example, the Supreme Court's treatment of "reverse discrimination" in the famous affirmative action case, *Regents of the University of California v. Bakke*, 438 U.S. 265 (1979).

4. Both Minnesota and Massachusetts include specific provisions distinguishing pedophilia from sexual orientation. Mass. General Laws Annotated, Chapter 151B, §4 (Supp. 1993), and Minnestota Statutes § 363.01 (Supp. 1993).

5. Given here is the exact wording of each question: "And what about a man who admits that he is a homosexual? (A) Suppose this admitted homosexual wanted to make a speech in your community, should he be allowed to speak, or not? (B) Should such a person be allowed to teach in a college or university, or not? (C) If some people in your community suggested that a book he wrote in favor of homosexuality should be taken out of your public library, would you favor removing this book, or not?"

5

The Idaho Anti-Gay Initiative: A Chronology of Events

Suzanne McCorkle and Marshall G. Most

THE 1994 IDAHO ANTI-GAY INITIATIVE CAMPAIGN

Four phases marked by significant events emerged from an analysis of press coverage of the Idaho anti-gay initiative campaign: (1) January 1, 1993, to March 4, 1993—early phase to submission of the initiative for Constitutional review I; (2) March 18, 1993, to November 3, 1993—interim between Constitutional reviews I and II; (3) November 4, 1993, to June 1994—from Constitutional review II to ballot qualification; (4) July 1994 to November 1994—ballot qualification to the election. An understanding of the press coverage and campaign activities within each phase is necessary to fully understand the initiative as a political campaign.

PHASE 1: EARLY TIMES, INITIAL SUBMISSION (JANUARY 1, 1993–MARCH 4, 1993)

Throughout the early months of 1993, the status of gays in the military received regular national and local news coverage on the front page and in smaller inside stories (Brogan, 1993; Cassala, 1993; Thompson, M., 1993). As stars flocked to the ski resort in Sun Valley while boycotting Colorado's slopes because of that state's anti-gay initiative, Idaho tourism officials and resorts worried about consumer backlash from anti-gay legislation in Idaho ("Colorado Darkens," 1993; "Idaho Resorts," 1993; Popkey, 1993a). Fresh from a ballot defeat for anti-gay legislation in Oregon, Lon Mabon, chairman of the Oregon Citizen's Alliance, visited Idaho to open discussions about an Idaho anti-gay ballot initiative. Kelly Walton became head of the Idaho Citizen's Alliance (ICA) and promised "anti-special rights" legislation for Idaho would not be as restrictive as Oregon's Measure 9 (which described homosexuality as perverse). Walton asserted that gays were protected from discrimination under the Constitution and the initiative would merely restrict "special" rights (Eckart, 1993a, 1993b; Popkey, 1993b).

Idaho Citizen's Alliance documents began to circulate. A letter in December established the "Stop Special Rights" Political Action Committee. The fund-raising effort linked the Idaho Education Association with a homosexual agenda in Idaho. The Idaho Citizen's Alliance's Statement of Principles (1993, p. 1) directly copied the U.S. Citizen's Alliance: "We believe that there should not be laws granting civil rights protections based on behavior that is morally wrong or injurious to public health, nor should government legitimize such behavior." The ICA Leadership Manual (n.d., p. 1) dedicated the organization to "defend and promote traditional American values, God, family, and country, against a deadly onslaught of secular humanism, socialism, and moral degeneracy."

In vain attempts to stave off an initiative drive, several individuals and groups stepped forward with arguments against anti-gay legislation. In the context of the Martin Luther King, Jr. Day celebrations, Governor Andrus told Oregon anti-gay advocates to keep their petition drive out of Idaho, saying "No matter how it is packaged, it amounts to the same kind of intolerance and hatred that Idaho has rejected before and will reject again" (Arbanas, 1993a, p. A1). The minister of the First United Methodist Church in Boise, the associate executive presbyter for the Presbyterian Church, and the bishop for the Episcopal Diocese of Idaho announced their opposition to the proposed initiative, comparing the initiative to ethnic cleansing in Bosnia and the holocaust in Germany. Walton replied that the Presbyterian and Episcopal churches were "left-wing liberals" (Eckart, 1993c; Paull, 1993). The Boise City Arts Commission and Idaho Commission on the Arts both adopted resolutions criticizing the proposed initiative and expressing fears that an initiative drive would chill artists' freedom of expression in the state (Flagg, 1993).

Even before the initiative was registered with the state, opponents formed a new group, Idaho for Human Dignity, and named Brian Bergquist as its leader. The association's mandate was to oppose policies that deny civil rights to lesbians, gays, or bisexuals and to decrease discrimination based on sexual orientation. They selected a person-to-person strategy where volunteers would discuss issues with voters rather than use inflammatory persuasive language (Eckart, 1993d, 1993f). Opponents and reporters attempted to clarify the distinction between "civil" rights and "special" rights, explaining that gays were not protected from discrimination in either state or federal law and may be refused housing or fired merely on the basis of their presumed sexual preference. Bergquist claimed gays just wanted civil rights.

Walton argued the invitation of three lesbians to talk to a high-school class in Meridian was an ominous sign of a militant homosexual agenda rising in Idaho (Eckart, 1993e, 1993g).

The Idaho Citizen's Alliance titled their initiative the "Idaho Civil Rights Act" and filed it on March 4, 1993. *The Idaho Statesman* printed the first story linking the ICA to national conservative groups (Eckart, 1993h).

PHASE 2: FIRST CONSTITUTIONAL REVIEW (MARCH 18, 1993–NOVEMBER 3, 1993)

On March 18, 1993, Attorney General Larry EchoHawk released a finding that the anti-gay initiative denied basic constitutional rights to homosexuals and was "fatally flawed" as proposed law. Kelly Walton, chairman of the ICA, replied that the opinion was the result of "left-wing bias" and "political correctness" in the attorney general's office (Eckart, 1993i), setting the stage for arguments about the legality and potential litigation costs to the state if the initiative passed.

Various groups announced opposition to the initiative during this phase, including the Idaho Education Association. Proponents showed a videotape produced by a conservative California group, the *Gay Agenda*, which utilized footage from out-of-state gay-rights marches and celebrations (Woolsey, 1993a, 1993b). The tape would become a primary "education" tool for the pro-initiative side. Information that the video's out-of-state producers were anti-Mormon would become public during the week before the election (see Chapter 7).

In early April 1993, proponents of the initiative submitted a revised version which softened its language, changed its location from the criminal to the government and state affairs section of the Idaho Code, and added a ban on same-sex marriages (Eckart, 1993k). The thirty-three-member steering committee of Idaho Voices for Human Dignity announced they would serve as the umbrella organization in a fight to keep the initiative off the ballot (Eckart, 1993j). On April 21st, Ada County Commissioner Gary Glenn became the first elected official to go on record supporting the initiative and encouraging citizens to sign the petition drive (Eckart, 1993l).

On April 22, the attorney general's office posted the official name of the initiative to be placed on the petitions: "An act establishing state policies regarding homosexuality" (Eckart, 1993n, p. C1). Opponents began to describe those who would sign the petition as extremists (Eckart, 1993m). Proponents began the search for 32,061 signatures to qualify the initiative for the ballot.

In late April, Idahoans watched nearly nonstop CNN coverage of the national gay-rights march, along with its attendant displays and celebrations. The Idaho GOP declined to comment on the proposed initiative at its statewide conference, even though they endorsed the 1990 and 1992 national

GOP platforms' opposition to protected minority status for homosexuals ("GOP Bypasses," 1993).

In May the University of Idaho faculty added to their faculty handbook a ban on discrimination on the basis of sexual orientation, stating such discrimination "to be inconsistent with the kind of atmosphere intended at institutions of higher education" ("U of I Protects," 1993, p. C1). Kelly Walton interpreted the action as adding "sex orientation to [the university's] minority status list." The university statement would be used throughout the campaign as evidence of a movement to extend "special" protections to homosexual Idahoans (Bailey, 1993c; Popkey, 1993c, p. C1). In a high-school leadership class, Governor Cecil Andrus expressed his personal opposition both to teaching alternative lifestyles in the school system and to the initiative, saying, "The gays do not have minority status in Idaho now. Nobody has asked that they do have. . . . They're [the ICA] trying to create an issue out of a nonissue" ("Students Cheer," 1993, p. C3). Idaho Republican party chairman, Randy Smith, also declared that the proposed law was unneeded (Popkey, 1993c).

Newspapers began the inevitable pre-election polls and declared that 40 percent of Boiseans were unaware of the initiative. When asked in May how they would vote if the election were held that day, 17 percent of Boiseans would vote for, 44 percent against, 20 percent unsure, 17 percent didn't know enough to say, and 2 percent refused to answer (Eckart, 1993o). Businesses with a stake in tourism began to voice reservations about the initiative, citing potential boycott losses if Idaho were targeted as Colorado had been after passing anti-gay legislation ("ICA's Anti-gay," 1993). In May, the Idaho State Library Board declared the initiative too close to censorship. Walton replied that the first amendment had to be weighed against protection of children (Threlkeld, 1993a). Lon Mabon, head of Oregon's anti-gay efforts and the U.S. Citizen's Alliance, echoed the protection-of-children argument in a visit to Boise to kick off the signature drive, saying the issue boiled down to whether or not people wanted their children influenced toward homosexuality. Those against the initiative responded that most child molesters were heterosexual men and that pedophiles were rarely homosexual in their adult relationships (Foster, 1993).

May 15th saw 100 people on the statehouse steps in Boise for the ICA signature drive kick-off. Dallas Chase, a member of Idaho for Human Dignity, commented, "Hopefully, the majority of Idaho voters will see that they're preying upon people's primal fears and not addressing the real issues" (Eckart, 1993p). A Nampa homemaker in favor of the initiative said, "I want my children to grow up in a moral society. I don't want them taught anything other than what I teach them." Mabon declared he expected to win the ballot vote with a 65 percent majority (Eckart, 1993q, p. C1, 1993p). On May 27, opponents staged their own statehouse rally to inaugurate a "Don't Sign On" campaign. Among the 100 attending was Attorney General Larry

EchoHawk. Initiative opponents declared a strategy of grassroots discussions in homes and churches and a goal of raising $500,000 (Eckart, 1993r, 1993s).

In June Idahoans observed their fourth annual Freedom Parade as 550 people marched and celebrated in downtown Boise. One rally protester commented, "Hispanics are trying to fight for their civil rights and I don't think it's fair for gays and lesbians to gain recognition instead. They want (rights) for their sexual preferences." The next day, 150 people attended an interfaith candlelight vigil for human rights (Garber, 1993, p. C1; Peterson, 1993).

The state Human Rights Commission announced a unanimous stand against the initiative and the Idaho AFL-CIO voted to oppose the initiative because it would "encourage divisiveness and hatred in the work place and in the community at large" ("AFL-CIO," 1993, p. C3; Woolsey, 1993d). Republican First Congressional candidate, Helen Chenoweth, announced her endorsement of the initiative, saying, "I do not believe that we should have special civil rights for a behavioral practice, because it could be extended on to special civil rights for someone who is overweight or someone who is underweight. With this we are opening a Pandora's box" (Etlinger, 1993, p. C1). A poll in late June reported that 77 percent believed the initiative only would keep homosexuals from acquiring additional rights beyond those of other citizens and that 51 percent of the 598 Idahoans polled would vote for the initiative if the election were held that day ("Poll Shows," 1993).

In June, *The Idaho Statesman* featured initiative supporters and their feelings of being threatened by an increasingly permissive society. Some saw the initiative as a way to protect their children and the blood supply or to stop more militant gays from gaining ground in Idaho. A Boise State University Sociology professor interpreted these fears as leading to the scapegoating of groups perceived to be different (Eckart, 1993t, 1993u).

In August, the Idaho Supreme Court certified the ballot title drafted by the attorney general ("An act establishing state policies regarding homosexuality"). Both proponents and opponents had filed unsuccessfully to have the language slanted to favor their side ("High Court," 1993). North Idaho Voices for Human Dignity began their Don't Sign On campaign by differentiating between opposing discrimination and accepting homosexuality.

Signatures on the petition in North Idaho lagged behind projections but were booming at the Western Idaho State Fair in Boise. Literature at a large, prominently placed booth in the exhibition area chronicled events they claimed were attempts to secure special rights and to promote homosexuality in the schools. Signs at the booth proclaimed: "Protect Our Children," "Sign Here to Stop Homosexual Special Rights," and "Help Stop the Homosexual Agenda in Idaho." Proponents continued to argue in favor of the initiative by suggesting rights of groups were in competition; one signer commented, "I signed because I'm anti-gay. They don't need special rights. We're giving away too much. There are people on the poverty line who need far more than homosexuals" (Eckart, 1993v, p. C2). In a visit to Boise,

Haley Barbour, chairman of the Republican National Committee, called the Idaho initiative unnecessary: "If there are not special preferences, I don't know why you would try to rule out special preferences. . . . The first thing the Republican Party believes in is individual freedom and tolerance. People ought to be able to lead their personal life any way they want to, as long as they're not hurting other people." Walton replied by agreeing that there are no existing laws giving gays special privileges, but there would be if the initiative didn't prevent them (Popkey, 1993d, p. C3).

In September, the ICA announced it was halfway to the 32,061 signatures required to qualify the initiative on the ballot and *The Idaho Statesman* began printing the full text of the proposed law. One person who signed the petition declared, "I believe people should keep their own affairs to themselves. I don't go around bragging about being heterosexual." Another was told by those gathering signatures that hiring quotas for gays would be enacted if the initiative were not passed (Eckart, 1993w, p. C1).

Kelly Walton uttered a statement that would become a pivotal argument for the other side later in the campaign: "If it [court challenges of the initiative] costs a lot of money, so be it" ("Walton Shrugs," 1993, p. C2). About 150 political activists and citizens attended a conference sponsored by Your Family Friends and Neighbors on how to cordially dispel myths about gays and lesbians (Threlkeld, 1993b).

PHASE 3: SECOND CONSTITUTIONAL REVIEW TO QUALIFICATION ON THE BALLOT (NOVEMBER 4, 1993–JUNE 1994)

On November 4, 1993, Attorney General Larry EchoHawk issued an opinion that the proposed law would cost the state a minimum of $200,000 to defend, a defense which he believed would be futile because the revised initiative was unconstitutional. EchoHawk declared all seven sections would never be allowed to go into effect: "This initiative, while purporting to deny special or unusual protection to one group, in fact seeks to deprive this group of the full enjoyment of these essential principles" (Eckart, 1993x, p. C1).

In Oregon local elections, twenty-one communities adopted anti-gay ordinances. The leaders of Idaho's Episcopal Church declared against the initiative (Eckart, 1993y, 1993z).

The end of 1993 saw Walton arguing that the initiative would actually save money, even with the legal appeals, because "fewer people will get AIDS because of the educational effort that accompanies the initiative, so the state will save money by not paying for their treatment" ("Larocco," 1993, p. C2). State Republicans rushed to downplay Ucon Republican Stan Hawkins and Meridian State Representative Al Lance's declarations that they would introduce the anti-gay proposal as legislation (Bailey, 1993a, 1993b, 1993c). Legislators from across the aisle added their own colorful comments. Democrat House Minority Leader Jim Stoicheff commented: "I think most Idahoans aren't sympathetic to special rights for homosexuals, but we don't want to bury them up to their necks, pour honey on their heads and set the ants on them either" (Simpson, 1993, p. C2). A poll indicated only 9 of Idaho's 105 legislators reported favoring the ballot ("Survey," 1993).

The year 1994 began with *The Idaho Statesman*'s hopeful resolution that "Supporters of the Idaho Citizens Alliance's anti-gay initiative and their opponents forget the whole thing and save the rest of us a whole lot of trouble" ("Our View: A Few," 1994, p. A11). Their wish was not granted.

A poll taken in late 1993 by the Boise State University Survey Research Center found 54 percent of respondents against the initiative, 26 percent for, and 20 percent unsure. A poll in February, 1994 found 48 percent would vote against an initiative aimed at preventing homosexuals from being guaranteed rights, 36 percent would vote for, and 16 percent were undecided (Etlinger, 1994; Poll Shows, 1994).

A speech by Ada County Commissioner Gary Glenn became a rallying cry for initiative opponents. Glenn emulated the military metaphors in the ICA Handbook at an Idaho Family Forum banquet, saying, "As long as I have the privilege of holding elected office, I'm going to man a foxhole. If the ACLU and Brian Bergquist are listening, the last time I was tested with an M-16, I shot forty out of forty." Bergquist noted he was not personally threatened by the comment, but chided Glenn for fostering a climate of violence with his language. Glenn replied that it was just a metaphor, yet later sent Bergquist a letter of apology (Eckart, 1994a, p. C1; "Glenn Issues," 1994).

Republican gubernatorial candidate Larry Eastland "clarified" his earlier position that the initiative was unnecessary by declaring that he was for the initiative and would sign a petition ("Governor Hopeful," 1994).

By May, *The Idaho Statesman*'s reporting of the campaign began carrying its own graphic logo. Coverage throughout the summer included detailed legal analyses of the initiative's wording, community reactions, and features about personalities involved in leadership positions in the campaign (Eckart, 1994b, 1994c; Flagg, 1994b, 1994c, 1994e, 1994j). The issues in the initiative were detailed in some stories, including whether or not there was a gay agenda. One front-page story presented five key issues about the so-called the "gay agenda" in a claim-counterclaim format with interpretations of law at the end of each section: (1) The ICA claimed homosexuals support pedophiles because they let the North American Man/Boy Love Association (NAMBLA) march in their parades. An attorney replied that gays were divided on whether NAMBLA should be allowed in parades and that "gay people should not be deprived of civil rights based on who marches in a gay-pride parade, any more than heterosexuals should be deprived of civil rights based on the activities of violent pornographers." A local gay leader replied that NAMBLA had never marched in Idaho, would not be permitted in the future, and diverted attention "from the real issue—that the majority of child sexual abuse occurs among heterosexuals." (2) Proponents contended gays sought to overturn all sodomy laws. Idaho's sodomy law applies to oral and anal intercourse, whether among heterosexuals or homosexuals. Gays agreed that they wished to repeal sodomy laws. (3) Proponents pointed to a national 1993 March on Washington's list of seven demands that included gays as part of multicultural curricula and to lesbian parents speaking at a Meridian high-school parenting class as attempts to gain a foothold in schools and to make homosexuality seem normal. Gays replied that the lesbians were invited to speak about parenting, not gay lifestyle, that homosexuality was an inborn trait, and that denying discussion in the schools ignored the fact that there already were gay youth in the schools. (4) Proponents, citing a 1992 gay magazine called the *Advocate*, argued gays want to undermine man-woman relationships and replace them with homosexuality. If homosexual marriages were allowed, they contended, it would lower the value of heterosexual marriage. Gays replied that domestic partnership legislation was desired because gays generally were not promiscuous and desired stable relationships. (In 1994, no state allowed same-sex marriage, but thirty-five jurisdictions allow domestic partnership agreements.) (5) Granting civil rights protection to gays and lesbians would give them special rights not granted to others. Initiative advocates argued that landlords would have to accept gays as tenants when they did not want to and that adding gays to the list of protections devalued protections for ethnic minorities who had immutable characteristics. Gays argued, whether homosexuality is inborn or not, discrimination in employment or housing was wrong. Gays were seeking equal, not special, treatment. Equal protection legislation would not create hiring or other quotas (Flagg, 1994d, p. A1).

Also in May, the ICA announced endorsement of several Republican candidates; most of the candidates quickly distanced themselves from the endorsement as neither solicited nor desired ("ICA Endorses," 1994). To counter the idea that religious people should automatically support the ICA, clergy from several denominations announced opposition to the ICA. Later in the summer, press coverage would note a schism between fundamentalist and mainline Christian churches on the issue, with fundamentalists focusing on sin and others focusing on human dignity and rights ("Clergy Announce," 1994; Roberts, 1994a).

On June 1 a total of 1,167 people attended the fifth annual Lesbian, Gay, and Bisexual Freedom Day parade. Some of the forty protesters yelled epithets of open hatred and displayed a sign "Only good queer is a dead queer." Parade speaker Brian Bergquist led the crowd in blowing a kiss to the ICA protesters. Over 100 people called to protest the issuing of a gay parade permit (Flagg, 1994g, 1994h, 1994i). The Idaho Library Association announced the results of a study it commissioned which estimated the costs of implementing the library section of the initiative at $14 million for internal review of books, magazines, and microfilm and for the creation of separate areas for "objectionable" materials. Librarians expressed concern over who would decide which materials "addressed homosexuality" and that materials like encyclopedias and the Bible could be restricted. John Slack, ICA communications director, labeled the figure outrageous propaganda (Flagg, 1994f). The ICA would feature the "large costs are propaganda" argument in an advertisement the week before the November election.

On June 29, Don't Sign On preempted the ICA's thunder by announcing that proponents had secured enough signatures to qualify the initiative for the ballot. Kelly Walton walked by thirteen people holding letters that spelled out "It's discrimination" on his way to deliver the signed petitions to the secretary of state's office (Flagg, 1994k, 1994l, 1994m; Prichard, 1994c).

PHASE 4: THE ELECTION CAMPAIGN (JULY 1994–NOVEMBER 1994)

In July of 1994, the campaign for and against the rights of homosexuals in Idaho began in earnest. Don't Sign On began searching for a new name (eventually becoming to the No-On-One Coalition) and new strategies to oppose the initiative ("Don't Sign," 1994). Before stepping down as the campaign leader, ICA founder Kelly Walton declared that if the initiative were voted in and the Idaho Supreme Court declared it unconstitutional, the justices opposing it should be removed ("Kelly Walton," 1994).

Walton was replaced by Bill Proctor as head of the ICA. In August, reporters discovered Proctor served sixteen months in prison during the 1980s for cocaine possession. Proctor said God turned his life around and that people's lives can change (Flagg, 1994o, 1994p, 1994r).

Opinion leaders began to declare for or against the ballot measure. Senator Larry Craig joined the rest of the Idaho congressional delegation in opposition to the initiative ("Crapo Says," 1994; Flagg, 1994n). Barry Goldwater opined that anti-gay initiatives would encourage discrimination against people in the workplace, promote censorship, and comprise government meddling in the private lives of citizens (Bradley, C., 1994).

The religious community began to respond to parishioners' questions about the initiative. The Catholic Church in Idaho declared against the initiative as discriminatory, while noting that legislation to create a protected class based on sexual preference also would be opposed (Eckart, 1994d). Evangelical ministers statewide declared for the ICA; Presbyterians and the Catholic sisters of the Monastery of St. Gertrude at Cottonwood declared against, and ministers from various faiths gathered in local communities to oppose or support the initiative ("66 Evangelical," 1994; "Church Leaders," 1994; Cottonwood, 1994; Flagg, 1994q, 1994s; Roberts, 1994b). The Church of Latter Day Saints took no official stand (counties with substantial Mormon populations later voted heavily against the initiative, see Chapter 10).

Initiative opponents revealed details from an ICA debate manual. Mary Rohlfing, co-chair of Idaho for Human Dignity, compared the manual's rhetoric to Nazi propaganda about the Jews. Brian Bergquist, co-chair of Don't Sign On, commented on the double standards in the manual and the discourse of the ICA: "The danger to Mr. Walton is that out of one side of his mouth, he says he loves gay and lesbian people, and out of the other side of his mouth, he provides his supporters with a manual that is filled with out-and-out lies." The anti-gay guide called opponents "promiscuous sodomite activists." It further declared that contraception was wrong, gays should enjoy getting beat up by homophobes because they were masochists, and that homosexual males were thirty-four times more likely to commit mass murder and ninety times more likely to molest children. The manual claimed gays wanted the closing of all churches that opposed them, the total destruction of the family, and the conversion of young men by forced sodomy ("Anti-gay Manual," 1994, p. C4). In August, Secretary of State Pete Cenarusa refused to include a rebuttal statement by the ICA in the voter pamphlet because of inaccuracies and inflammatory language ("Secretary of State," 1994).

In September, questions were raised on the potential for a boycott of Idaho potato products and tourism. Ballot measure supporters denied there would be any consequence. Initiative opponents claimed Idaho's easy identification with potato products and low population would magnify the effects of possible boycotts. The Sun Valley-Ketchum ski area businesses began a low-key opposition to the initiative. The Idaho Hospitality and Travel Association declared the proposition bad law and bad business (D. Gallagher, 1994; "Travel Group," 1994). Major companies with Idaho-identified national markets quietly began crisis plans in the event of the initiative's passage.

At an anti-initiative rally in September, Governor Andrus spoke bluntly against Proposition One saying, "We reject hatred whenever and wherever it appears, and it appears in this proposition" ("400 Rally," 1994, C1). The No-On-One campaign announced a list of forty statewide leaders who agreed to sit on their advisory board, including businesspersons and elected officials.

Throughout the fall, No-On-One called registered voters to determine their feelings about the initiative: 59 percent were undecided (Flagg, 1994t). To better inform voters, both sides brought national speakers to the state in October. Former ghostwriter for Jerry Falwell and gay human rights activist, Mel White, campaigned against Proposition One. Paul Cameron, accused of nonscientific research and ousted from several professional associations including the American Psychological Association, campaigned for the initiative. Cameron's controversial conclusions that gays die younger, suffer more diseases, ingest feces, and molest children were widely quoted by anti-gay activists throughout the campaign ("Ex-Falwell," 1994; Flagg, 1994v; "Sides Urge," 1994).

Colorado's anti-gay voter initiative was declared unconstitutional by their Supreme Court on October 11, 1994. Idaho ACLU attorneys suggested the Idaho law had similar flaws (Flagg, 1994u). News stories attempted to explain to the general public the difference between affirmative action laws and non-discrimination status (Flagg, 1994w).

As election day neared, both sides unveiled expensive media campaigns. The ICA bought $20,000 worth of statewide air time for eight commercials. No-On-One spent $200,000 for four ads. Kelly Walton (ICA) and Dennis Mansfield (Idaho Family Forum) debated Brian Bergquist (No-On-One) and Mary Rohlfing (Idaho for Human Dignity) on public television (Flagg, 1994x; "Opponents Fire," 1994).

The week before the election, polls showed the ballot measure losing by 10–20 percent margin. Rallies were held to get out the vote. A diverse group of religious and political leaders and private citizens spoke out against the initiative (Flagg, 1994y). The Reverend Jesse Jackson and Coretta Scott King urged voters not to pass initiatives that restricted rights (Sonner, 1994). An ICA advertisement argued it was unfair for gays to have rights when Blacks suffered real discrimination to gain their rights.

In last-minute sparring covered in election day news, ICA leaders claimed election fraud in the instructions given to elderly absentee voters on what a "no" vote on the ballot measure meant. Opposition leaders disavowed knowledge of the practices and replied, "We've not intentionally confused [anyone]. We think the initiative itself achieves that" (Flagg, 1994z).

Election day produced a Republican sweep of the nation and Idaho. The Proposition One vote was so close that two days elapsed before the outcome was certain. The initiative failed by 3,098 votes. About 420,000 Idahoans voted, of that number about 11,700 chose not to vote on Proposition One. ICA chairman, Kelly Walton, declared, "We won the war last night, but we lost the skirmish" (Flagg, 1994aa).

6

Fear and Loathing on the Editorial Page: An Analysis of Idaho's Anti-Gay Initiative

Suzanne McCorkle and Marshall G. Most

INTRODUCTION

On November 8, 1994, a voter initiative in Idaho to prohibit the state from establishing civil rights for homosexuals and to specify restrictions on libraries was defeated by 3,098 votes. The 420,000 Idahoans who voted on the anti-gay initiative split 50 percent to 50 percent, with another 11,700 voters skipping the question (Flagg, 1994aa).

A broad coalition of civic and religious organizations opposed the measure. The initiative was supported by a group modeled after Oregon's Citizen's Alliance, which sponsored a more restrictive anti-gay initiative during that state's 1992 election. The campaign for and against Idaho's initiative was protracted heated, and expensive.

While all aspects of initiative campaigns are worthy of scrutiny, this study[1] focuses its attention on one aspect of an election which is difficult to isolate—the reasoning behind an individual citizen's views on the issues. While most citizens formed opinions as they listened to public debates, examined leaflets, and viewed advertisements, other citizens shared their reasoning within running debates inside the editorial pages of the states' newspapers. The letters to the editor section of virtually every newspaper in the state was filled with opinions and testimonials related to the initiative. This study will examine the arguments and logical reasoning, or lack thereof, in letters to the editor in Idaho's largest newspaper concerning the 1992 anti-gay initiative.

REVIEW OF LITERATURE

Letters to the Editor as Argumentation

Existing research has examined newspaper coverage of the gay community (Bernt & Greenwald, 1992); however, it mainly addressed news—portions of the paper written by journalists. Research has not addressed the opinion/editorial pages, wherein lie debates from the general public. Likewise, studies of argumentation, values, and reasoning within print and electronic media focused on news and other noneditorial coverage (Al-Enad, 1991; Chaisson, 1991; Corrigan, 1990; Pritchard & Berkowitz, 1991; Riffe, Aust, & Lacy, 1993; Weiss, 1992). Those studies targeting the content of editorial opinion offered only thematic analyses of letters to the editor or examined argumentation used in journalists' editorials, not letters from readers (Boeyink, 1992/93; Lambkin & Morneau, 1988; Morello, 1991).

Several scholars have debated the representativeness of opinions expressed in letters to the editor. Two studies refuted the common notion that letters were not representative because writers were atypical or editors selectively chose the letters to be printed. Both studies concluded letters can be a valid measure of public opinion when the issue is perceived as highly salient, large numbers of citizens contribute letters, and several outlets were surveyed (Hill, 1981; Sigelman & Walkosz, 1992).

No studies have been found that analyzed letters to the editor beyond thematic levels or have been conducted on public argument within the gay-rights issue.

Anti-Gay Initiative Argumentation

Scholarship analyzing gay and anti-gay discourse can be grouped into two clusters: (1) rational argument and other perspectives that conducted microscopic analyses of arguments within the context of political campaigns, and (2) rhetorical perspectives that focused on persuasion or values argumentation related to entire campaigns.

Several studies utilizing a rational discourse perspective examined persuasive video- and audiotapes produced by the religious right. M. J. Miller (1994) applied a Burkeian pentadic analysis of anti-gay audiotapes. Netzhammer (1994) identified the normative, linguistic construction within the tapes. Taylor (1994) identified cinematic codes of homosexuality. Slagle (1995) examined the rhetorical differences among the gay liberation and queer nation movements. Sanger (1994) compared the arguments and rhetorical strategies in two anti-gay videotapes. Sanger's analysis is particularly useful as it revealed one type of anti-gay argumentation. He found *The Gay Agenda* to be an unambiguously explicit and inflammatory videotape appealing to the fears of those who already were convinced that homosexuality was disgusting and immoral. A later videotape, *Gay Rights, Special Rights*, was similar in content but carried a patina of rational argument. The video functioned both to incite citizen fears and to provide voters who did not wish to view themselves as homophobic the illusion of a reasoned argument for anti-gay feelings. Viewers were able to picture themselves as saviors of "true" (Black) minority's rights.

Several scholars studied the 1992 Oregon anti-gay-rights campaigns. Palmer (1993) matched the Oregon Citizen's Alliance language with Edwin Black's definition of paranoid rhetoric—seeing the world as replete with secrets and deep, sinister meanings. Palmer analyzed how the Oregon Citizen's Alliance (OCA) utilized argument by definition in the campaign, defining homosexuality in different ways for different audiences. Mayhead (1993) examined the use of causal argumentation in the OCA campaign rhetoric. She concluded that the OCA advanced several undocumented and faulty causal arguments. In response to the faulty causal arguments, opponents offered alternate causality arguments; for example, homosexuals were born and, therefore, could not be recruited. Initiative opponents also offered their own potentially faulty arguments: censorship will occur, loss of civil rights will occur, the initiative will negatively impact the workforce. In a study based on Toulmin's theory that different fields of reference require different types of evidence and argument structure, Bowker (1993) identified the Oregon YES campaign as grounded within a field relying upon traditional authority (the Christian Bible) and as projecting the opposition into a field dominated by grotesque and repulsive behaviors. Bowker concluded that the fields of Christian-Right rhetoric remain the same regardless of the issue.

Douglass (1993) analyzed the Oregon 1992 campaign and concluded that rational argument was advanced by the No On Nine group, while proposition advocates utilized a narrative strategy relying on value structures within narratives. Fielding (1993) examined the military's value argumentation against homosexuals in the United States Army case *Ben-Shalom v. Marsh*.

Finally and most relevant to this study, Tarbox (1995) explicated how the wording of a ballot initiative, specifically the 1992 Measure 9 in Oregon, determined the shape of public debate concerning the issue. Tarbox discussed the tension between the slogans, hoopla, and personally persuasive measures used to secure signatures on petitions—the center of public discourse—and the official wording on the initiative which could become law.

RESEARCH QUESTIONS, GOALS, AND OBJECTIVES

This investigation of a seldom-studied site of public argumentation—the letters to the editor section of newspapers—was undertaken to reveal how individuals engage controversial issues, how they utilize reasoning and evidence, and how they construct arguments. The study focused upon the most open public forum in print media. Hence, the first goal of the study was to reveal general typologies and methods of public argumentation and, consequently, to further knowledge in the field of argumentation concerning citizen argument on controversial issues. The second goal was to uncover topic-specific methods of public argumentation on the issue of the anti-gay rights initiative in Idaho.

To examine the public's view of the 1994 Idaho anti-gay initiative, we ask: How did the general public advance arguments for and against the anti-gay initiative in letters to the editor in Idaho's largest newspaper? The research was further advanced through several subquestions: (1) What issues were identified in arguing for or against the initiative? Did the issues in letters to the editor vary across time, and by siding or by gender of the author? (2) What evidence was offered in support of arguments for or against the initiative? Did the evidence in letters vary by issue, across time, by siding, or by gender of the author? (3) Which letters contained reasoning fallacies? Did the fallacies in letters vary across issue, time, by siding, or by gender of the author?

Based on previous rhetorical analyses of the Oregon Citizen's Alliance presented in the review of literature, we advanced several predictions about trends in public argument on the Idaho anti-gay initiative as represented in letters to the editor: (1) Persons for the initiative will identify different issues than those against the initiative. (2) Persons for the initiative will use different types of evidence than those against the initiative. (3) Persons for the initiative will commit more fallacies than those against the initiative.

Before beginning the study of the letters to the editor, we reviewed the context in which the letters were written. News articles, commentary, and other data from January 1993 to election day of 1994 were analyzed to determine critical time periods within the campaign. Four time frames were determined: (1) January 1, 1993, to March 4, 1993—early phase to submission of the initiative for Constitutional review I; (2) March 18, 1993 to November 3, 1993—interim between Constitutional reviews I and II; (3) November 4, 1993 to June 1994—from Constitutional review II to ballot qualification; (4) July 1994 to November 1994—ballot qualification to the election. The chronology, appearing in Chapter 5 in this volume, served as the basis for the determination of expected issues and themes within letters to the editor.

METHOD AND PROCEDURES

Based on the past research and on the trends discerned from the analysis of the chronology, a coding instrument was developed and tested for intercoder reliability.[2] Each letter was coded against the following categories:

theme, evidence, citation, fallacy, initiative siding, homosexuality siding, and various demographic items (see Table A.4).

Theme was an emergent variable. Each editorial was read to determine if one or more themes were present. Each editorial could contain from zero to five themes. Initial thematic categories were determined from the analysis of newspaper coverage of the campaign. Using the procedures established by McCorkle and Mills (1992), subsequent categories were added when the "other" category showed a substantial loading of a repeated theme. The themes included gays in the military, homosexuality as genetic or socially derived, the gay political agenda, gays as pedophiles and unhealthy, morality of homosexuality, legality or constitutionality of the initiative, economic effects of the initiative, general arguments about nondiscrimination, general arguments in favor of discrimination, refutation of past letters, place of religion in the initiative debate, and other (see Table A.4 for additional details concerning each of the categories in the coding instrument).

Evidence was a preset variable. Editorials were coded for the presence of zero to six items of evidence. Evidence categories included personal testimony, quotation from the Bible, reference to the Bible, quotation from other text sources, quotation of other people, reference to past letters to the editor, examples, statistics, comparison, general Bible paraphrase, and other.

Citation was a preset variable. Editorials were coded for the presence of zero to six occurrences of citation. Citation categories included Bible chapter and verse, print sources, research reports, specific persons, paraphrase of unknown medium, broadcast sources, and other.

Fallacy was a preset variable. Each editorial was coded for the presence or absence of from zero to eight fallacies. Fallacies were operationally defined based on Toulmin, Rieke, and Janik's (1984) theoretical framework. Toulmin's fallacies were supplemented with other categories discussed in Kahane (1992) and Freeley (1993), then converted into twenty-six discrete fallacy categories: begging the question; red herring; straw-person; appeal to authority; argument against the person; argument from ignorance; appeal to ignorance; appeal to the people; appeal to compassion; appeal to force and/or threats; hasty generalization; fallacy of accident; false cause; slippery slope; false analogy; poisoning the well; equivocation; pseudoquestions; appeal to tradition; false dilemma; irrelevant reason/non sequitur; fallacies involving statistics; no fallacies are found in this letter because no argument was attempted; emotional slanting; argument attempted but incomplete or insufficient by virtue of missing grounds, unsubstantiated grounds, or missing warrant; and argument present without fallacies.

Siding was a preset variable with two dimensions. Each letter was coded as (1) pro-initiative, anti-initiative, or can't tell/did not mention the initiative; and (2) pro-homosexual, anti-homosexuals, tolerant of homosexuality, or no determinable position on homosexuality.

In addition to the thematic coding, each editorial was coded for the demographic variables that were determinable from the newspaper: gender of author, city of writer, and date of publication. Date of publication was utilized to determine the campaign phase. Additional demographic information was obtained from information self-disclosed within letters (see Table A.4).

RESULTS

Six hundred and forty-five letters from *The Idaho Statesman* were published during the collection period which, at first reading, seemed relevant to the initiative or general issues related to homosexuality. A quasirandom sample, indexed to include a significant portion of letters within each month during the collection period, of 521 letters was coded. After discarding letters which were not relevant (they had no discernible side on the initiative *and* no discernible side toward homosexuality *and* no theme), 422 editorials remained to comprise the database for this study.

Sixty-nine percent of letters carried a Boise address, 25 percent were addressed from Southwest Idaho, and the remainder were authored by writers from other parts of the state. Ninety-seven percent of letters appeared on the editorial page; 3 percent were published in the religious section. Most authors of letters were male (57 percent), 33 percent were female; 2 percent were authored jointly by males and females, and 8 percent of names had indeterminable sex identification.

Fifty-six percent of letters either made no mention of the initiative or were neutral, 16 percent overtly stated support and 28 percent overtly stated opposition to the anti-gay initiative. Twenty percent of letters either stated no position on homosexuality or were neutral toward homosexuality, 34 percent were negative, 17.5 percent were favorable, and 28 percent were tolerant of homosexuality. Letters negative toward homosexuality stayed relatively stable in numbers across phases; letters tolerant or favorable toward homosexuality increased from phases one to three and decreased slightly in the last phase.

Self-identification (beyond the name and city of residence which were required by *The Idaho Statesman*) in letters was rare—occurring in only forty-seven of 422 letters. The most frequent self-identifications were as Christians (n = 11) or gay, lesbian, bisexual, or homosexual (n = 15).

Letters in the sample were proportionately drawn from the phases of the initiative campaign: 23 percent phase 1 (January 1, 1993–March 4, 1993), 23 percent phase 2 (March 18, 1993–November 3, 1993), 30 percent phase 3 (November 4, 1993–June 1994), and 25 percent phase 4 (July–November 1994).

Most letters evidenced one (47 percent) or two (41 percent) themes. The most frequently appearing themes were general arguments about nondiscrimination (34 percent), refutation of past letters (21 percent), whether there was a gay political agenda or plot to gain special rights status (18 percent), whether gays were pedophiles, practiced unhealthy sex, had an unhealthy lifestyle, or recruited others into their lifestyle (16 percent), whether passage of the initiative would have negative economic, social, or political effects (15 percent), whether homosexuality was evil or sinful (15 percent), whether homosexuality was genetic or a social/personal choice (10 percent), and themes generally favoring discrimination (10 percent). All other themes occurred in less than 10 percent of the letters.

The theme most frequently occurring first in the letters were general nondiscrimination (20 percent), refutation of past letters (14 percent), and whether there was a gay agenda (12 percent). Themes occurring in the second position in letters were general nondiscrimination (24 percent), whether gays were pedophiles (13 percent), refutation of past letters (11 percent), negative economic effects (11 percent), and whether homosexuality was a sinful state (11 percent). The forty-six letters containing themes in the third position were overwhelmingly dominated by negative economic effects (22 percent).

Fifteen percent of letters made no attempt to offer evidence in support of their claims. Of those offering evidence, the most frequent types of evidence offered were general references to non-Bible facts or sources (26 percent), examples (26 percent), comparison (22 percent), citation of previous letters (18 percent), direct quotation of non-Bible sources (14 percent), and personal testimony (13 percent). All other evidence categories were utilized by fewer than 10 percent of the letters coded.

Among the letters which contained evidence (n = 358), the first evidence used most frequently was general reference to a non-Bible source (20 percent), reference to previous letters (19 percent), example (19 percent), and comparison (13 percent). The second type of evidence (n = 196) offered within a letter most often was comparison (21 percent), example (20 percent), general reference to a non-Bible source (19 percent), and direct quotation (13 percent). When three pieces of evidence were offered in a letter (n = 73), the third place was dominated by general reference to non-Bible sources and example (25 percent each), comparison (18 percent), and direct quotation (11 percent). The twenty-four cases where four pieces of evidence were offered were dominated by the use of example (33 percent). Only three letters used five instances of evidence; no letter offered six usages of evidence.

Most letters (60 percent) did not cite any sources of their facts; among those who did cite, the most frequent sources were printed materials such as books (21 percent of all letters using citation), paraphrases of unknown sources (11 percent), and specific people (7 percent).

Virtually all (95.5 percent) letters contained at least one logical fallacy. The most frequently occurring argumentation errors committed in letters were the fallacies of incomplete argument (60 percent). For example, letters claimed but did not offer elaboration upon statements such as "The differences between the two are too obvious to recount"; or "This community does not want 'equal rights.' They want minority status, giving them 'special rights' and are depending on your publication to help them attain them."

The second most frequently occurring fallacy was pseudoquestion(s) (31 percent) which included unanswerable, loaded, or falsely premised questions or the asking of so many questions that they could not possibly be answered within the space allocated. For example, letters asked the following: "Why the media bias?"; or "My question is this Why not? just give up your cellular, Dennis [Mansfield]? I mean, after all, you do make your regular phone bill checks out to U.S. West, do you not? If you are really serious in making a point, you should cease altogether with phones in your home and office, right?"

The third most frequently occurring fallacy was emotional slanting (28 percent), which included loaded language and buzz words such as "We will not be sucked in by this whirlpool of fear if we stop to realize that the people being targeted and dehumanized are really our family, friends, co-workers and neighbors, contributing members to society and our culture"; and "Idaho's Christians must have the courage to say 'no' to the seductive call of political power games and to choose dialogue persuasion and example."

The top three fallacies were followed in order of occurrence by straw person (20 percent), poisoning the well (15 percent), false analogy (13 percent), hasty generalization (10 percent), and appeal to authority to stop argumentation (10 percent). All other categories of fallacies occurred in fewer than 10 percent of the letters. The top three fallacies dominated regardless of the order in which the fallacy appeared in letters, excepting letters that contained six fallacies (n = 32), where technical insufficiency (22 percent) was followed by straw person, false dilemma, and pseudoquestions (each with 13 percent). Most letters contained from one to three fallacies.

An inverse relationship was found between siding on the initiative and siding on homosexuality (n = 422, p ≤ .000).[3] Not surprisingly, those who were negative toward homosexuality were for the initiative and those who were favorable or tolerant toward homosexuality were against the initiative.

A significant difference was found between siding on the initiative and the phase of the campaign (p ≤ .000). The number of letters that were neutral on the initiative or indeterminable steadily decreased from eighty to twenty-five from phase 1 to 4, while letters which were sided for or against the initiative steadily increased from twelve to seventy-six from phase 1 to 4 (see Table A.5).

While the "political agenda/special rights" theme did not change in usage according to the writer's views toward homosexuality, other themes were used more or less depending on one's siding on homosexuality. Those who were negative toward homosexuality used the themes of pedophilia, sinful morality, and prodiscrimination more than those who were favorable or tolerant toward homosexuality. Those who were favorable or tolerant of homosexuality selected the themes of negative consequences of the initiative, nondiscrimination, and refutation of past letters more than those who were negative toward homosexuality. Those who were neutral or had indeterminable positions toward homosexuality more often opted for the themes focusing on the legality of the initiative or negative economic effects than those who were either favorable or opposed to homosexuality (see Table A.6). The remaining theme categories either had small overall usage or little separation in usage by attitude toward homosexuality.

Likewise, several argument themes were used differently depending upon the writer's opposition or support of the initiative. The military theme was presented only by those who were neutral or did not reveal a position on the initiative. Because the group that did not overtly declare a side on the initiative dominated the editorial pages, few significant results are determinable on siding and theme usage. However, those against the initiative dominated the legality theme, negative economic or social effects, and general nondiscrimination. Those favoring the initiative used the political agenda/special rights theme, pedophilia theme, sinful moral state theme, and general prodiscrimination theme.

Only three themes varied in their usage throughout the campaign phases; other themes were selected by writers relatively consistently across the campaign phases. Letters regarding gays in the military only occurred in phases one and two. While not statistically significant, the theme of whether homosexuality was genetic or a choice decreased in frequency from phase 1 to 4 and the themes of legality and economic consequences of the initiative increased from phase 1 to 4 (see Table A.7).

The use of evidence in letters to the editor did not differ in a statistically significant way when comparing the writer's position as negative, favorable, or neutral toward homosexuality. However, those letters that were favorable or tolerant toward homosexuality were slightly more likely to cite previous letters, to use comparison, to use personal testimony, to use statistics, and to directly cite non-Bible sources than were letters negative toward homosexuality.

Those whose position on the initiative was neutral or not determinable used the majority of all types of evidence, compared to those both for and against the initiative, including 70 percent of Bible paraphrases and 78 percent of general Bible references.

Evidence usage remained relatively stable throughout the phases of the initiative campaign. However, usage of comparison steadily decreased through the phases and direct quotation of non-Bible sources increased during the last two phases.

Usage of fallacies generally did not vary in a statistically significant way according to the writer's views of homosexuality or siding on the initiative. Fallacies that appeared in letters more than twenty times were examined further for patterns of usage. In particular, notice was given to fallacies where one opinion group committed 50 percent or more of the total times a fallacy was utilized. For example, writers against the initiative used 55 percent of the twenty-two total cases of appeal to the people fallacy. Those tolerant or favorable toward homosexuals used over 50 percent of the thirty-two total occurrences of red herring, argument against the person (59 percent, n = 32), appeal to compassion (63 percent, n = 27), hasty generalization (50 percent, n = 42), and emotional slanting (55 percent, n = 118). Those opposed to homosexuality used appeal to authority (54 percent, n = 41) and poisoning the well (51 percent, n = 65).[4]

Those against the initiative were more likely to use the fallacy of incomplete argument (p ≤ .006, n = 255). While not significant, those favorable or tolerant toward homosexuality used incomplete arguments more than those who were opposed to or had indeterminate positions on homosexuality.

As reported earlier, males were more likely to write letters than females. When mixed-sex group-written letters and letters from persons with indeterminable gendered names were deleted, 381 letters remained. Males were more likely to write letters with a political agenda/special rights theme (p ≤ .030); females were more likely to write letters with themes concerning negative economic or social effects of the initiative (p ≤ .001). Females were more likely than males to use personal testimony evidence (p ≤ .009).

No significant differences existed between males and females in usage of citations, siding on the initiative or siding on homosexuality. Females were more likely to utilize the fallacy of appeal to compassion than males (p ≤ .004)

The first public discourse trend predicted by past literature (persons for the initiative will identify different issues than those against the initiative) was supported. Trend two (persons for the initiative will use different types of evidence than those against the initiative) was not supported, as the data in this study did not provide a clear trend in usage of evidence. While the overall difference on siding and fallacy usage was not significant, those against the initiative committed a greater proportion of fallacies in one category (appeal to the people). Therefore, trend three (persons for the initiative will commit more fallacies than those against the initiative) was not supported and some evidence suggested the opposite.

DISCUSSION

The results reveal several interesting characteristics of letters to the editor. First, a majority of letters related to the initiative presented arguments without revealing the writer's position for or against the initiative. This may indicate writers believed their presentation would be more persuasive from a neutral or obscured standpoint or perhaps thought their side on the initiative was so obvious as to not require an overt statement.

The percentage of writers who overtly declared support (16 percent) or opposition (28 percent) to the initiative did not match the electoral outcome of 50 percent supporting and 50 percent opposing. The 12 percent difference between opposing and supportive letter viewpoints cannot be attributed to any particular cause. Past research has argued the representativeness of letter to the editor writers (Hill, 1981; Sigelman & Walkosz, 1992), even though only 9 percent of repondents in one national study report writing a letter to the editor (Milbraith & Goal, 1977).

Possible explanations must speculate about the characteristics of letter writers and of the populations who tend to oppose and support anti-gay initiatives. For example, a post-election Idaho Public Policy Survey (1995) indicated those with the highest education levels opposed the initiative; those with college education voted for it; and those with elementary education did not vote, leading to speculation that higher education may correlate with one's degree of articulation on the letter to the editor page. There are no data in this case, however, which permit correlating education and predisposition to write letters to the editor. Other explanations could include selection bias by the editorial staff or greater success by one side in motivating their supporters to write letters.

Attitude toward homosexuality may have been more central in letter authorship than siding on the initiative, as 34 percent of letters contained a discernible negative attitude and 45.5 percent contained a discernible favorable or tolerant attitude toward homosexuality. Those tolerant and intolerant toward homosexuality also do not match general public attitude as measured by the Idaho Public Policy Survey (1995), which found 27.7 percent of Idahoans strongly negative in their attitudes toward homosexuals and their lifestyle, 24.8 percent negative, 27.4 percent unsure, 17.8 percent positive, and 2.3 percent strongly positive. No reason for the disproportion in siding toward homosexuals can be determined; similar speculations to those presented for siding on the initiative merit exploration.

The dominant themes within letters concerning the Idaho anti-gay initiative may indicate where the general public anchored their opinions. Considering that more writers held tolerant opinions toward homosexuals, it is not surprising that letters arguing that "discrimination was bad" appeared most frequently and as the first theme presented within letters. The dominance of this theme is interesting in light of the No-On-One's discounting of discrimination and equality issues in favor of big government and economic issues—a deliberate move made after polling indicated publicity of information on discrimination actually had a reverse effect of solidifying opinion in favor of anti-gay legislation and that more pragmatic arguments concerning money and government intrusion would have greater success (Faber, 1996).

The themes favored by the No-On-One campaign—big government in-trusion and negative economic effects of passage—had a minimal overall presence in letters to the editor compared to other themes (excepting where these themes may have been included in letters categorized as refuting pre-vious letters). Legality appeared in only 6 percent of letters and economic effects in 15 percent. The decrease of genetic and choice arguments and the increase of legality arguments from phase 1 to 4 may indicate the shift of focus desired by the No-On-One campaign did occur. Economic effects did appear in the second, third, or subsequent positions within letters—indicat-ing a presence of the themes desired by the No-On-One campaign, but certainly not a dominance of the public discourse. If the No-On-One cam-paign had strong message control, meaning their official spokespeople kept to the plan and did not advance other arguments, then many of the letters in this study were written by individual citizens who were not officially af-filiated with the political campaign against the initiative.

The compartmentalization of the military issue (related to national poli-cies and news concerning the legality and desirability of gays in the military) to phases 1 and 2 indicated it played little or no role in public argument late in the campaign, and consequently may have had little impact on undecided voters.

The types of evidence selected in letters were those that carry less logical potency and validity. Those who declared a position on the initiative were less likely to use evidence than those who were neutral or had no discernible position. This may indicate those with fixed positions felt able to advance their "truth" without additional or outside support, an opinion congruent with Buell's (1975) findings that letter writers were more polarized on ide-ological issues than the general population. However, the 150-word limit enforced by *The Idaho Statesman* may also contribute to low usage of evidence and citation of sources.

Opinion toward the initiative or homosexuality was not significantly dif-ferent by gender, which is inexplicable when compared to the Idaho Public Policy Survey's (1995) finding that more males than females voted for the initiative.

The relative uniform application of fallacious argument regardless of po-sition on the initiative or views of homosexuality belies certain stereotypes of anti-gay advocates as an emotional, ignorant mass and of initiative op-ponents as an educated and reasonable elite. All perspectives abused the rules of rational discourse.

Because letter to the editor studies have not been conducted in other anti-gay initiative campaigns, we are unable to determine if the Idaho No-On-One group's decision to abandon the more technical and logically based discrimination and legal arguments in favor of more emotional arguments about big government and potential economic harms had an impact on the level of rational discourse in the campaign. Other studies (see Chapter 3 in this volume) would argue the less rational campaigns will be more success-ful—an argument that seems validated by the Idaho election results.

The results that virtually all letters contained at least one fallacy may be an effect of a dismal competence or valuing of logical argumentation, the value-centrality of some of the issues within arguments concerning homo-sexuality, or of word-limitation editorial policies. Since the most common error was incomplete argument rather than gross errors, that is, support, warrants, or other vital argument components simply were missing, the pres-ence of fallacies may indicate that editorial policies of word limits encourage or necessitate nonrational argumentation. Space limitation has been identi-fied in a survey of editors as the biggest problem associated with letters to the editor (Hynds, 1992). If the word limit is found in future studies to correlate to fallacy production, then the editorial pages with word limits may do more harm than service to enlightened public policy decision making.

CONCLUSION

Contrary to impressions in other rhetorical studies that anti-gay initiative advocates are emotional and base their opinions on folk wisdom and that opponents are rational and base their opinions on science, virtually all letter writers advanced fallacious, poorly evidenced arguments which lacked source citations. All perspectives abused the rules of logic.

If voters look to the letters to the editor page for reasoned discourse, they will be sadly disappointed. Contrary to popular opinion, all sides were de-ficient in their ability to forward reasoned arguments. The uniform presence of fallacies is not surprising, considering that while North American culture has valued of the appearance of logic and reasoning, schools and other in-stitutions do not systematically teach rationally based argument and decision making.

To the extent that the editorial page represents the themes that anchor public opinion, the editorial page may be a test of the range of emotional arguments and fallacious reasoning that are used by advocates in homes and other private arenas of talk about policy issues. If the editorial page is looked to for reasons to vote for or against value initiatives, then readers will cer-tainly be misinformed and misled. If word limitations on the editorial pages contribute to the general malaise of reasoned argument, they may be a det-riment to reasoned decision making.

NOTES

1. The research presented in this chapter was supported in part through a Boise State University Faculty Research Grant.

2. Holsti's (1969) conventions and coefficient of reliability equation were utilized. A minimal threshold of acceptability of 80 percent agreement was obtained. To sus-

tain the reliability of the study, the decision was made to use two coders on all letters, any discrepancies among coders were resolved by discussion.

3. All probability values reported in the study report Chi square values.

4. A secondary analysis was conducted after removing those whose attitudes were neutral or not determinable of fallacy compared to attitude toward homosexuality and fallacy compared to attitude toward the initiative. No statistically significant results were achieved during the secondary analysis.

7

In Their Own Words: Conversations with Campaign Leaders

Harvey Pitman

INTRODUCTION

Too often, our insights into the motives and strategies that drive political campaigns are deduced from the sound bites reported on television news or brief quotations in the traditional press. Through personal interviews, we gain a glimpse of the inner thoughts of leaders on both sides of a campaign. The most effective form of interviewing requires a willingness on the part of the interviewee to respond candidly to questions presented by the interviewer. Such is the pattern for what appears in this section.

The thoughts that follow arise from interviews with Kelly Walton, founder of the Idaho Citizen's Alliance, which supported the anti-gay initiative, and Brian Bergquist, leader of the Don't Sign On/No-On-One coalition, which opposed the initiative. Although interviews were edited to delete redundancy, their substantive content was not altered.

THE VIEW BEFORE THE ELECTIONS

Kelly Walton, October 12, 1994

Question: *What lead to the formation of the Idaho Citizen's Alliance (ICA) in the State of Idaho?*

Kelly Walton: When I moved back to Idaho in 1990, I had just experienced four years of political activity where I had gone to college in Oregon in the Portland area. I had become very involved in a grassroots organization over there, so I developed some skills in it [political work]. Frankly, when I moved to Idaho I really had no intention of duplicating the effort that I'd made over in Oregon. Maybe I was naive . . . but as I read the news, watched TV, talked with different people around the state it became very apparent to me that even though Idaho is much more conservative, the momentum, the direction the state is going [is] generally to the left. The state is becoming more and more liberal on that spectrum, and so that concerned me, and I wanted to start an organization that would confront the liberal movement at every phase. One of the most important issues in the right versus left debate is the issue of public condoning homosexuality, and I could see it coming in many, many other states and in Idaho as well. So I decided to make this the first issue that the ICA would address.

About the middle of 1992, I started getting lobbied by family and friends to consider doing [a campaign] again in Idaho, and it took me six months to make the decision, winter 1992/1993. And then on January 13, 1993, I had a press conference there at the Capitol in Boise and announced the formation of ICA.

Question: *Had it not been the anti-gay kind of movement, what other movement might you have picked up to demonstrate to the state that it's moving to the left—to the liberal side?*

Kelly Walton: Other issues that really concern me are education. We have the most powerful force in education today—the teacher's union. On a national level it's really advocating far left positions on all the issues. . . . The political power is still in the hands of the union, and they absolutely control the Democratic party, and for that reason, I think education would be very high on the list. . . . We're looking at that for the next election.

Question: *What was the primary goal of the initiative as you proposed it?*

Kelly Walton: Primary goal is to prevent homosexuals from attaining special legal privileges. Goal number two was to prevent the behavior being taught as normal and healthy to our kids in primary and secondary education.

Question: *Within that premise then, you feel that homosexuality as a style of life can be taught?*

Kelly Walton: Oh, yes. I really do. I'm not denying that a significant number of homosexuals have a genetic tie as well, but many, many homosexuals are recruited at a very young age, low teens, very, very typical. Yes, it's something that is mostly taught and caught.

Question: *Since you have formed the organization, from a global view how has it changed in size, composition, number of volunteers, purpose, or whatever?*

Kelly Walton: Well, ICA started from zero in January 1993. We got a mailing list of nearly 70,000, . . . primarily most of those people were signers. We've got about 61,000 signers. We turned in 57,000 and about 4,000 came in after the deadline. . . . We've got a list of volunteers and/or donors of about 6,000 people. . . . We have county directors who are active in just a little over half of the forty-four counties. I have three regional coordinators out of the four positions that are available. I do not have a regional [coordinator] at this point up in the Panhandle, but the other three areas of the state are represented by regional coordinators. I have an in-state executive director, Bill Proctor, who handles much of the day-to-day delegating and work at the Boise office and a state communications director, John Slack, and so we're starting to fill out our state executive board as well. I would say our network we have planned is no more than 10 percent complete. We're a very young organization, but we've really made good steps to get where we want to be in five to ten years.

Question: *As you look now at the campaign since you began it back there in the early 1990s, have you felt there are stages or "benchmarks" in your organization?*

Kelly Walton: The big high point was actually qualifying for the ballot on July 8. Six weeks out of July 8, we didn't know whether we would make it or not, but our volunteers came through. We had a total of 1,100 circulators averaging fifty names each to qualify and that was a real highpoint. You've got to realize, Harvey, the amount of political pressure that was being leveraged against us. Every editorial in the state, from the perspective of the newspaper ownership, was just browbeating us. Our opponents had the Don't Sign On. Nowhere in the history of the state of Idaho has so much effort gone into the prevention of a ballot measure getting on a ballot. The left of Idaho literally threw a tantrum over our purpose to get on this ballot, and so it was a major milestone to get over the top. I think one of the other real highlights I've had is the middle of May when we took our statewide tour of about ten days. I literally spoke [at] four meetings a day: breakfast, lunch, and evenings, sandwiching in interviews and everything else. To travel the entire state and actually meet many of my volunteers for the first time face to face—that was a real highpoint. [I] never had to stay in a hotel once, and they were wonderful folks, and we had a great time getting to know people and getting the petition sheets passed out and working for like-minded candidates like Helen Chenoweth and Larry Eastland for the primary.

Question: *What methods have you used to get your message to the public of the state of Idaho?*

Kelly Walton: Overall the media's reporting has been fairly objective, and I've been real pleased. When I read a reporter's work, my question at the end of the article is "Now do I have a hint as to how this person is going to vote?" If I don't, they did a good job. They covered both sides, they gave both sides' quotes that were accurate on information relayed, and I give the Idaho media a B+—it's been very good. The press conference has been used as a tool quite a bit, [though] not nearly as much as our opponents, primarily, because we've spent so much time actually making the news, making it valid rather than trying to create a spin or an angle, but the press conference has been a valuable tool. Direct mail is becoming more and more of a tool, . . . our list has increased threefold since May. . . . Just getting out, shaking hands face to face, and having some of our local coordinators host meetings that I and other leaders can come in and give has been a very valuable tool as well.

Question: *Have you had any efforts in getting the message to the public that have failed or that you have felt were least successful?*

Kelly Walton: One of the aspects of this whole debate that really caught me blind-side was the absolute power of political correctness on those people who tend to favor what we're doing. When we tried to host a rally we've been disappointed a few times on the number of people showing up. But as I analyze the situation, what I'm coming to is that people are afraid of confrontation. . . . There's no doubt how they're going to vote once they get in that booth, but they're a little hesitant to put a bumper sticker on their car. They're a little hesitant to tell a pollster how they're going to vote.

Question: *How successful has your group been in getting financial support?*

Kelly Walton: One of the things when you compare our effort to the other side's efforts, it's like the Alamo for the other side. . . . They feel their literal livelihood is at stake over this and for that reason they have been able to raise, I believe, $280,000 this year from forty-one different states around the nation. Our fund-raising efforts have been entirely in-state. . . . I find when I ask I receive. The more work I put into fund-raising, the more money we raise. Frankly, we have not spent the kind of energies the other side has, and it's shown in the contribution and expense reports to the secretary of state.

Question: *As you look now toward the next few weeks, which are critical for any public social issue campaign, what is the greatest need that your organization has between now and the day we all cast our ballots?*

Kelly Walton: Well, I think funding will continue to be a major part of the equation. We have reserved a lot of TV and radio, and we are on track to making those commitments financially. I think the volunteers are going to be very, very important in terms of getting their family and friends out to vote. So those are probably the two . . . funding and volunteer motivation. They're very important.

Question: *Would there be anything else that you would care to add in the way of an overall perspective of the total campaign at this point?*

Kelly Walton: I really feel that what we've done here is to give Idaho the opportunity to create a statewide community standard on this issue. We are not trying to persecute or pick on anybody. What we're trying to do is create an equal-level playing field. Everybody ought to be protected on the basis of their constitutional rights, not some special legal privilege that's granted when a group attains a minority-type status.

One thing I would like to say before the election is, if we happen to lose, and I am predicting a real horse race, this is not going to be a runaway. If we happen to lose, the other side can count on the same effort on the next election cycle. We are in this for the long term, and one temporary setback will not deter us. We will stay after it until we get it for the kids!

Brian Bergquist, September 12, 1994

Question: *From your perspective what led to the formation of the Don't Sign On or No-On-One group?*

Brian Bergquist: Don't Sign On or No-On-One, actually the earliest integration of it was Idaho Voices for Human Rights. It was really motivated more as a response to Lon Mabon and the Oregon Citizen's Alliance coming to Idaho and intending to set up shop here. They first came, I guess I would say, somewhat foolishly, to incorporate the week before the Martin Luther King celebration in 1992, which then provided a forum for the governor and the attorney general and a number of people to denounce what they saw as their long-term intentions. . . . I think the governor and attorney general speaking out early helped to empower people and [to help them realize] that it was in their best interest to get involved. Initially, it formed as The Voices for Human Rights, a group that probably had a much longer term agenda wanting to try to build some kind of a broader progressive movement in the state. . . . The filing of the initiative obviously was the specific motivator for formation of the Don't Sign On campaign, and its goal initially, obviously was to get people to not sign on to initiative petitions.

Question: *What would be the primary or subgoals for having the group?*

Brian Bergquist: I think those goals evolved over time so I'd start maybe at the Voices for Human Rights level. Initially I think the goal was to network progressive groups to get dialog going around the state to help pull people together and build some kind of statewide human rights framework that . . . would apply to other issues in the future, whether it's racism or economic oppression or whatever the human rights issue happened to be. . . . [The campaign message] evolved into a narrower focus with the Don't Sign On, partly due to the realities of the campaign disclosure laws and the needing to track all that money separately. . . . The complexities of that kind of jelled it into a more narrow focus to continue to educate people about human rights issues and discrimination and that type of thing. . . . And then No-On-One is even more tightly focused which is . . . getting people to vote no on Proposition One, and I think that our goals have shifted somewhat because the research we've done has shown that there's an amazing well of ignorance in Idaho. Something like 50 percent of the people believe that gay and lesbian people are currently covered under civil rights laws which, we think, is where the strength of the special rights argument comes from. If people think you are already covered under existing laws, you want something more, . . . what you want must be something beyond what they have.

Question: *Do you see a parallel to the ERA of a few years ago where so many of the Idahoans felt that women were equally protected under law?*

Brian Bergquist: Very much so. I think that we have this "divine reverence" for the Constitution as a document, and sometimes we forget that this is the same Constitution that allowed us to own other people and didn't allow women the vote, that it is not necessarily a perfect document, or it's a perfect document in that it allows itself to be corrected. Sometimes I think people may get so caught up in reverence for the document that they forget that the intent really is to include everyone.

Question: *Speak about the change in the organization, its size, maybe its composition, the types of people who are involved in it early and now.*

Brian Bergquist: Early on I would say that the primary folks involved were from two principal communities, one was from the gay and lesbian community in Boise and the other, I would say, was from the women's community; the people who had seen some more things done around abortion kinds of issues and saw the parallels there. . . . I think they saw some common ground there. Initially it was, I would guess, under a hundred people total of which maybe ten or twelve were active . . . there was tremendous skepticism that [the initiative] would ever get on the ballot. A lot of people perceived that the Citizens Alliance made some foolish public statements and that the great wise people of Idaho would rise up and reject them. . . . It was a challenge, because I think intellectually we all knew that they were going to get on the ballot, but the emotional reality is sometimes a little different. As Don't Sign On moved closer toward their signature deadline in early July, I think the numbers had grown. When they turned the signatures in, we probably had a core of 75–100 people who were pretty active, who wanted to go out to fairs and hand out literature . . . or talk to people who were thinking about signing petitions or do the same at the River Festival; it's a very diverse group; . . . it's everything from Democrats and Republicans. There are a lot more religious people involved; religious leaders who have spoken out, religious leaders who think it's important and have sermonized on it and against the initiative and have urged people to get involved—people who are willing to come down to just answer phones and do volunteer work . . . two months before the end of the Don't Sign On campaign we brought a professional fund raiser on board. And now as we're speaking on September 12 there are ten full-time people working for the No-On-One coalition—paid positions. I would guess we have an active volunteer list of about 400 people; we have offices in Coeur d'Alene and Pocatello as well as Boise.

Question: *Have there been other groups that have joined the movement Don't Sign On or No-On-One?*

Brian Bergquist: The Democratic party pretty much statewide both as a party and individual candidates have come out and a number of them have been involved. The person who is the chairperson for the Ada County Democrats, Les Bock, is the treasurer for the organization. There have been a number of business groups, Sun Valley/Ketchum Chamber of Commerce, there's a group in Boise that's more of a small group of presidents of corporations that have gotten together, and they're not sure what to do because it's such a new issue here that it's tough for businesses to get involved. . . . A lot of religious groups, the Catholics have come on board, the Methodist Church, the Episcopal Church, a number of groups like that, the Ada County Human Rights Task Force. The [Idaho Education Association] IEA has been involved but [they just allow] us to use their basement to make phone calls some times. They have a very large facility that they don't use at night, so we've done some phone banking there and that type of thing. Their support has been more in talking with their membership than about doing anything in a broader political sense. I wish they were as involved as the Citizens Alliance seems to think they are. The Idaho Women's Network has been has been real involved. . . . A group of artists kind of came together and helped us do a benefit this spring ["Lawn D'Art"] that raised about $16,000 which a lot of people saw as positive in a couple of ways. Good local artists rarely get a chance to have the exposure . . . it was real positive for them, but it also brought a lot of different people together and showed them the event in a different kind of way. And I think that our research has shown that the message . . . is probably a much more broad inclusive kind of thing, and my guess is that you'll be seeing more and more people feeling comfortable with where we are and jumping on.

Question: *Are there benchmarks? Are there periods that have been chalked up as very successful? Have there been other periods where you felt setbacks, lack of success, so far?*

Brian Bergquist: I guess our largest concerns so far have been just in fund-raising kinds of things. From what we've seen and what we've done, we're pretty pleased with what we have done with free media so far or earned media as our campaign manager calls it. . . . The feedback that we have gotten from some national groups . . . is that they think what were doing with earned media has been real effective and that we've been able to get the message out and work effectively with people.

Question: *And by earned media you are saying?*

Brian Bergquist: Press conferences, press releases, public events, anything that we don't have to pay to put on television but can get the message out there . . . there is still the aura of the new here so that almost anything anyone does . . . the media is willing to cover. We've often [felt] that if we could change our socks we could probably get a press conference out of it at this point.

Question: *Would you say then that the lack of skill in fund-raising has been your greatest obstacle?*

Brian Bergquist: I think so.

Question: *What have you found at this point to be your best form of media to get the message out. . . . For example, has TV been more effective—less effective, newspaper, flyer?*

Brian Bergquist: I think most of the flyers, brochures that kind of stuff is great if you're speaking in small groups to people doing one-on-one kinds of things. One of our fund raising mechanisms, which also has an education piece to it, is a house party. We basically find people in communities around the state who are willing to host a party. They invite 120 of their friends of which forty will show up, if they go through all the steps we outline for them. And then someone from the campaign comes and explains where the campaign is . . . that's the time when we hand out a lot of literature, so I guess when you're preaching to the converted, if you will, the literature, the handouts, and that kind of thing is effective in reinforcing the messages that are delivered that way. I think that the televised media has been generally pretty positive although we've had to work more there less hierarchally. There is less structure and control in television news, so it's tougher to make sure that people don't fall into the initiative to prevent "special rights for homosexuals" kind of description of the initiative and try to get them to work more toward a message which we think is either neutral or helps. . . . A lot of time the anchors write their own copy, and, depending what their mood is for the day, [that] is how they frame the issue. . . . We had some challenges with that with some of the print media, but we found you can go to them, explain what your concerns are, and a lot of times they'll try more to balance. . . . And the other positive thing with the print media here is that it really is a vehicle that gets out statewide. If there is an in-depth story in the *Statesman*, a lot of times it will be picked up by the Associate Press and go statewide.

One of our real challenges is that we haven't had huge sums of money, so we held off doing our polling as long as we could. . . . Our research showed us that when we were talking about discrimination, we were losing people . . . that we really needed to be talking about big government, and a government solution to people's personal lives and things that really relate more to the broad spectrum of the folks in Idaho. So a lot of our early free media was focused more around . . . discrimination and job discrimination and those kinds of things. A lot of the editorial boards have picked that up and have been beating that drum for us and now we're trying to change the song a little for them.

Question: *I'm hearing you say that one of your needs is to shift your message. As you look forward to the coming election, not so very far away, what . . . is your greatest need?*

Brian Bergquist: Cash!! From the best knowledge that we have the Citizen's Alliance is planning on running a ten-to-twelve-day media campaign right before the election, and we think our research has shown that a huge percent (something like 30–35 percent) of the electorate is confused about what voting yes means or what voting no means about what the initiative does. . . . Mediawise, early on, I think the first nine or ten months was mostly responsive; and starting probably this spring, we have started to be more proactive and going out and creating our own story that they can respond to as opposed to standing on the sidelines and waiting. I'm sure the next eight weeks will be a horse race of things. . . . We just got some interesting news this morning that Lieutenant Governor Otter has some properties and interests in Colorado, and they had a real nightmare with boycotts and things in Colorado. . . . He's very concerned about that issue. Our research shows that would move a lot of voters, but a lot of them don't think it would happen here so if we could get someone like a Butch Otter to get up there and say, "Shoot, I was in Colorado and I know what this is about and this is bad for us," that would be good and evidently he is interested in helping. And that's the thing that's been remarkable for me is the number of people who want to help, want to get involved from the entire ideological spectrum. It's not your normal progressive bunch of people that sit around the coffeehouse kind of thing; it's a real diverse group of people that helps a lot.

ELECTION EVE

Brian Bergquist, November 7, 1994*

Question: *Since we talked last, what landmark event have you experienced in the campaign?*

Brian Bergquist: Since then . . . I've been in Lewiston, Moscow, Coeur d'Alene, Idaho Falls, Blackfoot, Pocatello, Twin Falls, and Burley, in addition to Boise. Then we held a number of town meetings around the state and talked with people there, . . . to reporters and editorial boards and kind of made those connections with the press all around the state. . . . Our television commercials have been shot and tested in focus groups and narrowed down to the final three that we used and those have been running. . . . We've done some internal tracking polls on our own. We did one two weeks ago . . . showed us being ahead 44–34, . . . and there have been two other polls that have been done, one by Greg Smith, an independent pollster that showed us up by fifty-two to twenty-eight, and one that was done by a political media research at Washington, DC, which actually was the largest sample with 800 voters, that showed us up fifty-eight to thirty. The numbers, I'm sure, will change, but minimally we think that the trend line is moving in the direction it needed to move. Folks are seeing the commercials and are starting to understand Proposition One [the popular name given the ICA initiative].

*The ICA, citing their busy schedules, declined an interview during the week prior to the election.

Question: *What setbacks have you had in media relationships or coverage?*

Brian Bergquist: Our biggest setback in media has been one that is kinda beyond our control. . . . We had a lot lower level of television saturation than we'd really wanted. So we complemented that with buying some cable around the state and also doing additional radio in Boise and up north to kind of offset some of things there. Most of our earned media coverage has been pretty positive, and we don't really have any major concerns. . . . Jerry Evans, superintendent of Public Instruction, opposes Proposition One, and we've been playing phone tag for two weeks. . . . We would like to have [had] him come out against the proposition, because we know he does oppose it, but it really isn't commonly known. We figure he is respected as an apolitical figure. We did a press conference and a rally on Saturday where we had five or six hundred people at the rally which was very positive. We structured the content of the rally based on what our polling had shown us earlier in the week that the large numbers of undecided voters for this county are Republican women and senior citizens, so we had the Republican sheriff speak, Republican representative Jesse Berain, and a seventy-one-year-old grandmother, [a] Republican from Caldwell who came in from her church bazaar to do the speaking to kind of put that "faith and feel" on things . . . in words and language that they can understand.

Question: *What is the mood of your campaign and campaign staff here one day prior to election?*

Brian Bergquist: People are tired and there have been a lot of people who have been sick. I think when people are working ten- to twelve- to fourteen-hour days and six and seven days a week, after a while their resistance is low and when you're working in close contact with other people, it is inevitable. People are optimistic in a cautious kind of way. . . . I think we're feeling like, at least, we should be able to get 50 percent plus one at this point. I know that last Friday when the poll results came out that showed us that far ahead, that was really the first time that I was able to admit to myself that we might win. The early polling we did showed us so far behind the best face we could put on when we polled back in June or July was 45 percent yes and 37 percent no. . . . I'm guessing [the vote is] going to be more like fifty-six to forty-four—somewhere in that range.

Question: *How would you describe the people who fully support your campaign?*

Brian Bergquist: There are a lot of people that oppose the proposition and wouldn't necessarily support the campaign, if that makes sense. There are people who are voting no for various reasons. I think a lot of them are concerned. . . . I think they are caring people generally. Most of them are pretty hopeful people. I think that they view human nature in a pretty positive way. I think most of them are very accepting people, they take people at face value. . . . We call it the No-On-One coalition because about the only thing people could agree on was to vote no on [Proposition] One and how they got to that point is very different. There's a mom who . . . volunteers every day for three or four hours and comes and does things. She'll wash cups, vacuum the floors, and just do whatever needs to be done. There are college professors who will come in and phone bank at night . . . lawyers who volunteer their time—I mean it's a very broad section of people. That's one of the things that is pretty encouraging about it. And I would guess that it's probably two-thirds to three-fourth non-gay, one-third to one-fourth gay and lesbian. It's very broad-based support. I would say most of the people involved probably knew someone who was gay or lesbian or at least [those] actively working on the campaign knew someone who was gay or lesbian before they got involved. But as far as the folks voting no, they're a lot of them that don't really care for gay or lesbian people but just don't like the proposition more. Our real mission has been to create the safe ground that people can stand on . . . that they don't have to like . . . or dislike homosexuals. They can stand there and judge the proposition on its own merits, and that's been the real challenge: to create that safe space for people.

POST-ELECTION REFLECTIONS

Brian Bergquist, November 22, 1994

Question: *Name one or two prime reasons for the outcome of the election?*
Brian Bergquist: I guess if anything I would say that it was the planning and execution on the No-On-One side where early on we kind of laid out what we were going to do: television advertising, . . . calling people to persuade them, . . . going to do literature drops on their doors, . . . going to organize get-out-the-vote activities . . . my off-the-cuff glance at the Citizen's Alliance would be that they didn't do a lot of the long-term planning; and when they got past the signature gathering, it was kind of like, "Oh my gosh, we have to do a campaign now." They had to scramble to pull that together. They weren't quite as prepared to actually run a political campaign as they were to go out and gather signatures and do that.
Question: *What do you feel were the strengths of campaign?*
Brian Bergquist: We did do a pretty good job with the earned media both in the events that we had, the rallies, where the Saturday before the election we had five rallies around the state. . . . That played very strongly in local markets around the state, but also there was a piece we managed to work to get into the earned media that broke in Twin Falls the Friday before the election about the connection between the *Gay Rights/Special Rights* video that the Citizens Alliance used and a lot of anti-Mormon videos. That played real big in Eastern Idaho, and I think helped to perhaps open the eyes of some of the folks over there as to . . . where the Citizens Alliance ultimately [was] coming from. I think that those were all strong points.

The weakest point I guess in retrospect is that we should have had some stronger management internally. There were a lot of people who were okay.

We right now have a $50,000 debt that we are working to alleviate after-
wards. I guess since we won by 3,000 votes, I don't know where I would
have cut any of that, but it would have been better to have a handle on some
things a little more tightly going into it.... In talking with our national
media consultants, they said that we had some of the strongest message
discipline that they've seen of any campaign that they've worked with...
everything we did was moving people toward the message that we thought
needed to be moved.... I guess reading *The Idaho Statesman* this morning
where they say that Idaho is the state that has the smallest [number of]
democratic candidates of any state in the country in their legislature. The
analogy I used with people was if the tide was coming in, be happy, you're
still standing on the shore and look at all those out there swimming.

Question: *Your opponents. What were the strengths of their campaign statewide?*

Brian Bergquist: Probably their organizing in the evangelical community
in their work with the Christian Coalition and the focus on the family [and
the] Idaho Family Forum people to organize to get out the vote.

Question: *Did you feel that they had any advantage over you emotionally?*

Brian Bergquist: I guess the one piece that they had going for them was
the initial wording of some of things.... If you control that, you do pull
some of those emotional strings and fears. It's a lot tougher to sell truth that
people may not want to hear than it is to sell falsehoods that reinforce
people's biases and fears out there. That's a natural strength of whether it's
the Citizens Alliance or any group that is doing this kind of initiative where
there is so much misinformation you can use as a vehicle to achieve your
goal ... old wives tales kind of stuff out there that really doesn't relate to
reality.

Question: *Do you see, in their campaign, any weaknesses?*

Brian Bergquist: I was in Washington, DC this last weekend, and some
people were talking about how the biggest thing we have to fear [is] that
their side [may] actually get their act together and run a real campaign. So
many of their campaigns are so egocentrical driven that they don't profes-
sionalize them. The commercials they did, I didn't think were terribly persuasive. They didn't seem to have a common thread that tied them together
that would resonate with people. They weren't able to raise money effectively which impacted the television commercials and their inability to get
them out there. I don't know that they chose necessarily the best spokespeople for the organization. They tended to have people either who visually
were a little overpowering. I'm thinking of John Slack, who is six feet, four
inches, and [weighs] 280 and has a full beard ... or they chose people whose
backgrounds ... brought their credibility into question. So I think ... that
hurt them in some of the things they did in the free media ... people were
looking at the messenger rather than the message.

Question: *In hindsight, what one or two events during the campaign would you like to redo?*

Brian Bergquist: The television debate . . . we thought we had agreement on a format [but] when we went into it and got all set, we found out the format had been changed, and it was changed to a format heavily [favoring basic] questions pitched to Kelly Walton and Dennis Mansfield [head of the Idaho Family Forum], and they kind of got to respond in their [own] rhetoric, and then we were left to respond to their response. . . . Internally, better communication—we were kind of on three different computer platforms, so it was tough to share information sometimes. . . . Communication with the field offices was always a challenge, which is probably true of any campaign. . . . I guess the only other one would be an event that didn't happen that would have been nice to have had happen [had we not] started working on it too late. . . . The superintendent of public instruction, Jerry Evans, opposed the proposition but had never really been asked to come out and say anything or do anything. I think in a quiet way he is an opinion leader with people, and it would be kind of surprising to people that he would even have an opinion on this . . . and it was ten days out, and we tried to start working something with him. There wasn't enough time to work around his schedule, and I think that would have been a nice piece to have out there.

Question: *If you were going to get a call from me today from another state and we've had a Proposition One sent forth and we were going to be directing a campaign, what would be your advice?*

Brian Bergquist: When I was in Washington, [DC], people were truly stunned that we were able to win in Idaho. People have no concept of how it's even possible here (which may be more misperceptions about Idaho than anything else), but anyhow you need to have a [planning] board early on [with] some training in what it is to run a political campaign. They don't have to have a lot of previous political experience, but they need to understand the common goal of winning. If you're working heavily in the gay and lesbian community, some people there think it's about educating people, some people think it's about a whole variety of topics, politics is really about whether you win or lose. You need to get a board that can connect to that. Early on you need to hire someone who has political fund-raising experience, because political fund-raising is a very different animal than charitable fund-raising, which is where most people have experience. . . . And then make sure that you have fully analyzed the processes involved in putting the initiative on the ballot, who decides what language goes where, . . . what the appeal processes are, . . . how you can influence that. And I guess in going back if there were one thing I would change it would be to try to have had more persuasive impact. We didn't have any with the attorney general's office on the wording of the ballot title, that itself would have been something we [felt] should have . . . been amended.

Question: *What should happen next or will happen next?*

Brian Bergquist: "Will" is probably easier than "should." One of the challenges for the No-On-One coalition is that we really did bring together a very broad coalition of people whose sole point of agreement in a lot of cases was voting no on Proposition One, and how they got there is very varied and doesn't necessarily lend itself to a long-term coalition. . . . My guess is that we'll see something in the legislature this session that will deal with the "promoting of homosexuality in schools" piece of the proposition. Our goal is to hire a lobbyist, get in there, and try to . . . influence legislation in such a way that [it] was the least offensive possible and see if it could be modified so that there was no discussion of sexual orientation at all, . . . because my perception is that a lot of people hung their support for Proposition One on the schools issue—"I personally don't dislike homosexuals, but I just don't want them teaching *it* to my kids." And if that piece, the kid's piece, is no longer there, that may be a pretty critical pillar to pull out from underneath them and may make it a lot tougher for them to go back. And then if the schools piece passed, it may give them a face-saving device to say, "Golly, this is what we wanted all along, so we truly are victorious and we don't need to do this anymore and we can go on and search for a different witch to burn."

Kelly Walton, November 23, 1994

Question: *Name one or two of the prime reasons for the outcome of the election?*
Kelly Walton: The way I'm looking at it, I entered this effort from a part-time basis. I run a general contracting business over here and the last couple months . . . we ran it from a part-time basis, and our opponents took it so seriously that they actually hired out-of-state people full time to come in and to fight it. They outspent us about ten-to-one in the media, and for us to come up fifty-fifty with them in the vote clearly shows where the mainstream voters are. We just have to try it again, and this time I will be attempting to drop my responsibilities elsewhere and devote full attention to it; I'm very optimistic we can come out a winner next time.

We just had a few part-time volunteers taking on the entire homosexual political machine of the nation. The other side received contributions from over forty-one different states. It's very clear they have a network in place and that they're very good at raising money. We don't have to match the kind of money they are capable of raising and that's probably not possible. But all we have to do is work a little harder and get our message out. One of the other main factors besides my inability to go full time was the confusion factor. There were so many people [who] called our office after the vote and literally, many of them in tears, saying [they] voted the wrong way. [They] thought a no vote meant [they] were voting against the homosexual agenda. And so many people now realize what a no vote and a yes vote means and that was a major factor and much of the blame lays right at my feet. I was just not able to get the message out clearly enough, but I'm also placing a lot of blame at the attorney general's office. I think they purposefully wrote a very confusing ballot title. The actual wording of the initiative was not on the ballot. It was the attorney general's summary or ballot title and that played a major role in mass confusion around the state.

Question: *What do you feel were the strengths of your campaign?*

Kelly Walton: The basic strength is that inherently we represent the mainstream Idaho vote. Our polling numbers early on showed us at about the mid-sixties for support, and the other side was able to spend all their money on basically half-truths and lies throughout their campaign, and they were able to whittle it down to a fifty-fifty result. So our strength was we know the mainstream voter is with us, and we just have to work harder to battle the opposition's vast amounts of money and resources. Another strength is that we were able to focus on the main issues. The other side had to resort to ruses and red herrings; and so if truth is patient, we'll always win. It may just have to be a four-year project instead of a two.

We did very, very well in the areas that we primarily focused on and that was Southwest Idaho. I felt from the very beginning that was where the real battle would be and that if we could win that area we would win the state. Well, it was a false assumption, because out East there was so many confused voters, the issue literally did not get debated very much in Eastern Idaho.

Question: *What do you feel were the strengths of your opponents?*

Kelly Walton: Their basic strength lies in the fact that they treated this issue like it was their Alamo. They really felt that if they lose this that somehow homosexuals are going to get run out on a rail in Idaho. It's simply not true. We were just trying to maintain an equal-level playing field, but it's very, very clear now that we struck a cord. They kept saying "We don't want special rights," then why did they fight it so hard? It's very clear they do want [the] special rights we're talking about and they pulled out the stops. Many of their top supporters either quit or got leaves of absence from their jobs and I commend them for it. They paid the price, and they pulled out a squeaker of a win. Now they cannot feel very comfortable with only getting 50.37 percent of the vote after all the time and money they spent. And also, one of the main results is we were able to rob left-wing candidates of precious campaign money that was devoted to this initiative, and the election night results of the candidates clearly shows that to be true.

Question: *What is your perspective of their weaknesses?*

Kelly Walton: Their major weakness is they know they cannot focus on the main issue of the campaign which is, "Should Idaho be celebrating homosexuality?" They know if they focus on that issue with me in the debate they lose, because the mainstream voter is obviously against the celebration of homosexuality. None of us is saying homosexuality cannot be here. Whatever [people do] in the privacy of their own home[s] is their business, but we're opposed to them promoting that behavior to our kids and schools and for them to get minority rights like Blacks and Hispanics. So that's their main weakness—they can't focus on the main issue and as long as that's true, truth will eventually win out. One of their other main weaknesses is they're only well organized in the traditionally urban areas, and once we are able to spend the time to develop our organization throughout rural Idaho, not just in spotty areas, we will win overwhelmingly. Boise, Pocatello, and Moscow will not carry Idaho in the long term.

Question: *What role did money play in this outcome?*

Kelly Walton: It was major. If I could have had another $5,000 in radio spots, it would have gone the other way. They haven't turned in their final contributions report to the secretary of state, but I'm estimating it will be close to $700,000 as compared to—we'll be just under $200,000. It's real clear that money was a major, major factor. We're going to use that also to our advantage next time, because we'll be able to go through there and pick out the number and quantity of contributions that were out-of-state, and once the Idaho voters realize they have been duped by out-of-state homosexual money, they'll vote differently next time.

Question: *What one or two events in your campaign would you like to redo, to change or to modify?*

Kelly Walton: Probably the last minute, weekend hit against us on the film [*The Gay Agenda*] that some of our volunteers were using with regard to Jeremiah films who also produces, apparently, videos on the Mormon Church and other issues. That video, I did not realize that particular firm produced that stuff. I never watched the movie *Godmakers*, apparently a movie that's very derogatory towards Mormons, and Brian Bergquist mentioned that was extremely insensitive of us. I would agree with him had I really known the connection; but the media, especially in Southeast Idaho, did a very good hatchet job of connecting the two, and I feel that hurt a lot of the Mormons in the Southeast, so I'm going to agree with Brian that, yes, that was insensitive and that we will not be using that video in the future because it's very clear when someone looks at our organization many of our county directors do happen to be LDS (Latter Day Saints) and that would be the last thing this organization would try to do . . . something politically against that church. It's just ludicrous, but I do feel that had enough effect to swing the difference, and I apologize to any Mormon supporters if that seems insensitive, and we will not be using that film in the future.

Question: *If I were to call you from another state to seek advice from you how to run a similar campaign, what would be your advice to me?*

Kelly Walton: Secure early finances so the top leadership can go full time and work like you've never worked before, and the average state, especially out here in the West, will win this issue. It appears right now that all four U.S. Citizens Alliance affiliates in the West will be doing this again for '96. Nevada, Idaho, Washington, and Oregon. There are other states where people are inquiring about doing it, so it's a very valid question on your part, very timely.

Question: *Final question. What do you feel now either should or will happen next?*

Kelly Walton: Number one. I feel very good about the effort we put in. . . . I sleep very well at night knowing I gave it my best shot, and I also sleep very well at night knowing that our resources and our network and our number of volunteers are steadily growing, and we're much stronger for 1996 and we'll be doing it again. We're sending out a letter to all of our supporters very soon . . . outlining where we want to go and if they come on board with us we'll be doing it again.

8

Secular Anti-Gay Advocacy in the Springfield, Missouri, Bias Crime Ordinance Debate

Ralph R. Smith

A pattern of secular argument against positive government action on gay issues has developed during the past twenty years.[1] In secular argument, discouragement of homosexuality is advanced without religious reference and as a secular civic good. While this pattern is parallel to, consistent with, and implicitly grounded in religious anti-gay appeals, secular appeals do not directly rely on revealed authority or supernatural claims. Though religious claims about the sin of sodomy continue to be widely circulated, especially for mobilizing the evangelical community, secular discourse has become significant in public anti-gay advocacy (Judis, 1994; Wuthnow, 1994, p. 67). The cliché, "God created Adam and Eve, not Adam and Steve," is now strongly reinforced with the secular claim "no special rights." Civic appeals are viable without support from beliefs rooted in religious culture. "Order" and "decency" remain central terms in such secular discourse. Order can be sanctioned by reference to community tradition as well as by biblical injunction, and decency can be justified by social function as well as by divine mandate. By featuring a secular pattern of argument, anti-gay advocates avoid church-state questions, evade the imputation of religious zealotry, strive to create an image of rational civility, and reach beyond the evangelical community which forms the core support for anti-gay campaigns.[2] As Hardisty (1993, p. 9) observes, the "association of anti-homosexual organizing with religious (specifically Christian) principles is highlighted only when activists are targeting fellow Christians in order to recruit or educate them. When organizing in the wider political arena, anti-homosexual organizing is cast in secular terms. . . ."

This essay analyzes secular anti-gay appeals by examining the rhetorical pattern of anti-gay activists in a recent referendum campaign. In this referendum, anti-gay advocates defined terms such as "homosexual" and "rights" in ways to evoke fundamental fears. Presenting homosexuality as behavior rather than orientation, they argued that homosexuality disrupts civilization and causes revulsion in the "natural" person. Defining rights as minority privileges and protections, anti-gay advocates predicted a threatening authoritarian future if the gay movement succeeds.

The referendum that will be used throughout to exemplify secular anti-gay rhetoric took place during the winter of 1994 in Springfield, Missouri. Springfield, with a population of approximately 160,000, is located in a politically conservative region which consistently votes Republican. A number of educational institutions are located in Springfield, most notably a large public university, a nondenominational college, and several colleges associated with evangelical denominations. The world headquarters of the Assemblies of God is located there. The city is home to a regional newspaper owned by Gannett, three network-affiliated television stations, an independent station, a number of commercial radio stations, and a public-broadcasting station (Springfield Area Chamber of Commerce, 1994).

On October 4, 1993, the Springfield, Missouri, City Council, upon recommendation of the city's Human Rights Commission and following extensive testimony from citizens, approved a bias crime ordinance by a seven-to-two vote ("Hate Crime Ordinance," 1993). This ordinance provided sentence enhancement for persons convicted of assault or property destruction motivated by bias. Bias was defined in the ordinance (City Council, 1993) as "hostility or animosity towards another person by reason of the race, color, gender, religion, national origin, disability or sexual orientation of the victim."

Following the ordinance's passage, a local organization, Citizens for Decent Standards, gathered sufficient signatures to place on the February 8, 1994, special election ballot the question of whether the ordinance should be sustained ("Both Sides," 1993). Even though Missouri had not previously experienced an anti-gay referendum campaign (and has not since experienced one), Citizens for Decent Standards had agitated anti-gay causes in other contexts (Bradley, R., 1992; Rottman, 1991). From December through early February, the bias ordinance was extensively discussed in radio and television debates, letters to the editor, editorials, newscasts, and opinion columns. On election day, the bias crime ordinance favored by pro-gay advocates was repealed by 71 percent to 29 percent with one third of the eligible voters casting ballots ("Voters' Choice," 1994). This public debate illustrates secular anti-gay discourse because it produced an extensive body of recent anti-gay material and because it attracted and involved significant national anti-gay advocates, including Lou Sheldon and Paul Cameron, as well as important anti-gay national organizations such as Focus on the Family and the Traditional Values Coalition. Springfield's referendum debates provide an illustrative sample of main themes in current secular anti-gay discourse.

PUBLIC ARGUMENT AND ANTI-GAY APPEALS

The secular pattern of anti-gay argument has been forged and honed in public debates over same-sex public policy questions. In the past two decades, Americans have voted on more than sixty state and local ballot measures concerning civil rights laws for gays, exclusion of openly gay teachers, domestic partner laws, bias crime ordinances, and the like (Fight the Right Project Staff, 1994). These initiative and referendum campaigns, often losing battles from a gay perspective, have been viewed with suspicion by some in the gay community who reject the liberal equality paradigm developed through these civil rights plebiscites and who detect a number of negative consequences for gay people in organized electoral activity.[3] Other gay advocates see as beneficial the publicized challenge to hegemonic religious, legal, and medical discourses that represent homosexuality as sin, crime, and sickness (Ehrensaft & Milkman, 1979; Shilts, 1982, p. 218). They sense that productive confrontation is occurring between traditionalists and progressives.[4]

Campaign organizations in these contests employ the usual techniques of late-twentieth-century politics—advertising, video-tape distribution, rallies, direct and e-mail, personal contact, pamphleteering, and get-out-the-vote drives (Fight the Right Project Staff, 1993). In these referendum campaigns, no less than in campaigns for public office, debate, or the illusion of debate, assumes high visibility. Debate comes in a variety of formats, including mediated and non-mediated confrontation between opponents, talk-show exchanges, published opinion statements juxtaposing opponents, and exchanges in letters to newspaper editors. These debates, though not demonstrably influencing election outcomes, occur because they serve a variety of needs: media visibility for individuals who believe themselves marginalized, opportunity to wrestle publicly with the devil, occasion to exercise free expression, and a venue to correct error and offer new explanations.[5] Important for this analysis, such debates are sites of contestation in which opponents attempt to state arguments they believe most compelling for an uncommitted but interested public. Thus, while persuasive appeals surface in many formats during a campaign, reasons tend to appear in more lucid and evidenced form in public debate.

This is not to suggest that public argument on "gay rights" issues is impressively substantiated. One's imagination is challenged to understand as rational advocacy the farrago of claims that gay people are child-molesting, disease-transmitting, serial-murdering, feces-eating, family-corrupting humanist Nazis who, though infinitesimal in number and subject to early mortality at public expense, are destroying the republic by flaunting demands for special rights.

For many gay activists, debates are futile or counterproductive spectacles. From their perspective, individuals opposed to gay civil equality cannot be argued out of their emotional anti-gay biases (Bawer, 1993; Kirk & Madsen, 1989). The attempt may harden prejudice (Nava & Dawidoff, 1994, p. xiv). Further, reasoned discourse for the anti-gay advocate may only be "filler for the print media" (Mohr, 1988, p. 3).

Some rhetoricians and social scientists are no more sanguine about public moral argument. Pearce, Littlejohn, and Alexander (1987, p. 172) assert that such arguments degenerate into reciprocated diatribe because "disputants lack a common moral frame with which to understand the issues."[6] Sociologists such as Hunter (1991, pp. 128, 130) see opposing sides on gay issues as "worlds apart," making "any mutually agreeable resolution of policy, much less cultural consensus . . . almost unimagible."

While hyperbole and vilification systematically distort debate on gay issues, our attention is drawn to such encounters by the inevitability of debate, recognition that the goal is not conversion but influence on the uncommitted, and hope that "public advocacy crafts a viable collective morality" (Condit, 1987, p. 81).

THE STRUGGLE FOR DOMINANT MEANING

Debate on gay-policy issues is centrally concerned with definition. As Rubin (1993, p. 23) notes, "definitions and evaluations of sexual conduct are objects of bitter contest." Such definitional contests can be considered, in Bourdieu's (1991, p. 239) formulation, as the "symbolic struggle for the production of common sense or, more precisely, for the monopoly of legitimate *naming*." If language is understood as the means of bringing order to an otherwise chaotic existence, then contests to supply dominant meaning to key terms provide access to control over symbolic "machineries of legitimation" and powerful influence over social behavior. All sides in current moral argument recognize that "those who have the power to establish the language of public debate will have a tremendous advantage in determining the debate's outcome" (Hunter, 1994, p. 66).[7]

"Homosexuality," strategically defined as behavior, is the first of two terms central to secular anti-gay argument. Based on experience with anti-gay referenda in the 1970s, Brummett (1981) insightfully observes that both pro- and anti-gay rhetoric focus on who (agent) is doing what (act) and are diametrically opposed because pro-rhetoric emphasizes agent and anti-rhetoric features act. Thus, in anti-gay discourse, "actions are primary and *agents are derivative*" (Brummett, 1981, p. 293). By emphasizing homosexuality as act, anti-gay advocates frame homosexual behavior as nonprocreative, unnatural, freely chosen, and easily abandoned. This definition of homosexuality has remained stable over the years, surfacing recently in judicial opinions, anti-gay propaganda, and debate (Chinn & Franklin, 1992; Halley, 1991). Throughout the Springfield, Missouri, bias crime ordinance debate, anti-gay speakers returned repeatedly to the behavior theme: "This is a behavioral-based minority," "Homosexuality is defined by behavior," "Homosexuality is nothing but an act" (KOZK, 1993).

A second central term in anti-gay advocacy is "special rights," defined as government intervention on behalf of gay people. Special rights, presented by definition as a violation of "equality," is salient in arguments opposed to adding sexual orientation to existing civil rights or anti-discrimination laws and is also important in attacks on domestic partner and bias crime laws (Hibbard, 1994, p. 14; Mohr, 1994; White, 1994, p. 227). Recognizing that proponents of civil rights for gay people have adopted a minority identity position, opponents sought from the first to challenge gay minority status and to advance the thesis that protection for gay people necessarily entails less protection for others.

The special rights argument remains a dominant feature of anti-gay rhetoric. Taken in context, the phrase "special rights" becomes linked to the behavior-based definition of homosexuality in a secular rather than religious appeal. Anita Bryant, the first prominent anti-gay spokesperson in an anti-gay referendum, contended that "homosexuals should not ask for a special privilege ordinance to give community sanction to an act that God says is immoral" (as cited in Brummett, 1981, p. 297). This contention has been secularized into Sheldon's declaration that homosexuality should not be "elevated from [a] behavior based lifestyle to a legitimate minority with 'special rights' " (as cited in Gay Rights, 1993). On several occasions in the Springfield debates, the behavior/special rights appeal took narrative form: "Say that four or five or six men went up to a room and had sex with one another, and then came down to the street and said that we deserve special protection for what we've just done—that would be wrong" (KOZK, 1994).

Having defined homosexuality as act and government intervention as special rights, the secular pattern of argument advances to describe such acts and special rights as contrary to the public good in such a way as to evoke fundamental anti-gay images, a process of appeal which will now be examined in detail.

EVOCATION IN ANTI-GAY ADVOCACY

While gay advocates tend to limit discussion to cognitive-instrumental rationality, their anti-gay opponents, less mindful of fact and rigorous inference, seem to believe they are offering "good reasons" by making assertions and weaving narratives consistent with established norms and legitimatized expectations.[8] To use M. Edelman's (1964) classic distinction between referential and condensation symbols, gay advocates attempt to use referential symbols to establish objective situational elements. Anti-gay advocates tend to use condensation symbols which "evoke the emotions associated with the situation" (Edelman, M., 1964, p. 6).[9]

Such condensation symbols function to evoke images of order, decay, and chaos. Mathews and DeHart's (1990, pp. 133, 152, 136, 218) characterization of debate on the Equal Rights Amendment (ERA) applies equally well to controversies over civil rights for gays. They note that pro-ratificationists were dedicated to a rationalistic combination of style and substance designed to refute lies, misrepresentation, and ignorance. In contrast, antiratificationists "skillfully wove the symbols of the ERA into a web of apprehension, defensiveness, and anger." While ERA opponents made declaratory statements that were untrue, "as statements of *meaning* they were undoubtedly true." Antiratificationists made "moral statements by transforming metaphor and simile into empirical fact." Similarly, anti-gay secular discourse produces arguments designed to name, and thereby evoke, threats to order and decency.

Order is at the center of one extensive cluster of anti-gay arguments. These arguments support the conclusions that social approval/acceptance/legitimation of homosexuality will destroy the community. Such arguments are part of a long tradition. L. Edelman (1994, p. 130) asserts that the act of sodomy, defined ambiguously as all forms of nonprocreative sex, "has been viewed historically, at least in the West, as constitutively disruptive of essence. In this way it has proven to be infinitely adaptable as a figure for the disruption or destabilization of any foundational order." In recent anti-gay rhetoric, destabilization takes the form of the collapse of American civilization. Acceptance of homosexuality sanctions every form of deviance, disrupts the sexual order, prevents society from reproducing itself, destroys the family, facilitates child molestation, and spreads disease. In general, these familiar claims serve two purposes: (1) function as secular arguments apart from religious warrants; and (2) serve together to evoke a sense that same-sex eroticism is profoundly dangerous.

Fear of a wrathful god is unnecessary to advance these arguments. Religious anti-gay discourse can invoke Sodom's fire, Onan's sin, Leviticus, St. Paul, and death as the "wages of sin." However, in secular form, society dies of natural causes innate to human social life. Who sleeps with whom can produce naturally corrosive effects. Thus, as James Dobson, prominent anti-gay advocate and leader of Focus on the Family, states, "robbed of sexual standards, society will unravel like a ball of twine. That is the lesson of history. That is the legacy of Rome and more than 2,000 civilizations that have come and gone on this earth" (Dobson & Bauer, 1990, p. 55). Arguments to civic fear evoke a variety of connected images. Recognition of homosexuality will cause society to be chaotic, barren, corruptive, and diseased.

Traditionalist discourse emphasizes boundaries, constraint, and fear of moral collapse (Browning, 1993; Davies, 1982, p. 1032; Himmelstein, 1990, p. 105; Marty, 1984, p. 59; Wuthnow, 1983, p. 180). One would consequently expect a traditionalist view of homosexuality which focuses on the "inevitability of a symbolic order based on a logic of limits, margins, borders, and boundaries," expressed in a "language and law of defense and protection: heterosexuality both secures its self-identity and shores up its ontological boundaries by protecting itself from what it sees as the continual predatory encroachments of its contaminated other, homosexuality" (Fuss 1991, pp. 1–2). As Rubin (1993, p. 14) notes, there is strong expression of the need to enforce a line "between sexual order and chaos" arising out of fear that if "anything is permitted to cross this erotic DMZ, the barrier against scary sex will crumble and something unspeakable will skitter across." Thus, in anti-gay discourse, acceptance of homosexuality threatens the normative universe (Klatch, 1987, p. 47; Marty & Appleby, 1993). In one variant of this slippery-slope or domino theory, "if homosexuality is deemed normal, how long will it be before rape, adultery, alcoholism, drug addiction, and incest are labeled as normal" (Falwell, 1980, p. 183). In another variant, identified by Rubin (1993, p. 43), homosexuality is the first breach in the barrier against all forms of sexual deviance, including bestiality, pedophilia, and necrophilia. In the Springfield debates, both versions of the barricade against deviance theme appeared, with special emphasis on how sexual disorder disrupts the family (KOZK, 1994; Debate, 1994).

Procreative/nonprocreative is the most important boundary between ordered sexuality and moral chaos (Pronk, 1993, p. 234). Hence, it is the source of some of the most powerfully evocative traditionalist rhetoric through a play on the multiple senses of the term "reproduction." Weston (1991, pp. 24–25) correctly observes that reproduction functions as a "mixed metaphor [which] may detract from its analytic utility, but its very ambiguities make it ideally suited to argument and innuendo." Anti-gay advocates argue that because the homosexual act is not reproductive, society will end, the family will not survive, and most prominently, children will be seduced. In the Springfield campaign, some of the dimensions of reproduction were indirectly exploited by assertions that homosexuals are not "productive" (Summers, 1993). However, the most important evocation of reproduction came in the familiar slogan: "homosexuals don't reproduce, so they must recruit" (Bryant, 1977, p. 62; Falwell, 1980, p. 185; LaHaye, 1978, p. 93).

Recruitment is the rhetorical entry into an important set of appeals about child molestation. At the heart of much anti-gay rhetoric is the claim that children must be protected from predatory homosexuals, from visible homosexuals, or even from a knowledge of homosexuality's existence.[10] In the Springfield controversy, a variety of arguments evoked the homosexual threat to children. The term "sexual orientation" was construed to suggest that child molesters would be protected by approval of the bias crimes ordinance (Askew, 1993; McGrath, 1994). Narratives were spun about police reluctance to arrest child molesters (Testimony, 1993; Summers, 1994).

The corruption of society and its children by homosexuality is further objectified by evocation of the image of homosexuals as, in Rueda's (1982, p. 49) phrase, "a reservoir of disease for the rest of society." This image has, of course, been especially exploited in relation to AIDS. In the Springfield debates, two arguments were advanced which evoked the disease image. In the first, homosexuals were cast as people against whom discrimination was appropriate because they were already rejected, as a class, for organ and blood donations (Summers, 1994). In the second, the concept was advanced that because homosexuals are diseased, encouraging homosexuality would further enhance a serious public health problem (KSMU, 1994).

"Disease" provides a gateway into a second cluster of arguments that evoke repulsive and threatening images. Rubin (1993, p. 15) wisely observes that "most people find it difficult to grasp that whatever they like to do sexually will be thoroughly repulsive to someone else. . . ." Consequently, as Ruse (1988) argues, strong negative feelings about homosexuality, especially male same-sex eroticism, are aesthetic, not moral judgments—what he calls the "Ugh! Factor." Similarly, Nava and Dawidoff (1994, p. 5) conclude that the "revulsion many men and women feel at the thought of sexual activity between people of their own sex remains a formidable factor, which we call the Ick Factor. . . ." In anti-gay rhetoric, the notion often surfaces that same-sex acts are repulsive. Bryant (1977, p. 67) recounted that "I opened the mail one day . . . and there before my eyes was the most hideous thing I had ever seen—a picture of two nude men committing an act of homosexuality." Buchanan (as cited in Editors, 1992) finds that such visceral recoil from homosexuality "is the natural reaction of a healthy society wishing to protect itself."

To enhance such reactions, anti-gay advocates advance arguments based on depiction of behavior that is, at most, atypical: "stories detailing how gay men ingest pounds of feces during their lifetimes and pour urine on each other during parties" (J. Gallagher, 1994b). In the Springfield debates, homosexual acts were routinely characterized as "filthy," "vile," and "disgusting" (KOZK, 1993). One anti-gay advocate ("Testimony," 1993) suggested that citizens would not vote to protect homosexual behavior if they saw homosexual acts. The claim was made that gay behavior is dangerous to public health because coprophilia is central to homosexual behavior, and that fisting, rimming, and gerbiling are routine sexual practices among homosexual men (KSMU, 1994).

AUTHORITARIANISM IN ANTI-GAY ARGUMENT

Struggle over public policy in which fundamental values appear at stake creates the impression in major segments of the community that they are prospectively victims of unconstitutional imposition and that their own ways of living are being unfairly disadvantaged (Moon, 1993, p. 10). At the most general level, both traditionalists and progressives believe that the other side favors government intrusion into private life. As Hunter (1991, p. 128) concludes, the "enactment of law that endorses a shifting cultural climate will be perceived as an intrusion by those who resist the present cultural changes; the reversal of these laws . . . will be perceived as an intrusion by those who approve these changes. . . ."

Pro-gay advocates (Adam, 1987, p. 111; Cruickshank, 1992, p. 80; Russo, 1987, p. 248) have long charged that anti-gay supporters are authoritarian opponents of pluralism. This construction of anti-gay efforts is justified by linking anti-gay rhetoric with the new religious right which, in turn, is depicted as undemocratic, a view consistent with a general public understanding of fundamentalist religion as intolerant.[11] This depiction is reinforced by the gay community's perception of its history as one of oppression by government and church (Dawidoff, 1994; Halperin, 1990; Marcus, 1992; Norton, 1992). The gay projection of anti-gay authoritarianism takes many forms, including charges that anti-gays use homophobia as an entering wedge to deprive women or minorities of civil rights and the association of anti-gays with fascism through the example of Nazi persecution of homosexuals (Clark, 1994; Goldberg, 1993; Haeberle, 1989; Plant, 1986).

Anti-gay rhetoric includes appeals that mirror the characterization of traditionalists as authoritarians. Anti-gay advocates depict themselves as stigmatized and powerless, victims of harassment and violence who are subject to an increasingly authoritarian state controlled by elites bent on undermining free American institutions (Blunt, 1993; Herman, 1994, p. 96). Hawley and Proudfoot (1994), for instance, note a sense of beleaguerment among traditionalists, a feeling that they are victims of modernity, a "wounded majority [which] harbors what appears to be a 'minority complex.' " Within this framework, pro-gay government action threatens equality and free expression. At its most simplistic, this rhetoric equates gays with Nazis. While such a *tu quoque* argument may be lightly dismissed, it does point to a main current in traditionalist thought and toward a larger shift in anti-gay secular discourse toward terms associated with liberalism.

The argument that pluralism produces totalitarianism is at the heart of traditionalist rhetoric. In its most philosophical statement, this argument is produced as Neuhaus's (1984) "naked public square," the notion that the attempt to exclude traditional religion and morality from public life will result in "totalitarian monism." In a more aggressive statement, Schaeffer (1982, p. 29) argues that humanism "always leads to chaos. It then naturally leads to some form of authoritarianism to control the chaos." More narrowly, a humanist government is portrayed as undermining morality by promoting abortion, affirmative action, sexual permissiveness, and a secular school curriculum (Himmelstein, 1983, p. 16; Klatch, 1987, p. 6; Neuhaus,

1984). Within this general framework, a legal system that fails to suppress homosexual acts, or which recognizes the existence of gay people, is understood as dangerous government intrusion: the government is forcing approval of homosexuality, silencing protests against sodomy, and abridging parents' rights to protect and train their children. Expression of this understanding takes several forms. LaHaye (1978, p. 196) maintains that "leniency toward homosexuality will endanger the civil rights of the majority." Citizens will lose their free speech rights to denounce homosexuality as an evil, employers will be forced to give preference to homosexual applicants, property owners will be compelled to rent to homosexuals, and parents will be forced to send their children to schools that employ self-identified gay people (Cooper, 1992; Kane, 1993).

The general traditionalist fear of state intervention in community, church, and family is materialized, as noted above, in the image of the gay as fascist. The reference of vociferous anti-gay advocate Gene Antonio (as cited in People for the American Way, 1994) to the "homosexual gestapo" is not casual name-calling. It is rooted, Lake (1984, p. 430) perceptively maintains, in the broader notion that all forms of permissiveness lead to totalitarianism. As Dobson and Bauer (1990, p. 28) contend, "it will be helpful to remember that the Nazis also made up their rules as they went along." In anti-gay rhetoric, this line of thought leads to the conclusions that "homosexuals were an integral part of the Nazi Party throughout history," and that, like Nazis, homosexuals attempt to corrupt the young (Scott Lively as cited in Editors, 1994).

Ironically, the suggestion that civil rights for gays leads to fascism exemplifies an important trend in traditionalist rhetoric toward the invocation of liberal terms. Moen (1992b) notes that traditionalists increasingly use a vocabulary emphasizing rights, freedom, liberty, and choice. Through the lens of this vocabulary, anti-gay initiatives preserve the right to choose to discriminate against homosexuals. Referenda on civil rights measures for gays becomes an opportunity to preserve the liberty to discriminate and the freedom to teach an anti-homosexual "morality."

In the Springfield controversy, antiauthoritarianism was a key line of argument. The usual suggestions were made that anti-gay supporters were both marginalized and the victims of harassment. The bias crime ordinance was portrayed as an elitist attempt to suppress free speech and to suspend freedom of action for those morally opposed to homosexuality (KOZK, 1993). Pro-gay advocates were described as vicious name-callers seeking to silence their opponents (KOZK, 1994; Supporters Fight Back, 1994; Thompson, G., 1993). Emphasis was placed on the rights of citizens to protest homosexuality, of churches to condemn it, and of property owners to choose their tenants (Beck, 1994; Gillming, 1993). The struggle for gay rights was depicted as an assault on equality enforceable only by an intrusive government (KOZK, 1994).

CONCLUSIONS

The anti-gay shift from religious to secular appeals can be understood as a strategic response to the charge that only religious zealots oppose gay rights. A decision that pro-gay advocates must make is the extent to which they ought to generate rejoinders to specific elements of anti-gay secular argument. Pivotal to this decision is whether one understands anti-gay argument as a smokescreen for visceral prejudice against homosexuality or as a genuine expression of confusion and discomfort over the relationship of the individual to the community.

Students of public policy discourse can contribute to shaping pro-gay responses to anti-gay secular discourse. Possibly the most important issue that they can address concerns the connections between public policy debates and culture. In the microcosm of the Springfield, Missouri, debates, no less than in national clashes between pro-and anti-gay movements, advocates draw on their cultural repertoire to define, evoke, and threaten. To understand this process, we should begin to interrogate the notion that each side in such a debate is, in Hunter's (1991, p. 128) words, "using a different form of debate and persuasion." Whether this is true may partly be determined by observing the struggle for dominant meaning, assessing the extent to which each side relies on instrumental or evocative arguments, and by comprehending what debate reveals about the relation of individuals to government.

On a more specific level, because sexuality is so central to culture, debate on same-sex issues provides a way to examine the relationship between the normative universe(s) out of which arises both our rhetoric and specific laws to regulate sexuality. For example, the struggle for dominant meaning allows us to explore the cultural basis of change in the key terms such as "rights," "equality," and "natural," which frequently appear in public debates (Condit, 1990; Condit & Lucaites, 1993, pp. xii–xiii).

NOTES

1. For brevity, the term "gay" and its variants (anti-gay, pro-gay) is used throughout to stand for the longer term "lesbian, gay male, bisexual, and transgendered persons."

2. For an early and blatant example of the strategic substitution of secular for religious appeals, see Medhurst (1982). Heinz (1983) examines the church-state question. For an insightful view of religious zealotry and emergent civility, see Hunter (1987, pp. 152, 184, 212). Branham and Pearce (1987) discuss the new Christian Right's rhetoric of civility. Marty (1984, p. 67) stresses the necessity for evangelicals to reach beyond their own community.

3. Herman (1994, pp. 4–8 *et passim*) provides an excellent analysis of the civil rights strategy. D'Emilio (1992, p. 181) traces the evolution of the gay movement toward a civil rights emphasis. Problems created by organizing the gay movement

around civil rights campaigns are discussed in Cagan (1993). On the limitations of reform strategy, see Bronski (1984, pp. 197–200), and Ehrensaft and Milkman (1979). For an attack on the reform strategy, see Mieli (1980, p. 82). Altman (1987) summarizes problems created by the encapsulation of the gay community.

4. On positive aspects of referendum campaigns, see Parks (1981), Licata (1981), and Gallagher (1994a). Bray (1994) and Redwing (1994) discuss the connection between rights initiatives and gay-movement building.

5. Cohan (1992) summarizes the determinants of outcome with respect to gay equality. On the importance of self-representation in these debates, see Editors (1993). Gross (1991) emphasizes the importance of self-representation. Olson and Goodnight (1994, p. 252) believe that "performed arguments" reveal "specific social conventions as unreflective habits." Bourdieu (1994, pp. 163–164) stresses the general importance of public discussion of moral belief. Siegel (1991) argues that opportunity for expression is especially important to gay advocates since many of the forms of oppression against which they are arguing consist essentially of limits on free speech. On the importance of media exposure, which is gained through debate, see Gitlin (1980, p. 3), and Molotoch (1979, p. 73). Hall (1993, p. 40) emphasizes being heard as a legitimate political voice, while Wuthnow (1994, p. 98) stresses the need for moral advocacy groups to dramatize their positions.

6. Vanderford (1989) reinforces this interpretation. Mansbridge (1986, p. 118) provides further explanation of the causes of oversimplification and antagonism in moral debate.

7. Hunter's analysis is similar to W. S. Brown's (1982) description of attention switching, the application of a linguistic template that leads advocates to understand an argumentative situation.

8. This general distinction is made by Habermas (1981, pp. 14–15).

9. For the similar notion of "supersaturated symbolic act," see K. M. Brown (1994, p. 182). Jamieson (1992, p. 101) insightfully describes evocative rhetoric.

10. Rubin (1993, p. 6), Herman (1994, p. 99), Eberly (1992, p. 207). Watney (1991, pp. 399–400) describes child seduction as a premodern fear, Chauncey (1994, p. 359) stresses an increasing fear of gay molestation, and Oberschall (1993, p. 354) provides strategic reasons for anti-gay concern with molestation. For the threat of gay visibility as key to understanding fear of child seduction, see Greenberg (1988, p. 471) and Conrad (1983, p. 168). Fischli (1981, p. 311) examines the strategic power of the seduction argument.

11. For a classic statement on the opposition between democratic pluralism and the monistic views which characterize fundamentalism, see Lipset and Raab (1970). Hunter (1983b) analyzes liberal objections to right-wing authoritarianism. Diamond (1989) and Cantor (1994) provide examples of such objection. For negative public perception of religious moralism, see Hunter (1983a). A. J. Reichley (1987, p. 92) summarizes public opinion on the repressive nature of the religious new right, while Hadden and Shupe (1988, p. 223) highlight media's role in promoting a negative image.

9

Direct Democracy and Minority Rights: Opinions on Anti-Gay and Lesbian Ballot Initiatives

Todd Donovan and Shaun Bowler

Direct democracy has been criticized as a process that can produce outcomes that are inherently antidemocratic or explicitly antiminority. Democratic theorists have often granted little credence to the idea of governance via massed-based, direct democratic practices. Mill, De Tocqueville, and Madison each raised concerns about the potential for majority intolerance of minority rights. Other critics question if mass attitudes reflect the attachments to democratic norms that are necessary for a well-functioning, massed-based democracy (Adorno, Frenkel-Brunswick, Levinson, & Sanford, 1950; Lipset, 1963; McCloskey, 1964; McCloskey & Brill, 1983; Stouffer, 1955). These studies suggest that elites are more supportive of civil liberties than the mass public. One major contemporary study of tolerance concluded that there has been little increase in tolerance since the 1950s (Sullivan, Pierson, & Marcus, 1979). Sounding similar themes, some scholars criticize the direct-citizen initiative as providing an unchecked institutional vehicle for directing tyrannical, majoritarian hostility against minorities (Bell, 1978; Fountaine, 1988; Linde, 1993).

The history of direct-democracy practice in the twentieth century does indeed include numerous examples of abuses of minority rights. Californians, for example, voted to repeal housing integration ("fair housing") legislation passed by the state legislature in the 1960s (Wolfinger & Greenstein, 1968) and made it illegal for Japanese to own land in the 1920s. Voters in Washington, Colorado, and California repealed busing programs designed to integrate public schools (Cronin, 1989). Western U.S. history provides numerous examples of citizens initiatives directed against Asians, immigrants, non-English speakers, Catholics, and other groups. The institutions and policies associated with *direct* democracy thus present democratic societies with a fundamental test of tolerance: What happens when relatively small, unpopular groups become the topic of policies that are selected by majority popular vote?

This chapter examines the politics of opinion surrounding citizen initiatives directed against gays, lesbians, and bisexuals. At first glance, the surge of these initiatives in the 1990s seems to lend support to the majority-tyranny critique of citizen-initiated policy making. They also raise important questions about how direct-democracy institutions might translate intolerance of minorities into public policy. However, we present indirect evidence that the mass public might respond to elite cues about tolerance.

In previous decades, an occasional state ballot might have included initiatives dealing with gay-rights issues. As Table A.1 illustrates, the decade of the 1990s represented an upswing in the number of state-level ballot issues addressing the rights of homosexuals, with near-identical anti-gay initiatives circulating in several states simultaneously. In 1992, Colorado voters approved Amendment Two, an initiative that overturned local ordinances protecting against job discrimination on the basis of sexual orientation. That same year, another initiative qualified for the Oregon ballot (Measure 9, later defeated) that included policies similar to the Colorado initiative. The Oregon measure also would have amended state laws to declare homosexuality "abnormal, wrong, unnatural and perverse ... behaviors" and equated homosexuality with pedophilia. In 1994, initiatives designed to curtail civil rights extension based on sexual orientation circulated in nine states and qualified for the ballot in Oregon and Idaho.[1] Petitions circulated for two anti-gay-rights initiatives in 1995 in Washington state, and another measure designed to repeal local gay-rights ordinances appeared on the Maine ballot. Most of these initiatives involve attempts to prevent state and local governments from protecting gays, lesbians, and bisexuals from employment and other forms of discrimination.

In addition to raising questions about the compatibility of majoritarian institutions with minority rights, the frequent occurrence of these initiatives also present questions specific to direct democracy regarding the decision processes that voters use to evaluate these measures. In addition to standard demographic questions of "who supports" these initiatives, we are faced with the question of how voters respond to complex, noneconomic initiative measures in general. Unlike tax issues (a more frequent topic of ballot initiatives), voters have a more difficult time using such measures as narrow self-interest or personal financial status to sort through questions about gay rights. An examination of these anti-gay initiative efforts also allows us the opportunity to evaluate when the process of direct democracy might come to be used to limit minority rights.

These ballot questions can be seen as placing voters in a position of deciding on fairly complex issues. The initiatives can also place voters in a situation where their established values and attitudes toward gays might be challenged by campaign information. Most, if not all of these initiatives place voters in a position of deciding upon the nature of minority group rights, of judging affect for a traditionally unpopular group, and assessing claims of discrimination against a group (or the alleged threat presented by the group).

Decisions are likely complicated by at least two major forces that shape opinion about the subject matter contained in most anti-gay-rights initiatives. National opinion surveys indicate that a substantial majority of Americans view homosexuality, in the abstract, negatively. On the other hand, when presented with a more concrete situation, a substantial majority of Americans are opposed to job discrimination on the basis of sexual orientation. Ballot questions about the rights of homosexuals tap into both abstract and concrete political issues. To add further difficulty, campaigns over the issues can present a discussion of relatively complex legal concepts that are at the center of debate, including the definition of minority status, discrimination, and protected class. Initiative proponents can add yet another level of complexity to the issue by presenting these themes in the language of special rights, affirmative action, and job quotas.

STANDING OPINIONS VERSUS SHIFTING OPINIONS

As much as most individual voters pay little attention to politics and have enduring predispositions that affect how they evaluate abstract policy issues, scholars note that aggregate public opinion often reflects rational responsiveness to concrete political situations (Page & Shapiro, 1992). Similarly, a major theory of mass opinion suggests that when abstract issues (like "homosexuality") are actually translated into concrete situations like a gay-rights ballot decision, we might expect that voters would depart from predispositions they have about an abstract concept and react to cues (endorsements, public positions) given by political elites (Zaller, 1992).

Thus, knowing something about the rigidity of opinions on these ballot issues can tell us something about how voters respond to the issue during an initiative campaign. If we view gay-rights questions as an enduring symbolic issue tapping abstract themes, we might expect that many voters avoid applying conceptual sophistication when sorting through the merits of ballot issues dealing with gay rights. This being the case, voting might be structured by "gut responses" where views about the issue are ingrained over such a long period of time (Carmines & Stimson, 1980) that no amount of new information is likely to affect voter choices. Without new information, such voters might have nothing to cue their decisions but their affect, that is, feelings, toward the group made the subject of the policy.

Magleby (1984) referred to a category of ballot measures where aggregate opinion distributions reflect something akin to gut responses, or "standing opinions." These measures pass or fail based on enduring "deep attachments" that voters have to positions on issues such as the death penalty or legalization of drugs. With individual opinions being inflexible, aggregate opinion shifts very little over the course of campaigns on these measures (Magleby, 1984, pp. 170–171). Since Carmines and Stimson emphasized that issues associated with racial minorities are affected by easy, gut-response issue voting, we might expect that opinions on policies dealing with the rights of sexual minorities could also be structured by similar attitudes that produce standing opinion distributions.

Magleby, however, suggested that California's 1978 initiative directed against homosexual teachers was an issue where voters might not have had such deep, inflexible attachments to a specific issue position. Rather, he categorizes the teacher initiative as being of the type where opinions were fluid and vote intentions changed over the course of the campaign as civil rights issues were framed (1984, pp. 170–171). In other words, mass opinions about policies directed against homosexuals appeared to have responded to information from the initiative opponent's campaign.

Conversely, there is also evidence suggesting that attitudes about homosexual rights are grounded in deep attachments and distaste for homosexuals. Sniderman, Brody, and Tetlock (1991, pp. 47–49) found homophobia to play a significant role in how citizens with low education reason about AIDS policy, and found that for well-educated and low-educated citizens homophobia has a direct effect on attitudes about civil liberties of homosexuals. Gay-rights ballot issues can thus place opinions about narrow civil rights issues in conflict with opinions and evaluations of homosexuals. Magleby also illustrated that opinion on some civil rights propositions (California's Proposition Fourteen of 1964 repealing the state's open housing law; Massachusetts' Question 1 of 1976 about the Equal Rights Amendment) were characterized by inflexible, standing opinions that did not seem to shift over the course of a campaign in response to arguments about civil rights. From the perspective of an evaluation of the prospect for minority tolerance under direct, majoritarian democracy, the distinction between standing opinions or fluid opinions is critical.

At issue here is the question of how malleable opinions about anti-gay ballot issues might be. If opinion on anti-gay propositions is inflexible and subject to "gut-response" voting based on affect for the minority group, we might expect that anti-gay activists might easily pass policies that are abusive of gay rights in jurisdictions where the majority is critical of homosexuals. This would confirm the fears of direct democracy's critics—that the institution is incompatible with minority rights. If, conversely, opinion shifts and is malleable during initiative campaigns, we might expect that some members of the majority are open to suggestions that there are unacceptable costs or risks involved with the proposed initiative. This would suggest that the initiative process need not necessarily be viewed as being a vehicle for translating majority distaste for minorities into public policies incompatible with minority rights.

OPINION ON HOMOSEXUALITY AND CIVIL RIGHTS

For anti-gay-rights activists, there is a potentially large reservoir of majority distaste for gays and lesbians that might be tapped during an initiative campaign. Table A.3 reports trends in responses to annual National Opinion Research Council (General Social Survey) questions designed to measure tolerance of homosexuality. A clear majority of Americans disapprove of homosexuality. The trend over time, however, reveals that mass opinions about homosexuality are potentially fluid. These data suggest that, at least at the national level, opinions about homosexuality are not fixed but appear to be evolving toward greater tolerance.[2] By the mid-1990s, a growing proportion of Americans are likely to respond that homosexuality is "not wrong at all."[3]

These ballot questions, however, are not simply a referenda on homosexuality. The contemporary crop of initiatives and initiative proposals also deal with specific questions of civil rights. Table A.3 lists responses to questions that measure attitudes about the civil rights and liberties of gays and lesbians. The data in Table A.3 indicate that since the early 1980s Americans have become much less likely to respond that books about homosexuals should be removed from libraries, that homosexuals should be banned from college teaching, and that homosexuals should be barred from public speaking.[4] Furthermore, other data illustrate that three quarters of Americans are opposed to job discrimination against gays and lesbians. A CBS/*New York Times* poll from February of 1993 found that three of four respondents stated homosexuals should have equal rights in job opportunities. A 1992 CNN/Gallup poll also found that 74 percent of respondents felt "homosexuals should have equal job opportunities."

Nevertheless, political acceptance of gays and lesbians is low, compared to many other groups in America. Table A.8 lists feeling thermometer scores from the 1992 American National Election Study post-election survey. Feeling thermometer questions allow respondents to rate a group at 50 if the respondent is neutral toward the group, 100 if they feel positive about the group, and 0 if they feel negatively about the group. Twenty-two percent of respondents gave gays and lesbians (as a group) the most negative rating possible (zero). Comparatively, other targets of recent initiatives (people on welfare and illegal immigrants) were rated zero by only 3.5 percent and 15.4 percent of respondents, respectively.

Thus, the mass public appears to have a firm (and somewhat increasing) commitment to broad concepts of civil rights for homosexuals and a corresponding disdain for gays and lesbians as a group (although there are signs of greater acceptance). On the surface, some of these opinion data suggest that initiatives directed against gays might be widely popular. How then, do voters approach ballot issues that merge issues of civil rights and homosexuality?

VOTING ON BALLOT PROPOSITIONS

A large body of literature suggests that individuals decide how to vote on ballot propositions in response to symbolic themes evoked by the ballot subject or the campaign. Sears defines political symbols as "emotion based on some enduring predisposition rather than on tangible costs and benefits of the matter to which the symbol refers" (Sears, 1993, p. 114). Studies within this literature indicate that, even where ballot choices are defined narrowly in terms of personal tax burdens, symbolic factors might exceed self-interest as the motive for voting (Lowery & Sigelman, 1981, p. 972; Sears & Funk, 1990, p. 170). Other studies indicate that self-interest might structure voting on propositions when the monetary costs and benefits of a proposition are clearly identifiable to distinct segments of the electorate (Bowler & Donovan, 1994c). Self-interest has been found to be associated with support for certain policies, with interest being deflected somewhat by long-term, symbolic predispositions (Tedin, 1994).

There is little reason, however, to expect motivations based on self-interest to be a major factor structuring voting on anti-gay initiatives. Clearly gays, lesbians, and many others are likely to feel that these initiatives would have a direct, immediate impact on their lives. For most voters, however, changing laws dealing with the civil rights extended to gays and lesbians represent a policy that is unlikely to alter the status quo in a manner that is immediately perceptible to them. Thus, for most people, instrumental motivations are not likely to structure the vote on anti-gay initiatives. Vote motivations on initiatives dealing with the rights of gays, lesbians, and bisexuals are not likely to be analogous to vote motivations on other material issues. Questions about taxation and spending define large groups of winners and losers in clear, pocketbook terms. Civil rights issues dealing with small minorities have less tangible personal content to most voters. The minority targeted by an initiative might evaluate the proposal in terms of how it affects their interests. However, when targeted minorities are fairly small, narrowly self-interested motivations are not likely to be a dominant factor in structuring the vote.[5]

This being the case, it is reasonable to expect that many voters act in response to other factors. These might include, but are not limited to, enduring symbolic predispositions and information received during the campaign. Operational definitions of symbolic factors will be offered in the analysis below. It is unknown, however, how much room there is for opinion fluidity or for campaign information to affect predispositions that voters might have about homosexuality. As the data and discussion above indicate, tolerance of gays and lesbians is increasing yet gays and lesbians continue to be viewed unfavorably. From a normative perspective, democratic practices that are compatible with minority rights require either that majority opinions and predispositions recognize minority interests, or that majority opinion can be moved to recognize the costs of policies that affect minority rights. This perspective suggests empirical tests that might provide a basis for evaluating direct democracy's compatibility with minority rights. First, we must examine if aggregate opinions shift over the course of anti-gay campaigns. Second, at the level of the individual voter, it suggests that we examine factors that structure the vote decision.

OPINION CHANGE, POLITICAL AWARENESS, AND ANTI-GAY RIGHTS INITIATIVE CAMPAIGNS

We might expect that some direct-democracy voters are influenced by cues from elected elites or that they absorb and process information from campaigns. This might be particularly true of initiative voting, since standard decision cues such as party are absent (Bowler & Donovan, 1994b; Magleby, 1984). Lupia (1994) demonstrates that where voters can obtain information about who is backing or opposing a ballot initiative, they are able to make decisions that emulate the behavior of well-informed voters. Bowler and Donovan (1994b) also found that partisan voters' opinions about initiatives were likely to be influenced by positions taken by political elites and political groups. All of this suggests that many voters can respond to cues from political elites. For this reason, we expect that levels of political awareness are associated with opinion, particularly if political elites are taking public positions on the ballot measures. If we assume that the politically aware are more likely to be exposed to campaign information and elite positions, we might expect that political awareness structures vote intentions (Banducci & Karp, 1993). We can examine this issue with aggregate-level and individual-level opinion data.

We assume that, given the media attention directed to officials elected from large constituencies (or statewide office) that many voters will become aware of the positions elites take on anti-gay initiatives. At the aggregate level we might expect that, if voters are cued by elite positions on these anti-gay initiatives, the existence of consensus or conflict among political elites is likely to affect the distribution of mass opinions on the initiative. This assumes, of course, that some direct-democracy voters respond to more than just enduring feelings about gays when evaluating anti-gay initiatives.[6] Specifically, where political elites' positions on propositions are divided, mass attitudes might reflect greater polarization on the ballot question (Banducci & Karp, 1993; Karp, 1994; Zaller, 1990, 1992). Conversely, where political elites are in consensus, opinions might move toward the elite position (regarding information and opinions about homosexuality, see Zaller, 1992, pp. 316–321). In the case of elite consensus, voters might be expected to receive similar cues (for tolerance) from politicians often at odds with each other over many issues. If voters respond, mass opinions should be less polarized and could reflect greater tolerance.

Lacking panel data from anti-gay-rights initiative campaigns and lacking direct measures of voter awareness of elite positions on these propositions, we can only indirectly test hypotheses about the effects of elite positions on anti-gay initiatives. First, trends in aggregate opinion distribution from cross-sectional surveys taken over the course of three anti-gay initiative campaigns are examined: California's Proposition Six of 1978 (the anti-homosexual teacher initiative), California's Proposition Sixty-four of 1986 (the AIDS quarantine initiative), and Idaho's Amendment One of 1994 (an initiative banning civil rights protections for gays).[7] These cases provide some variation in the level of opinion consensus among liberal and conservative elites.

The teacher initiative was placed on the ballot by the efforts of a conservative California state senator, John Briggs. Proposition Six would have permitted (if not required) school boards to fire "any teacher who advocated, solicited or promoted public or private homosexual activity" (Cronin, 1989, p. 96). Initiative proponents attempted to frame the question as one of protecting school children from being approached or influenced by homosexual teachers. The text of the measure appears to have authorized districts to fire teachers known to be gay, regardless of their classroom behavior. Early polls indicated that over 60 percent of registered voters intended to vote in favor of the Briggs initiative when given a brief explanation of the measure. A fairly active campaign was fought by proponents and opponents alike. Advocates of Proposition Six spent slightly over $1 million, and opponents spend just under $1.3 million.

However, over the course of the campaign California's governor and former governor (the liberal Jerry Brown and conservative Ronald Reagan, respectively) united in opposition to the initiative (Cannon, 1978; Cronin, 1989, p. 96). Many of these elites, including Reagan, announced public positions early in the campaign (Jacobs, 1978). Each of the state's U.S. senators publicly voiced opposition, as did the Democratic party; the State GOP chair, Mike Curb; and the highest ranking elected state Republican—GOP attorney general (and candidate for governor) Evelle Younger ("Homosexual Teachers," 1978; Ramirez, 1978). Other visible nonelected conservative elites such as antitax crusader Howard Jarvis and Catholic Archbishop John Quinn also voiced opposition to Proposition Six nearly a month before the election ("Catholic Leaders Blast," 1978; Poll Showing Growing Shift, 1978).

As Table A.9 indicates, there was substantial movement in response to survey questions measuring support for Proposition Six over the course of the campaign. This occurred as some voters were likely exposed to campaign messages from each side, with the vast weight of information from paid ads coming from the "no" side. Opinion was fairly fluid, but liberal and conservative political elites eventually reflected a consensus position against the initiative. These data illustrate that opinion moved in the direction of the positions taken by elected officials.[8] Since many direct-democracy voters might decide on the basis of positions taken by political elites (Bowler & Donovan, 1994b) and since political elites from each party were in consensus in this contest, the fact that opinion shifted to the "no" side is not entirely surprising. One interpretation might be that some voters learned that civil rights and job discrimination issues outweighed any personal disdain they might have had for homosexuals as a group (or as teachers). Thus, initial levels of support could reflect anti-gay predispositions that have not yet been displaced by campaign information and cues from elites.

Whatever the reason, a substantial opinion shift occurred, illustrating that public predispositions about homosexuals held by the majority were not necessarily a dominant factor in affecting the election outcome. In the end, support was reduced to 41 percent. Magleby notes (1984, p. 183) that with this initiative, civil rights issues were not clearly defined as an operative issue until the latter stages of the campaign. Thus, we suggest that opinion was fluid as elite positions and opposition campaign messages about potential civil rights abuses cued voters in the late stages of the campaign.

The potential for abridgment of civil rights was much more apparent from the outset with the framing of California's Proposition Sixty-four, an initiative backed by Lyndon Larouche's political organization. The measure would have declared carrying the AIDS virus a contagious condition and subjected carriers to quarantine and state regulation. Opponents declared that the initiative intentionally targeted gay men[9] (being one of the primary groups affected by the disease) and was a threat to public health (since it would have discouraged AIDS carriers from seeking treatment). Most importantly, the issue was framed as a gross infringement on the civil rights of AIDS victims.

Furthermore, major political elites such as each party's candidate for California's U.S. Senate seat (Alan Cranston and Ed Zschau) and both candidates for governor (George Deukmejian and Tom Bradley), were opposed to the initiative (Delson, 1986; Richards, 1986). Liberal and conservative elite opposition became evident before the initiative officially qualified. In addition to health care officials and elected elites such as San Francisco mayor Diane Feinstien and Democratic assemblyman Willie Brown voicing early opposition, Clair Burgenar, the chair of the state GOP, spoke out against the measure in late June (Shilts, 1986). Very few political elites in California could be found voicing even conditional support for Larouche's initiative, with GOP U.S. Representative William Dannemeyer being the only official endorsing the initiative until the week of the election when

Sacramento's John Doolitle and three other San Diego area state legislators endorsed Proposition Sixty-four at the last minute (Grey, 1986; Hastings, 1986).

The dissemination of paid campaign information was also heavily one-sided. Apart from money spent to qualify the initiative ($230,000), only $137,000 was actually spent on campaigning by supporters. Opponents were far more active, spending $2.7 million in a campaign against the measure (spending data from Price, 1988, p. 484). In the end over 70 percent of voters rejected the initiative. As data in Table A.9 suggest, in a case where nearly all major elected elites clearly lined up against the initiative at early stages of the campaign, mass opinion among California voters was highly stable, tolerant of minority rights, and never polarized.

A different scenario developed in the case of the 1994 Idaho anti-gay initiative. The Idaho measure would have repealed and blocked state and local laws prohibiting discrimination against gays, lesbians, and bisexuals in Idaho. It was championed by the Idaho Citizen's Alliance and its leader, Kelly Walton. Walton was a former official in the Oregon Citizen's Alliance (OCA), a conservative group associated with the national Christian Coalition ("Who's Who," 1993). Oregon's anti-gay Measure 9 of 1992 was designed and promoted by the OCA. As with the California initiatives, many elected officials, religious leaders, and community leaders did come out strongly against Idaho's Proposition One ("Our View: Future," 1994).

Unlike the California initiatives, there was a less cohesive elite-level mobilization against the Idaho initiative. One of the state's two incumbent U.S. House of Representatives members, Republican Michael Crapo, initially stated he could support the initiative—although he later came out against it ("Crapo Says," 1994). Crapo and Dirk Kempthorne, one of Idaho's two Republican U.S. Senators, reportedly advised the state GOP to avoid taking a position against the initiative (Liechtiling, Mazzochi, & Gardiner, 1993, p. 16). The Idaho State GOP never took a position against the initiative, and Larry Eastland, a GOP primary candidate for governor[10] made issue of this fact in defense of the initiative (Prichard, 1994b). The state's second U.S. Senator also hesitated in voicing opposition to the initiative after it had qualified for the ballot ("Our View: Future," 1994).

Several political elites did voice opposition, including Larry EchoHawk, the Democratic candidate for governor, and Republican Phil Batt (Prichard, 1994a). Batt eventually received 52 percent in the general election and was elected governor. Newspapers ran editorials against the initiative, and opponents were able to transmit anti-initiative information by spending over $700,000 (widely outspending proponents in an inexpensive media market). In the end Proposition One was defeated; however, opinion was highly polarized, with only 3,000 votes separating supporters and opponents.

These cases are illustrative of how one minority that is relatively unpopular has fared recently when made the subject of policies through direct, majoritarian democratic institutions at the state level. A review of these cases suggests that when elites are fairly unified in condemning proposals, election results reflect that direct democracy outcomes need not be abusive or intolerant of the minority group. In these cases, mass opinion at the time of the election is less polarized, if not moving toward a more tolerant position. Where major elected officials are divided or silent, however, outcomes might differ as mass opinion is more polarized.

These aggregate data suggest, but do not establish, that elite positions matter. We should note that in each case opponents outspent proponents. However, in the case where opinion change might have been greatest (Proposition Six), spending was most closely balanced. Spending alone, then, might not fully explain opinion change and opinion formation on these issues.

Direct-democracy processes might avoid majoritarian abuses of minorities if voters are aware of the political positions of elites. Without this, or with divided messages from elites, voters might be left with little more than their existing feelings toward homosexuals when making ballot decisions. As Tables A.3 and A.8 demonstrate, most voters have negative feelings about homosexuality and homosexuals. Yet most of the time most voters oppose statewide anti-gay initiatives, particularly where political elites are united in opposition. At the individual level, this suggests that voters who are aware of positions that political elites take on initiatives (other things being equal) could be less likely to support anti-gay initiatives. Political awareness, or we might also call attentiveness to politics, should thus condition support for these initiatives. An individual-level test of the effects of political awareness can be conducted by modeling support for anti-gay initiatives. In addition to indicators of awareness, several measures of symbolic predispositions are used below to estimate support for three statewide initiatives dealing with the civil rights of gays.

INDIVIDUAL-LEVEL SOURCES OF SUPPORT FOR ANTI-GAY INITIATIVES

Opinion data adequate for this task are available from California's Proposition Sixty-four of 1986 (the Larouche AIDS quarantine initiative); California's Proposition 102 of 1988 (the Dannemeyer initiative) and from Colorado's Amendment Two initiative campaign of 1992.[11] The Field Institute conducted surveys during each California campaign. The Colorado survey was conducted by John McIver and the University of Colorado Social Science Data Lab.[12]

Like Proposition 64, Proposition 102 was placed on the California ballot by the efforts of conservative activists and paid signature gatherers (Price, 1988, p. 484). Two years after the defeat of Proposition 64, an Orange County member of the U.S. Congress, William Dannemeyer, sponsored

Proposition 102, an initiative directed against AIDS carriers. The measures would have required state officials to compile names of AIDS carriers and remove them from some jobs. The initiative was seen as part of Dannemeyer's broader anti-gay political interests. These interests are reflected in a book (Dannemeyer, 1989) where he argued that a dangerous homosexual movement in the nation was seeking to destroy religion and America (Lesher, 1994).

The Colorado initiative is important to examine since the substance of Amendment Two is fairly representative of initiatives that have circulated and qualified in western states since 1992. Indeed, there is evidence that anti-gay-rights advocates from various states built upon the Colorado measure and subsequently coordinated initiative-drafting and qualifying efforts across state lines (Boxall, 1994). The Colorado initiative repealed local laws (including an ordinance passed by Boulder voters in 1987) that offered protections against job discrimination based on sexual orientation and other factors.[13]

Political awareness was measured indirectly for this analysis in two of the three races, and not measured in a third (Proposition 102). In the October 30, 1986, survey of voting intentions in California, voters were asked if they had heard of four initiatives other than Proposition Sixty-four. We measure awareness as an additive index of responses to these questions, assuming that the politically aware will have heard of more ballot propositions. Voters who reported hearing of more initiatives were given higher scores on the awareness variable (four being the highest possible score).

In Colorado, our surrogate measure of awareness is a variable indicating if the respondent watched the presidential debates. Respondents reporting that they watched the 1992 presidential debates were coded as one, those not watching were coded as zero. Each of these measures represents general attentiveness to political information. We can be fairly confident that the measure of awareness in California captures something independent of education and more akin to attentiveness to politics and elite positions since the Pearson's correlation between education and the awareness index is a low .15 in the 1986 sample.

We also assume that symbolic predispositions affect voter decisions about ballot initiatives, particularly since these initiatives lack a clear fiscal impact for large segments of the electorate. By symbolic predispositions we mean those broad categories of strong, non-self-interested attitudinal predispositions that can motivate voter decisions. Such predispositions are typically acquired early in life, with classic examples including racial prejudice, patriotism, and religious convictions (Sears, 1993, pp. 120–124). These predispositions are often measured with indicators of ideology, partisanship, and attitudinal references. Such variables reflect the long-standing, affective orientations that structure how individuals react to actual political issues (Jacoby, 1994, pp. 345–346; Sears, Lau, Tyler, & Allen, 1980).

For this reason, we include a measure of partisanship where respondents are coded one if Republican and zero if otherwise. We also include a measure of ideology where self-identified liberal respondents are coded one, and others zero. We expect liberals to have greater tolerance of minority groups and expect (at least in Colorado) that GOP identification will increase support.[14] Given the design of these surveys, we are unable to use direct measures of symbolic motives and attitudes that might be the most precise representatives of support for anti-homosexual initiatives. Affect, or feelings toward gays and lesbians as a group, was not recorded, but the 1988 California poll did include a question asking respondents if they "identified with the Gay/Lesbian community."[15]

Each survey provides some additional (albeit surrogate) measures of symbolic predispositions that might be associated with affect toward gays, lesbians, and bisexuals. The California polls of 1986 and 1988 asked respondents if they identified themselves as "born again" Christians. Other things being equal, we might anticipate that these Christians are more likely to have values that lead them to hold civil rights protections for gays, lesbians, and bisexuals in low esteem, and to consequently motivate them to support anti-gay initiatives. Direct measures of religious identification are not available from the Colorado poll. However, Colorado respondents were asked to identify "the most important problems" facing their state. We create a variable that identifies voters who say family values are the most important problem in Colorado or the United States. Another variable represents those respondents who said they would be opposed to abortion under many circumstances. This is also used to tap fundamentalist attitudes in the Colorado sample. An additional variable measuring antiminority sentiments in California was created that indicated those respondents who supported the "Official English" initiative (Citrin, Reingold, Walters, & Green, 1990) that appeared on the ballot that year.

Education has also been found to structure attitudes about homosexuality, to affect tolerance, and to affect how individuals reason about policy (Sniderman, Brody, & Tetlock, 1991). For these reasons, we anticipate that the higher educated are less supportive of these initiatives. It has also been noted that contemporary anti-gay initiatives are framed in a language of scarcity and job quotas, such that "special rights" are being extended to one group (gays, lesbians, and bisexuals) at the expense of others.[16] The California initiative of 1986 was not contested under these terms, but the Colorado initiative was. We might expect that voters who perceive that their personal economic condition had deteriorated[17] would thus be more supportive of anti-gay initiatives that use the language of "special rights." For comparative purposes, we include similar measures of economic concerns when estimating support for Proposition Sixty-four.[18]

Age, race,[19] gender (1 = woman, 0 = man), and income are included as additional control variables in models estimating support for these initiatives.[20] The first model reported in Table A.10 estimates vote intentions on California's Proposition Sixty-four using reported vote intentions recorded a few days prior to the election. The second model estimates support for Proposition 102 early in the 1988 fall campaign.[21] The final model estimates vote intentions for Colorado's Amendment Two. Since each survey uses a different mix of questions, the models differ slightly from each other. Logistic regression is used to estimate models of support since the dependent variable is dichotomous.

FINDINGS FROM SURVEYS

Results presented in Table A.10 indicate that there were some common determinants of support for each of these initiatives. Most noticeably, education clearly structured the odds of supporting each initiative.[22] The significant coefficients for education indicate that when other variables in the model are held constant statistically, support was weakest among the most educated respondents. The models also illustrate that income does not appear to have an effect on vote intentions. Age and gender were only significant in the estimation for Proposition 102 (at the early stage of the campaign, older voters appeared more supportive of the Dannemeyer initiative and women more opposed). The direction of the coefficient for African-American voters was negative and not significant in the models of vote intentions on Proposition Sixty-four, and positive and insignificant for the other initiatives. It thus appears that African-Americans are no more or less likely to favor these initiatives than other voters.

In Colorado, where one element of the issue was framed by initiative proponents as "no special job rights for gays," economic discontent was not associated with support. When we consider partisanship, Republican identifiers in Colorado were clearly more supportive of Amendment Two. In California, however, Republican partisanship was not associated with support for Proposition 64 or Proposition 102 (despite Proposition 102 being authored by a GOP congressman). Given the position of "traditional values" advocates in the Colorado State GOP by 1992, it is not entirely surprising that there was a more pronounced effect of GOP partisanship in the 1992 Colorado vote than in California in 1986 or 1988.[23] In comparison, the Dannemeyer forces in California never were strong enough to affect the party statewide, with Dannemeyer failing to win in state primaries.

The coefficients for the other indicators of symbolic predispositions support the hypotheses that enduring, deep attachments (or gut feelings) are likely to structure voting on these issues. In each estimation, liberals are consistently less supportive (although the effect is significant only with Proposition 102). In California, self-identified born-again Christian voters were much more supportive of the Larouche and Dannemeyer initiatives. Support for the official English initiative was also associated with support for the

Larouche initiative. In Colorado, measures of family values concerns were not significant, yet Colorado voters who opposed most forms of abortion (a measure used here as a surrogate for fundamentalism) were significantly more supportive of Amendment Two.

Finally, the indicators of political awareness are associated with opposition to the Larouche initiative and to Colorado's Amendment Two. In terms of questions about direct democracy's propensity to turn mass opinion about unpopular groups into public policy, this is perhaps the most interesting finding here. It provides some indirect evidence of the potential for elite cues to move some voters away from their initial predispositions about groups made the subject of policies that limit civil rights protections. At the end of these election campaigns, voters who were more attentive to politics were more likely to hold tolerant opinions. This suggests a process where voter attitudes are shaped by information received during the campaign, with opinions possibly moved toward the tolerant positions advocated by elites.

This interpretation of the awareness effect is a substantial modification of what Zaller's full theory of mass response to political information might suggest. Zaller (following Converse, 1962) notes that the most attentive voter should be *more* resistant to elite messages than other voters since she has a greater store of political information. Having no data on the opinions of attentive voters prior to the campaigns, this chapter cannot assess which interpretation is most accurate. However, initiative campaigns are likely to be quite different than the (partisan) candidate races that Converse and Zaller focus on. Here, even highly informed voters could be unaware of the details of initiative proposals prior to a campaign. As attentive voters, they could be more likely to seek information about the details and consequences of initiatives or at least seek out cues on the positions of elites. Results in Table A.10 are consistent with such a process. However, the data might also fit another explanation of the process of mass response to anti-gay and lesbian initiatives. For example, it might be that attentive voters were simply more tolerant of gays or more resistant to denying civil rights protection from the start of the campaign. Without a panel survey design, we cannot definitively determine how (and when) voters respond to elite cues.

DISCUSSION AND CONCLUSIONS

What does this say about critics' fears that state-level direct democracy will allow unchecked majorities to run roughshod over unpopular minorities? We might see these results as offering only partial solace to those who fear that direct democracy is explicitly antiminority and abusive of minority rights. Regardless of electoral outcomes, the fact that such policies appear regularly on ballots and in petition drives might cause great stress and public stigmatization for groups made the subject of the proposals. The existence of initiatives that fail might nevertheless polarize mass opinions about gays, lesbians, and bisexuals, particularly if elites are not in consensus on such measures. Campaigns might also create situations that generate greater hostility directed at groups targeted by the initiative. Furthermore, it must be noted that the Colorado anti-gay initiative passed, and that the Idaho initiative lost by only 3,000 votes. These facts do not appear consistent with a political process that acts to protect the rights of unpopular minorities.

That being said, some of the findings presented here suggest that there is certainly some potential for state-level direct democracy outcomes to be tolerant of gays and lesbians.[24] Most of these initiatives have failed to gain enough signatures to qualify for state ballots (see chapter note 1), and the Colorado initiative is only one of two to have received a majority vote at the state level between 1978 and 1995.[25] Aggregate data presented here suggest that voters do change opinions that, initially, can be seen as intolerant of gay rights. Individual-level data illustrate that the politically aware (those assumed to be attentive to elite messages that call for tolerance) were less supportive of an anti-gay rights initiatives and an AIDS quarantine initiative.

We suggest that these findings reflect a process where, prior to an election, mass attitudes about a gay-rights issue might not reflect high levels of tolerance. Many undecided voters, however, are likely to search for information cues such as elite positions and endorsements when making their decisions late in the campaign. When campaigns against anti-gay initiatives are one-sided (dominated by opponents) and elites are in consensus in opposition, we might expect outcomes to be tolerant of minority rights. Where elites' messages are less clear and forthcoming in opposition, or where there are numerous anti-gay initiative proponents holding public office or assume visible roles within major political parties, we might expect more opinion polarization and a greater likelihood of these policies passing. Still, many factors that might be considered static or representative of relatively inflexible "deep attachments" are important vote determinants. Relatively inflexible symbolic predispositions reflected in the form of religious identification, ideology, and partisanship shaped votes in California and Colorado.

One final problem with this analysis of direct democracy relates to the extent that we might generalize beyond these results. There has been some variability in the content of these initiatives over time and across states. In some cases, the potential for abridgment of civil rights is more clearly framed in the ballot language. Oregon's Measure 9, for example, included hostile, pejorative language directed against homosexuals. In such a case, voters who are disposed toward protecting civil rights (even of unpopular groups) might have less difficulty in forming choices that are tolerant of gays, lesbians, and bisexuals. Pejorative and condemnatory language thus might cue voters to the potential civil rights issues in the text of the initiative proposal. When attacks on rights are presented in the text of the initiative more subtly, civil rights issues might be made less explicit and voter responses that might typically be triggered by concerns for protecting rights could be less frequent. At this point, little is known about how a slight change in subject matter (or ballot title) could elicit a different response from a given voter. It remains to be seen how initiative proponents' attempts to alter the wording of these initiatives (while retaining much content) will result in changes in voter responses.

NOTES

1. In 1994 petitions were filed in Arizona, Florida, Idaho, Maine, Michigan, Missouri, Nevada, Oregon, and Washington. A petition organization announced plans to file an anti-gay initiative in Ohio but never filed with the state. The 1994 Florida petition was invalidated by the state court. In 1995, two additional anti-gay, lesbian, and bisexual initiatives were circulating in Washington. There were active "do not sign" campaigns against the petitions in several states. Among other things, the failure of these petition efforts might reflect the "do not sign" efforts, tolerance in the mass electorate, and/or weak organization efforts by initiative proponents.

2. Sniderman, Brody, and Tetlock (1991, Chap. 3) found a similar trend in California opinion data suggesting changing attitudes about homosexuality and discrimination. They concluded that a liberal trend on antidiscrimination laws was evident from 1977–1985 (see also Page & Shapiro, 1992, pp. 98–100). W. G. Mayer notes (1992, pp. 184–185) that cross-sectional data illustrating change over time can mask the liberalizing effect of generational replacement and the growing conservativism associated with the aging of older cohorts. Respondents from younger cohorts measured in later surveys are more tolerant; however, tolerance appears to diminish within older cohorts as they age.

3. It is interesting to note that the major nonincremental change in attitudes occurred between 1991 and 1993—after anti-gay initiatives in Oregon and Colorado received national press coverage.

4. Other factors might be affecting response patterns over time. We cannot account for the possibility that survey respondents might adopt more socially acceptable responses while retaining anti-gay attitudes.

5. We might also expect that other minorities could evaluate such initiatives in self-interested terms. The editors, for example, note that majorities of LDS (Mormon) voters in parts of Idaho opposed that state's anti-gay initiative. One explanation of this would be the sense among the LDS minority that "you will be next." Alternatively, LDS members might generally be more tolerant than other voters, or more fearful of using state laws to censure minority group behavior.

6. This assumption reflects loosely the model of John Zaller (1992) and V. O. Key's assumption (1961, p. 2) that "the voice of the people is but an echo." Zaller adds to Key's assumption his own expectations that voters have political predispositions that are shaped by campaign information. For an example of an application of the logic in the context of direct democracy, see Karp (1994).

7. These cases were selected by matter of convenience. There are not many multiple cross-sectional surveys available for analysis on this topic. The AIDS measures did not mention homosexuality specifically, but it and other California AIDS ballot measures were seen by the media and proponents alike as being directed against gay men (see, for example, Lesher, 1994).

8. Care should be used when interpreting questions measuring movement in support for ballot initiatives. Such questions might overestimate initial levels of support by attributing opinions to people who have not yet heard about the initiative (see Bowler & Donovan, 1994b).

9. The Larouche initiative was very similar to other AIDS regulation initiatives introduced in California.

10. Eastland finished second in a four-candidate primary race.

11. These are some of the only cases where surveys of scholarly quality were conducted at or near the time of an election including statewide anti-gay propositions. Although the AIDS-oriented initiatives were not explicitly anti-gay, Propositions 64 and 102 were seen as targeting gay men (unlike Proposition 96 of 1988).

12. The authors of this chapter bear all responsibility for any errors in interpreting these data.

13. The 1994 Idaho and Oregon initiatives would also have prevented state and local governments from recognizing same-sex marriages and domestic partnerships and barred discussion of homosexuality in public schools. They would also have allowed employers to consider sexual orientation as a factor in employment decisions.

14. The party hypothesis is time bound. The strength of "traditional values" forces in the state Republican parties was stronger in Colorado in 1992 than California in 1986. Furthermore, there might be a measurement problem with the ideology variable. Self-identified conservatives holding libertarian ideas might be equally or more tolerant than self-identified liberals.

15. The question allowed these responses: "totally," "quite a bit," "some," and "not at all." We use this as an ordinal variable coded such that the 1 = "totally," 2 = "quite a bit," and so on. Having friends or family who are gay, lesbian, or bisexual is another variable likely to reduce support. Measures of this are also not available.

16. See also "Survey of Voter Attitudes" from the National Gay and Lesbian Task Force (NGLTF), June 9, 1994. Results available from the NGLTF, Washington, DC. Or at: ftp.QRD.org in pub/QRD/orgs/NGLTF/1994. Access date November 12, 1995.

17. For Colorado the estimations reported use a dummy variable measure of perception that present personal economic conditions are "worse off" than four years before. Alternative estimations using variables created from responses to open-ended questions where respondents voiced sociotropic economic concerns produced similar results.

18. The October 30 California estimations use a dummy variable where 1 = expectation that personal finances will be worse off in the future. The November 4 exit survey used wording similar to the Colorado estimation (1 = present conditions worse than before). An alternative hypotheses holds that negative economic evaluations are associated with more negative voting on proposition since voters might be more risk aversive in bad economic times. This effect should be more apparent with aggregate data, however (Bowler & Donovan, 1994a).

19. For the California and Colorado estimations, race is coded 1 = Black, 0 = otherwise. In the Colorado analysis there were only six Black respondents. All models were re-estimated with a dummy variable representing all non-Whites, with no change in the substantive findings.

20. See note 5 for additional reasons why race might structure opinions about these initiatives.

21. We should note that at the time the Proposition 102 poll was done, most respondents favored the proposal. It failed in November, receiving only 34 percent support.

22. See note in Table A.10 explaining the logit coefficients.

23. Substituting a dummy variable representing Bush voters to the Colorado estimates indicates a positive relationship between support for Bush and support for Amendment Two.

24. As Madison anticipated, a greater danger to minorities can exist in smaller, more homogeneous jurisdictions. Scores of anti-gay initiatives (many invalidated by courts and state legislatures) have passed in local contests. As of 1993, the National Gay and Lesbian Task Force reported that anti-gay initiatives had passed in nine of nine counties and in thirty-five of forty-five cities since 1974. One year after Oregon's Measure 9 failed 44 percent to 56 percent eighteen Oregon cities had anti-gay initiatives before their voters; seventeen passed.

25. In 1988 Oregon voters passed an initiative with 52 percent in favor (later overturned by the courts) that revoked the governor's executive order banning sexual-orientation discrimination in the state executive branch (Mason, 1994).

10

The Correlates of Tolerance: Analyzing the Statewide Votes on Anti-Gay Initiatives

Stephanie L. Witt and Leslie R. Alm

Voters in four states—Colorado, Idaho, Oregon, and Maine—have voted on statewide anti-gay initiatives in recent years.[1] Oregon voters have considered two different measures, one in 1992 (Measure 13) and one in 1994 (Measure 9). With the exception of Colorado's 1992 vote on Amendment Two, all of the statewide anti-gay initiatives have failed at the ballot box. Colorado's Amendment Two was later struck down by the U.S. Supreme Court (see Chapter 11). Table A.11 displays the election results for the four statewide votes considered in this chapter. This analysis uses county-level data to evaluate the votes on four of these anti-gay initiatives (the 1992 Oregon initiative is not used).[2]

The literature on public opinion and attitudes towards gays suggests that certain voter characteristics correlate with tolerance toward gays. An important empirical question is whether or not voters take those predispositions with them into the voting booth when considering anti-gay initiatives. By comparing socioeconomic, political, and religious characteristics of county populations with the county's vote on the anti-gay measure, we can begin to assess the relationship between tolerance and this divisive social issue.

SOCIOECONOMIC CORRELATES OF TOLERANCE

Studies have shown that tolerance for homosexuals is greater among those with higher education levels. This applies in regard to the granting of civil liberties to gay people (Dejowski, 1992), support for gay marriage (Wonn, 1996), and the general support of gay rights (Schneider & Lewis, 1984).

Similarly, people with higher incomes are also more tolerant of gay people (Schneider & Lewis, 1984; Wonn, 1996). Age, on the other hand has been found to be negatively related to tolerance of gays, meaning that older people tend to be less tolerant than younger people (Dejowski, 1992; Wonn, 1996). People from rural communities, or similarly, smaller communities, are also less tolerant of gays and gay rights than their urban counterparts (Dejowski, 1992; Pratte, 1993).

POLITICAL CORRELATES OF TOLERANCE

The Democratic and Republican parties have taken divergent stances on the issue of gay rights in recent years. The 1992 Republican platform opposed gay rights while the Democratic platform endorsed the end to the ban on gays in the military (Lowi & Ginsberg, 1996). The Republican party has attracted many voters in recent elections for whom family values or social issues in general (such as anti-abortion and anti-gay-rights stances) are most important (Kellstedt, Green, Guth, & Smidt, 1994).

RELIGIOUS CORRELATES OF TOLERANCE

Previous research has indicated that Protestants are less tolerant of gays than either Catholics or Jews (Dejowski, 1992). There are, however, important distinctions among the many Protestant denominations. Those who are members of denominations classified as conservative theologically or evangelical in orientation, such as the Southern Baptists or the Nazarenes are less tolerant of gays than other mainline protestant denominations such as Presbyterians or Episcopalians (Kellstedt & Green, 1993; Roof & McKinney, 1987).[3] The Christian Right, often noted for its advocacy of the anti-gay initiatives (see Lunch, 1995), is usually associated with the conservative Protestant denominations. The political movement of the Christian Right, however, is distinct from these denominational barriers and includes many other actors, such as Pat Buchanan, a Catholic (see Green, 1995a for a description of the Christian Right; or Chapter 2).

An important distinction to make in regard to Protestant denominations is the inclusion or exclusion of members of the Church of Jesus Christ of Latter Day Saints (LDS, also known as Mormons). While many studies omit this group as a minor sect, research by and Roof and McKinney (1987) reports that LDS adherents have very high scores on civil liberties scales in regard to gays. This becomes relevant when examining the vote on anti-gay initiatives because LDS adherents comprise approximately 24 percent of the population of Idaho (Bradley, Green, Jones, Lynn, & McNeil, 1992).

METHODOLOGY

The dependent variable used in this analysis is the percent yes vote on the anti-gay initiative for each county in the four states in which there has been a statewide vote (Colorado, Idaho, Oregon, and Maine).[4] All of the anti-gay initiatives discussed in this analysis were worded so that a yes vote indicated support for the anti-gay position. Election results were provided by the secretary of state's office in each of the four states.

Socioeconomic information about the counties was obtained from United States Census data. Education is measured by the percent of people in the county with a Bachelor's degree in 1991. The county's average per capita income in 1990 is used to measure income. An additional measure of the relative income of the county was also used: the percentage of families living below the poverty line in 1989. A measure of the urban-rural nature of the county is obtained by using the percent of the population living in urban areas in 1990. The median age of county residents in 1990 measures age.[5]

The political variable used in this analysis is the percent vote for President Clinton in each county in 1992. This is intended to serve as a surrogate for Democratic vote in the county.

Religion is measured using Bradley, Green, Jones, Lynn, and McNeil's 1992 breakdown of churches and church membership by state and county. The number of LDS adherents was obtained from this source for each county. A compilation of the number of conservative Protestant adherents in each county was created by using the classification of denominations developed by McKinney and utilized in Roof and McKinney (1987). The inclusion of these two measures of religion is based first upon the high civil liberties score and concentration of LDS adherents in Idaho as well as on the importance of conservative Protestants in the political mobilization of the Christian Right (Rozell & Wilcox, 1995; Chapter 2).

ANALYSIS AND DISCUSSION

A multiple regression was conducted to assess the impact of the independent variables listed above on the county's percent yes vote on the anti-gay initiative. Table A.12 displays the results of that regression. The model explains 59.3 percent of the variance in the dependent variable. The F statistic was 26.88, significant at $p \leq .000$.[6] Education, income, the percentage of LDS adherents in the county, the percent of families in poverty in the county, and the presidential vote in 1992 were all statistically significant in explaining the variance in the yes vote on the anti-gay initiatives (see Table A.12). These relationships confirm the importance and direction of the relationships suggested by the previous studies mentioned above. Higher education levels in the county were correlated with fewer yes votes on the anti-gay initiative. Higher income levels in the county were correlated with fewer yes votes on the initiative. Higher percentages of LDS adherents in the county were correlated with fewer yes votes on the anti-gay initiative. Higher percentages of votes for Clinton in 1992 were correlated with fewer yes votes on the anti-gay initiative. Conversely, the higher the percentage of families living in poverty in the county, the higher the number of yes votes on the anti-gay initiative. Only the median age in the county, the percentage of conservative Protestants and the percentage of those living in urban areas were not significant at the p<.05 level. It should be noted that while these relationships were not statistically significant in this model, they were in the expected direction.

Several aspects of these results are unexpected. The variable that has the strongest impact on the percent yes vote on the anti-gay initiative (Beta = −.6319; significance = .000) is the political variable: the percent vote for Clinton in the 1992 presidential election. While political party preference was expected to be related to one's stance on the anti-gay initiative (see literature review above)—it is somewhat surprising that it is the most explanatory variable in the equation—especially given the literature indicating that political parties are weakening and voters are more often "independents" (Ladd, 1995). This finding does, however, replicate the results of Haider-Markel and Meier (1996), which also found the presidential vote to the the strongest predictor of votes against lesbian and gay rights.[7] They suggest that the importance of morality in the Bush campaign may explain the importance of this variable. Another explanation of this finding may lie in the consistent Republican voting of evangelical Christians. Previous stud ies estimated that 63 percent of evangelicals voted for Bush in 1992 (Kellstedt, Green, Guth, & Smidt, 1994), and that 75 percent of evangelicals voted Republican in the 1994 elections (Green, 1995a). Recall that the relationship between the vote for Clinton and the yes vote on the anti-gay initiative was negative, meaning that as the vote for Clinton went up, the yes (anti-gay) vote on the initiative went down.

Particularly surprising is the weaker-than-expected relationship between the percentage of conservative Protestants in each county and the percent yes vote on the anti-gay initiatives. The bivariate relationship between the percentage of conservative Protestants in the county and the percent yes vote on the anti-gay initiative as measured by a Pearson's correlation coefficient is .46, significant at p<.000. When taking all of the other variables into account in the multiple regression, however, the significance of the percentage of conservative Protestants fades. This may be indicative of the complexity of the issue and the cross-pressures felt by voters. It may also indicate that while the percentage of conservative Protestants in a county may be large enough to advocate on behalf of an initiative, they may not represent a bloc large enough to impact the ultimate vote. The initiative process, after all, allows a relatively small group to force a vote on its issue with a minimum number of signatures and without possibility of compromise.

Another surprising finding is the direction and significance of the relationship of the percentage of LDS adherents in the county to the yes vote on the anti-gay initiatives. The relationship is negative, indicating that as the percentage of LDS adherents in a county goes up, the yes vote on the anti-gay initiatives goes down. Despite well-known opposition to gay rights and intolerance of practicing homosexuals within the church, it appears that LDS voters voted no on the anti-gay initiatives.[8] This would reaffirm the earlier work of Roof and McKinney, in which LDS adherents scored high on civil liberties scales (1987). The data in this analysis cannot explain this pattern. It may be, however, that the pre-election revelation that the Idaho Citizen's Alliance was distributing the video *The Gay Agenda*—whose producers also made anti-Mormon films—hurt the initiative's chances with LDS voters (see Chapter 7 this volume). It may also be that early Idaho persecution of LDS adherents instilled a strong belief in civil liberties (see Wells, 1978).

The findings in a study such as this are suggestive. It is impossible to know what each voter contemplated while voting. Given that advocates on both sides of the issue concede that significant numbers of voters were confused about what a yes or no vote meant (see Chapter 7), the voters themselves may not have known what they were doing. Based on the brief review of the literature included in this chapter and the above analysis, however, it does appear that, in the aggregate the correlates of tolerance apparent in public opinion measures extend to votes on anti-gay initiatives.

NOTES

1. The text of the anti-gay initiatives in Colorado, Oregon, Idaho, and Maine are in Appendix B.

2. The 1992 Oregon election was not included for two reasons. First, the second initiative more closely resembles the state's other measures. Second, only one Oregon election was included in the multiple regression model that follows to avoid double counting the Oregon countries' characteristics in the equations.

3. We acknowledge that frequency of church attendance is an important determinant of attitude and behavior. For example, Kellstedt, Green, Guth, and Smidt (1994) found that regular church attenders were more conservative in their attitudes about abortion and gay rights than other evangelical voters (see also Legge, 1983). Unfortunately, data at the county level do not provide this level of information, so a measure of church attendance is not included in our analysis.

4. Colorado has sixty-three counties, Idaho has forty-four counties, Oregon has thirty-six counties, and Maine has sixteen. All of the counties are included in the analysis.

5. The use of data from different years results from using the most recent data available for all of the counties. Not all data is available for every year.

6. An analysis of several measures of collinearity (tolerance, variance inflation factors, eigenvalues, and condition indices) for this regression equation suggests that no serious collinearity exists for any of the independent variables in the model (Lewis-Beck, 1980; Norusis, 1993).

7. The Haider-Markel and Meier (1996) study did not include Idaho's 1994 or Maine's 1995 vote on anti-gay initiatives.

8. The Church of Jesus Christ of Latter Day Saints' (LDS) ability to have a strong impact on Idaho politics has been documented previously. See Witt and Moncrief (1993) for a discussion of the impact of LDS legislators and constituents on abortion politics in Idaho, and Blank (1978) for a more general discussion of the role of the LDS church in Idaho.

11

Romer v. Evans: The Centerpiece of the American Gay-Rights Debate

Sean Patrick O'Rourke and Laura K. Lee Dellinger

INTRODUCTION

"When seven gay-rights activists met on a May afternoon in 1992, sipping weak coffee in a down-at-the-heels conference room on East Colfax Avenue [in Denver, CO], they launched a lawsuit likely to reach the velvet curtained chambers of the U.S. Supreme Court." So wrote Michael Booth, a staff writer for the *Denver Post* newspaper in 1993 (Booth, 1993b). Booth was referring to a group of civil rights activists, now known collectively as the Colorado Legal Initiatives Project (CLIP). CLIP had gathered to discuss legal strategy in response to the possible passage of a Colorado anti-gay-rights ballot initiative in the fall of 1992.

The initiative, known as Amendment Two because of its place on the ballot, was proposed by Colorado for Family Values (CFV), a right-wing offshoot of the better known Traditional Values Coalition of Anaheim, California. Joining with a cadre of other right-wing organizations (including the Traditional Values Coalition, Focus on Family, Concerned Women for America, Summit Ministries, and The Eagle Forum), CFV filed the initiative petition on July 31, 1991, and the signature drive along with a "no special rights" campaign began. By March 20, 1992 CFV had collected 85,000 signatures, enough to qualify for the Colorado ballot. Activists and legal experts on both sides of the issue agree that, prior to Amendment Two, no measure had ever been attempted in the United States that had as great potential negative impact on the basic civil rights of the gay, lesbian, bisexual community.

CFV proposed Amendment Two largely in response to existing antidiscrimination ordinances in Denver, Boulder, and Aspen, and a proposed ordinance in CFV's base city of Colorado Springs—home to more than eighty conservative groups where more than one third of the 350,000 residents claim to be "born again Christians." The various ordinances CFV sought to invalidate in various Colorado cities quite simply prohibited discrimination based on sexual orientation. The practical effect of the measure was to make it legal and constitutional to discriminate against men and women who are—*or who are thought to be*—homosexual or bisexual, by repealing existing ordinances and policies in Colorado that protect gay men, lesbians, and bisexuals from discrimination in housing, employment, and public accommodation. The measure also prohibited the future passage of antidiscrimination laws protecting homosexuals by state or local government and prevented all governmental bodies from considering any claim of sexual-orientation discrimination. In addition, the amendment would have changed insurance code provisions and invalidated Governor Roy Romer's Executive Order prohibiting discrimination in state employment. But the most far-reaching effect of Amendment Two was to make it impossible, indeed illegal, for government to respond to existing or future discrimination which gay, lesbian, or bisexual Coloradans might encounter by constitutionally prohibiting their right to make a claim.

CFV's prodiscrimination rhetoric had one central theme: "no special rights." Those who fought for the passage of Amendment Two based their campaign on the premise that gay, lesbian, and bisexual Coloradans enjoyed "special rights" because of the ordinances enacted in various Colorado cities. To be successful, they had to convince a public—70 percent of which support equal rights for gay people (Lake Research, 1995)—that the gay community was, in fact, seeking something *more* than the rest of the citizenry enjoyed. Elizabeth Birch, executive director of the Human Rights Campaign, noted that it was to CFV's advantage "that the majority of Americans do not know that no federal law protects lesbian and gay people from discrimination. Indeed," Birch said, "most people do not know that it is perfectly legal to *fire* someone for being gay in the forty-one states that do not have civil rights protection based on sexual orientation" (Birch, 1996).

CFV's "no special rights" campaign appeared to have succeeded. And on November 4, 1992, six months after CLIP's first meeting, what many in Colorado's human- and gay-rights communities viewed as their worst nightmare of came true, and Colorado became the first state in the nation to pass an anti-gay rights ballot measure. Although the margin of victory was narrow—53.4 percent—the amendment attracted national attention from the anti-gay rights proponents as well as from gay-rights advocates and activists around the nation.

THE ROAD TO THE COURT

Human-rights activists were confident that Amendment Two was unconstitutional before it ever qualified for the ballot. And as the battle for votes was being waged (and won) by CFV's "no special rights" campaign, CLIP, along with Lambda Legal Defense and Education Fund, the ACLU (American Civil Liberties Union), GLAAD (Gay and Lesbian Alliance Against Defamation), Equality Colorado, and many others were quietly working out the details of their legal strategy.

Nine days after its passage, Amendment Two began the long journey to the U.S. Supreme Court when CLIP filed the case of *Evans v. Romer* in Denver District Court. Just over a month later, the legal team filed a motion for an injunction claiming that Amendment Two was likely to be ruled unconstitutional on the basis of the equal protection clause of the Fourteenth Amendment to the Federal Constitution. The injunction, granted by Judge Jeffrey Bayless on January 15, 1993, kept Amendment Two from being enforced until a trial on its merits could be held. The state appealed the decision, but on July 19, the Colorado Supreme Court upheld the injunction (six to one), affirming the lower court's opinion that equal participation in the political process is a fundamental right and that Amendment Two "fences out" an identifiable group of people from participating in that process. The state of Colorado appealed the decision to the U.S. Supreme Court, which refused to hear the case. Meanwhile, a trial on the merits was held before Judge Bayless in District Court between October 12 and 22, 1993. Two months later, in his December 14 ruling, Judge Bayless found Amendment Two unconstitutional. The ruling was affirmed nearly one year later by the Colorado Supreme Court (six to one). Linda Greenhouse, of the *New York Times*, summarized the Colorado High Court's ruling when she wrote that "any legislation that infringed on the fundamental right to participate equally in the political process by 'fencing out' an independently identifiable class of persons, must be subject to 'strict judicial scrutiny,' meaning the challenged legislation must be shown to be necessary to support a compelling state interest and must be narrowly tailored to meet that interest" (Greenhouse, 1995).

As the legal battle dragged on in Colorado, anti-gay-rights groups across the nation used the Amendment Two victory as impetus for furthering their agenda. And the public was caught in the cross-fire.

Fred Brown, writer for the *Denver Post*, noted in December 1993 that the public seemed to be confused about the effect of Amendment Two. Brown wrote, "throughout the months of debate and public opinion sampling on Amendment Two, it has been clear that Coloradans are convinced they were voting *against* 'special rights' for gays and lesbians, not that they were voting against laws to protect homosexuals from discrimination" (F. Brown, 1993).

Further evidence of public confusion is reflected by research conducted by Talmey Drake Research & Strategies Inc. Their 1993 survey concluded that 71 percent of Coloradans believe that it should be illegal to fire a person based on sexual orientation (F. Brown, 1993). Yet Coloradans had just approved a ballot measure that had the practical effect of *making it legal to do just that*. As Amendment Two was making its way through the state courts, citizens in Telluride (February 2, 1993) and Crested Butte (April 5, 1993) passed ordinances *prohibiting discrimination based on sexual orientation*. Obviously, confusion over the effect of Amendment Two was widespread.

Anti-gay rights activists across the nation continued to make the most of the public confusion by "circulating petitions for anti-gay rights laws in eight states, setting the stage for public votes on proposals ranging from Amendment Two clones to wholesale declarations of public morality" (Booth, 1993a). The states of Arizona, Florida, Idaho, Michigan, Nevada, Oregon, and Washington were all engaged in initiative petitioning and "[n]ational political lobbies on both sides of the issue call[ed] 1994 a test year that [would] decide whether the anti-gay movement gains momentum" (Booth, 1993a).

In the middle of this divisive battle over citizens rights, activity grew to an all time high in Colorado's gay community. Gay organizations and activities flourished, "including a gay rodeo, gay mountain climbing club and a gay wine tasting club" (Brook, 1996). Ground Zero, a gay-rights organization, published what began as a two-page tabloid covering the Amendment Two battle, then exploded into a twenty-page full-color monthly with more than 1,200 subscribers. In January of 1996 Ground Zero began producing a four-page insert to *The Colorado Springs Independent* newspaper.

As the citizens of Colorado and the nation continued to debate the issue of discrimination against homosexuals, the state of Colorado made its final appeal to the U.S. Supreme Court, which granted *certiorari* on February 21, 1995, and heard argument in October of 1995, just two months shy of the three-year anniversary of the passage of Amendment Two.

THE *ROMER* DECISION

The Supreme Court handed down its decision in *Romer v. Evans* on May 20, 1996. In a six-to-three ruling, the Court affirmed the ruling of the Colorado Supreme Court and held that Colorado's Amendment Two violated the equal protection clause of the Fourteenth Amendment to the Federal Constitution. The decision, the most significant gay-rights action taken by the Court in ten years, is noteworthy both for its constitutional significance and its passionate rhetoric.

Justice Kennedy began the opinion of the Court[1] by invoking Justice Harlan's eloquent dissenting opinion in *Plessy v. Ferguson* (1896). Harlan urged, Kennedy asserted, that the Constitution "neither knows nor tolerates classes among citizens," words that, according to Kennedy, are "now understood to state a commitment to the law's neutrality where the rights of persons are at stake" (*Romer v. Evans*, p. 1623). This principle, enforced by the equal protection clause, required the Court to declare Amendment Two unconstitutional.

Kennedy's opinion pivots on two central points. At the first he considered Colorado's argument that Amendment Two "puts gays and lesbians in the same position as all other persons," and that the measure "does no more than deny homosexuals special rights" (*Romer v. Evans*, p. 1624).

Kennedy relied upon the "authoritative construction" of the Colorado Supreme Court, which determined that the change in legal status effected by the law was "sweeping and comprehensive" (*Romer v. Evans*, p. 1624). Given this construction, Kennedy reasoned, Colorado's assertion that Amendment Two does no more than deny homosexuals special rights was "implausible" (*Romer v. Evans*, p. 1624). "To the contrary," he wrote,

the amendment imposes a special disability on those persons alone. Homosexuals are forbidden the safeguards that others enjoy or may seek without constraint. They can obtain specific protection against discrimination only by enlisting the citizenry of Colorado to amend the state constitution or . . . by trying to pass helpful laws of general applicability. This is so no matter how local or discrete the harm, no matter how public or widespread the injury. We find nothing special in the protections Amendment Two withholds. These are protections taken for granted by most people either because they already have them or do not need them; these are protections against exclusion from an almost limitless number transactions and endeavors that constitute ordinary civic life in a free society. (*Romer v. Evans*, p. 1627)

Far from denying only special rights then, Amendment Two imposed a "special disability" and was therefore held unconstitutional.

The second point around which Kennedy's opinion pivots is the established analysis demanded by "even the ordinary equal protection case" (*Romer v. Evans*, p. 1627). Often called the "rational relation" or "rational basis" test, the inquiry is whether a law that neither burdens a fundamental right nor targets a suspect class bears a rational relation to a legitimate state interest. If so, the law passes constitutional muster.

In *Romer* the Court found that Amendment Two failed the test on two grounds. First, the Court held that the amendment imposed a "broad and undifferentiated disability on a single named group" (*Romer v. Evans*, p. 1627), a targeting of a suspect class that was "at once too narrow and too broad" (*Romer v. Evans*, p. 1628). Because the amendment singled out a specific trait and denied citizens with that trait rights "across the board" (*Romer v. Evans*, p. 1628), it burdened the disadvantaged group far more than the rational relation test could bear. Its reach was not narrowly limited to only what was needed to ensure citizens' freedom of association (Colorado's stated rationale) but rather had the effect of disqualifying an entire class of citizens of the equal protection of the laws.

Amendment Two also failed the test because it raised an inference that the law was the product of an illegitimate state interest. In Kennedy's words, it raised "the inevitable inference that the disadvantage imposed is born of animosity toward the class of persons affected" (*Romer v. Evans*, p. 1628).

The Court concluded that Amendment Two, "in making a general announcement that gays and lesbians shall not have any particular protections from the law" violated the equal protection clause because it inflicted on them "immediate, continuing, and real injuries that outrun and belie any legitimate justifications that may be claimed for it" (*Romer v. Evans*, p. 1627).

The Court's decision did not go unchallenged. Indeed, in the annals of anti-gay-rights rhetoric, Justice Antonin Scalia's[2] dissenting opinion ranks among the most strident of judicial examples. Scalia took issue with the majority's discussion of Colorado's "special rights" argument and its rational relation analysis. He also disputed the Court's assessment of constitutional precedent and claimed that the decision reached far beyond the judicial realm.

On the special rights argument, Scalia took issue with the majority's reading of the Colorado Supreme Court's interpretation of Amendment Two. He focused on that portion of the earlier opinion that took notice of Colorado laws that proscribed discrimination against persons who are not suspect classes (such as discrimination based on age, marital or family status, and veteran status), and argued that Amendment Two's impact was not as far reaching as the majority asserted. In fact, Scalia argued, Amendment Two did no more than mandate that homosexuals take recourse in the usual, more general political decision making, a mandate that does not abridge the equal protection clause. The majority's claim to the contrary is unsupported by precedent, Scalia argued, "which is why the Court's opinion is so long on emotive utterance and so short on relevant legal citation" (*Romer v. Evans*, p. 1630). Scalia and the dissenters therefore rejected the majority's special rights analysis, and asserted that the people of Colorado had "adopted an entirely reasonable provision which does not even disfavor homosexuals in any substantive sense, but merely denies them preferential treatment" (*Romer v. Evans*, p. 1637).

Similarly, Scalia rejected the Court's rational basis analysis. Relying on the Court's decision in *Bowers v. Hardwick* (1986) upholding Georgia's antisodomy law, Scalia claimed that the long history of legislation criminalizing or otherwise disfavoring homosexual conduct provided an adequate and legitimate rationale for Amendment Two. Indeed, the "moral and social disapprobation of homosexuality" has itself been an important part of the nation's legal history and expression of that view may well be, he implied, a political right.

Finally, Scalia characterized the circumstances that gave rise to Amendment Two as a "culture war" (*Romer v. Evans*, p. 1637), a war best waged in the legislature and other political venues. The Court's "novel and extravagant constitutional doctrine" (*Romer v. Evans*, p. 1637) notwithstanding, the *Romer* decision, in Scalia's opinion "has no foundation in American constitutional law" (*Romer v. Evans*, p. 1637).

THE REACTION TO *ROMER*

The response to the Court's decision was as divided as the original initiative campaign. While the decision itself was clearly viewed as a victory by Amendment Two opponents, not everyone in the human rights community agreed on the significance. The ACLU, in a statement given by Matthew Cole, director of the groups Lesbian and Gay Rights Project, applauded the High Court's decision saying, "this ruling should bring an end to the anti-gay initiatives that have been proposed in states, cities and towns across the country over the past several years . . . it establishes as a general principle that lesbians and gay men are entitled to the same constitutional protections granted to everyone one else" (Coles, 1996). Elizabeth Birch, the executive director of the Human Rights Campaign, the largest national lesbian- and gay-rights organization, called the ruling "an outstanding moral victory" but said the decision did not advance equal rights for gay and lesbian Americans, rather "[i]t merely ensures that Colorado—and every other state—cannot pass laws to deny gay and lesbian Americans equal access to the democratic process" (Birch, 1996).

Others found the Court's decision wanting. Syndicated columnist James J. Kilpatrick nominated Justice Kennedy's effort the year's "worst opinion from the Supreme Court" (Kilpatrick, 1996). Lon Mabon, leader of the Oregon Citizens Alliance, called the decision "an attack on the moral foundation of American culture" (Bates, 1996), and Gary Bauer, president of the conservative Family Research Council, called May 20, 1996, "a very dark day for the liberty rights of the America people" (Asseo, 1996).

While the importance of *Romer v. Evans* is evident, the decision raises at least as many questions as it answers. It seems already to have shifted the debate over gay rights from workplace and public accommodation issues to marriage and personal relations, and it raises questions about the status of existing criminal sanctions against avowedly homosexual conduct. In short, *Romer v. Evans* seems destined to live on as a centerpiece of the American gay-rights debate.

NOTES

1. Kennedy's majority opinion was joined by Justices Stevens, O'Connor, Souter, Ginsburg, and Breyer.
2. Scalia was joined in dissent by Chief Justice Rehnquist and Justice Thomas.

Appendix A: Tables

TABLE A.1
Anti-Gay/Lesbian/Bisexual Initiatives in the West

Year	State	#/Type	% for	Short Subject/Title
1992	AZ	ICA	dnq	Repeal and block laws prohibiting discrimination against lesbians, gays, and bisexuals*
1978	CA	P6 IS	41	Homosexual teachers*
1986	CA	P64 IS	29	Acquired Immune Deficiency Syndrome
1988	CA	P69 IS	32	Acquired Immune Deficiency Syndrome
1988	CA	P96 IS	62	Communicable Disease Tests+
1988	CA	P102 IS	34	Reporting Exposure to AIDS Virus+
1992	CO	A2 I	53	No Protection Status Based on Homosexual, Lesbian, or Bisexual Orientation
1994	ID	IS	49	Repeal and block laws prohibiting discrimination against lesbians, gays, and bisexuals*
1994	NV	IS	dnq	Repeal and block laws prohibiting discrimination against lesbians, gays, and bisexuals*
1988	OR	M8 I	57	State shall not "forbid the taking of any personnel action against any state employee based on the sexual orientation of such employee"

Year	State		Type		Description
1992	OR	M9	I	43	State shall not recognize categorical provisions such as "sexual orientation," "sexual preference," and similar phrases that include homosexuality
1994	OR	M13	IS	44	Shall constitution bar governments from creating classifications based on homosexuality or spending public funds in a manner expressing approval of homosexuality?
1994	WA	608	IS	dnq	State shall be prohibited from according rights or protections based on sexual orientation, and schools from presenting homosexuality as acceptable
1994	WA	610	IS	dnq	Shall rights based on homosexuality; homosexual custody of their own children; and governmental approval of homosexuality be prohibited?

dnq = did not qualify

Type: ICA = Initiative Constitutional Amendment; IS = Initiative Statute

*not official ballot title or state summary
+issue did not address homosexuality directly
Source: Assembled by Donovan and Bowler from state ballot listings.

TABLE A.2
Signature Requirement of States with Initiatives by Stringency and Type of Signature Requirement

State	Signature Requirement		
	Statutory Initiative	Constitutional Initiative	
North Dakota	2%	4%	Resident Population
Massachusetts	5%	5%	Vote for Governor[1]
Colorado	5%	5%	Vote for Secretary of State
California	5%	8%	Vote for Governor
Oregon	6%	8%	Vote for Governor
Missouri	5%	8%	Vote for Governor[2]
Washington	8%	--	Vote for Governor
Montana	5%	10%	Vote for Governor[3]
South Dakota	5%	10%	Vote for Governor
Ohio	6%	10%	Vote for Governor[4]
Nebraska	7%	10%	Eligible Voters[5]
Michigan	8%	10%	Vote for Governor
Arkansas	8%	10%	Vote for Governor
Florida	--	8%	Votes in President Election[6]
Illinois	--	8%	Vote for Governor
Oklahoma	8%	15%	Votes for office with highest number of votes in last election
Alaska	10%	--	Total Votes[7]
Arizona	10%	15%	Vote for Governor
Idaho	10%	--	Vote for Governor
Maine	10%	--	Vote for Governor

Nevada	10%	10%	Total Votes[8]
Utah	10%	--	Vote for Governor[9]
Mississippi	--	12%	Vote for Governor
Wyoming	15%	--	Total Vote[10]

1. No more than 25 percent of the signatures from one county.

2. 5 or 8 percent of the vote each from 2/3 of the congressional districts.

3. 10 or 5 percent of the vote each from 2/5 or 1/3 of the state legislative districts.

4. 1/5 percent of the vote from each of 1/3 of the counties.

5. 5 percent of the vote each from 2/5 of the counties.

6. 8 percent of the vote from 1/2 of the congressional districts.

7. From 2/3 of the election districts.

8. 10 percent each from 3/4 of the counties.

9. 10 percent each from 1/2 of the counties.

10. From 2/3 of the counties.

Source: Adapted from Magleby (1995) and Kehler and Stern (1994).

TABLE A.3
National Trends in Public Attitudes about Homosexuality

	1984	1985	1987	1988	1989	1990	1991	1993	1994
Homosexuality is:									
Always wrong	73.2	75.3	76.2	76.8	74.2	76.3	75.5	66.3	66.5
Almost always wrong	5.0	4.0	4.1	4.7	4.1	4.8	4.1	4.3	4.0
Sometimes wrong	7.4	7.0	5.8	5.7	6.0	6.1	4.4	7.3	6.2
Not wrong at all	14.3	13.7	11.9	12.8	15.7	12.8	16.0	22.0	23.3
Number of cases	1412	1481	1750	937	980	872	926	1012	1884
Homosexuals should be allowed to teach:									
Allow	61.3	59.7	58.4	59.5	66.6	65.9	65.8	71.7	73.0
Not allow	38.7	40.3	41.6	40.5	33.4	34.2	43.2	28.3	27.0
Homosexuals should be allowed to speak . . . :									
Allow	70.6	69.1	69.2	72.6	78.4	76.6	77.8	80.8	81.3
Not allow	29.4	30.9	30.8	27.4	21.6	23.4	22.2	19.2	18.7
Books about Homosexuality should be removed from the library:									
Remove	38.7	42.9	41.8	37.3	33.8	34.1	29.4	30.5	29.1
Not remove	61.3	57.1	58.2	62.7	66.2	65.9	70.6	69.5	70.9

Source: NORC General Social Survey. Items not used in 1992, 1986, and 1983.

TABLE A.4
Coding Categories

Category Name	Definition	Coding Choices
Theme	An overtly expressed subtopic, including a claim and support within the greater issue of the initiative or the practice of homosexuality. The same words may be used in more than one theme.	(1) Whether gays should serve in the military. (2) Whether homosexuality is genetic, social, or a personal choice. (3) Whether there is a gay political agenda or plot to gain special rights status. (4) Whether gays are pedophiles, practice unhealthy sex, have an unhealthy lifestyle, or recruit/seduce others into their lifestyle. (5) Whether homosexuality is evil or sinful in a moral sense. (6) Whether the initiative is legal/constitutional. (7) Whether passage of the initiative will have negative economic, social, or political effects. (8) Other (specify). (9) No discernible themes in the letter. (10) General arguments about nondiscrimination. (11) General arguments in favor of discrimination. (12) Refutation or ridicule of past letters.
Evidence	Subsets of themes that present evidence to support the letter's argument. The same words may not be used in more than one piece of evidence.	(1) Citing a previous letter to the editor as a basis of rebuttal. Must be more than just merely stating the previous letter's name and date. (2) Comparison: Drawing similarities/differences between two groups, practices, or historical events. (3) Example: Giving a specific instance of an event or occurrence, real or hypothetical.

TABLE A.4—continued

	(4) Direct Quotation--non-Bible: Using the exact words of a person or sources within quotation marks.
	(5) Direct Quotation--Bible: Using the exact words of the Bible within quotation marks, with or without an exact chapter and verse citation.
	(6) Personal Testimony/Self as Expert: Giving personal testimony from one's own experiences.
	(7) Statistics: Presentation of numerical data.
	(8) Other (specify).
	(9) No evidence.
	(10) Reference to non-Bible, not a quote or citation but a general reference like "Bible says."
	(11) Reference to Bible, not a quote or citation but a general reference like "Bible says."
	(12) Reference to Bible, paraphrase verse(s), with citation of chapter or verse.
Citation of Sources Statements of the source of information or evidence. The same words may not be used in more than one citation.	(1) Bible chapter and verse.
	(2) Print source: Book article, pamphlet.
	(3) Research report: (If a study plus where published, mark as 2).
	(4) Specific person (other than self).
	(5) Other (specify).
	(6) No citation of sources.
	(7) Paraphrase of an unknown medium.

Fallacies

A fallacy is an error in reasoning as defined by one of the categories below. The same words may not be used in more than one fallacy.

(1) Begging the question: Circular definition where the thing is defined as being itself or where claims are supported by repeating the claim in another way. Code the subtypes of begging the question, red herring, and strawperson as separate and unique fallacies.

(2) Red herring: A fallacy of misdirection where a topic that has no relevance to the main point is brought up.

(3) Strawperson: A fallacy of misdirection where a case is made for a position that nobody in fact holds, usually oversimplifying the issue. The opposition's position is restated in a way that makes it easy to refute. [i]

Initiative Siding

An overt statement of position on the anti-gay initiative.

(1) Overtly in favor of the initiative: Mentions the initiative by name within the letter and states that it should be passed or that homosexuals should not be given special rights.

(2) Overtly against the initiative: Mentions the initiative by name within the editorial and states the initiative should not be passed or that the initiative does not award special rights.

(3) Neutral or can't tell: Doesn't mention the initiative.

Homosexuality Siding	An overall tone toward homosexuality inferred or stated in the letter.	(1) Negative toward homosexuality or homosexuals: The overall tone of the letter labels homosexual acts and/or homosexuals as deviant, sinful, unhealthy, or plotting against other people.
		(2) Favorable toward homosexuality or homosexuals: The overall tone of the letter labels homosexuals as much like anyone else, denies that homosexuals are deviant, sinful, unhealthy, or plotting against other people.
		(3) Tolerant of but not overtly favorable toward homosexuals.
		(4) Neutral or can't tell.
Geographic Area	Geographic area of the address listed for the letter's author.	(1) Boise.
		(2) Southwest Idaho--not Boise.
		(3) Idaho Falls or Pocatello.
		(4) Southeast Idaho--not Pocatello or Idaho Falls.
		(5) Central Idaho--not Moscow.
		(6) Moscow.
		(7) Coeur d'Alene.
		(8) North Idaho, not Coeur d'Alene.
		(9) Outside Idaho.
		(10) Can't tell/other.
Sex of Author	The gendered identification of the letter writer's first name.	(1) Males(s).
		(2) Female(s).
		(3) Multiple names including both male and female.

	(4) Can't tell.
	(5) No name given.

Demographic Self-Identification	Several unique categories based on the author's disclosure of the characteristic within the letter or signature, each coded separately as "Present" or "Absent."	(1) Christian. (2) Religious person, but not Christian. (3) Atheist or nonreligious person. (4) Gay, lesbian, bisexual, homosexual. (5) Parent of gay, lesbian, bisexual, or homosexual. (6) Current or past member of the military. (7) Child of gay, lesbian, bisexual, homosexual. (8) Minister or religious leader. (9) Democrat. (10) Republican. (11) Person who lived in Idaho for more than five years.
Month	Month of publication.	(1) January to (12) December.
Year	Year of publication.	(1) 1993. (2) 1994.
Newspaper	Section in which the letter was published.	(1) Editorial page. (2) Religious section.

Continuation of Coding Choices for Fallacies:

i (4) Appeal to Authority: Using an authority to stop discussion. The fallacious argument is that because authority "X" says something, it is the last and indisputable word on the subject.

TABLE A.4—continued

(5) Argument Against the Person: The opposition's arguments are rejected merely because of who they are or the group they belong to without any examination of the worth of their argument. The character of a person or his/her group membership is essentially connected with his/her claim. At its worst, the fallacy is mere name-calling.

(6) Argument from Ignorance: Reasoning from opposites to say that something is true because its opposite cannot be proven.

(7) Appeal to Ignorance: Reasoning that the absence of evidence for a claim is proof that the claim is false.

(8) Appeal to the People: Justifying a claim on the basis of its popularity. Just because many people believe a thing (i.e., opinion polls), does not make it "true." Also code here popular appeal where advocates seek support because of their own ordinary humanity and bandwagon appeals.

(9) Appeal to Compassion: The traditional sob story used to obscure an issue or playing upon emotions as the primary reasons to support a claim.

(10) Appeal to Force/Threats: Implying that persons will be harmed if they don't/do refrain from doing a particular thing. Threats can be physical, moral, or psychological.

(11) Hasty generalization: Jumping to conclusions based on too few specific cases or when a conclusion is dawn from atypical conclusions.

(12) Accident: Misapplication of a rule. An argument is advanced without considering reasonable exceptions, that is, not allowing seeing-eye dogs into places where dogs are not allowed.

(13) False Cause: Confusing temporal succession with causal sequence or mistaking one event to be the cause of another.

(14) Slippery Slope: Objecting to an action on the grounds that the action will inevitably lead to other less desirable actions, which ultimately leads to some horror at the bottom of the slide.

(15) False Analogy: Comparing things that do not have sufficient literal similarities where occurrences in one area are erroneously argued as the same as in the area compared to.

(16) Poisoning the Well: Making a claim in such a way that no possible evidence can be brought

against it. Arguers simply refuse to acknowledge that counterwarrants or evidence could exist and dismiss nay-sayers as acting in bad faith or unable to be in a position to understand the claim.

(17) Equivocation: Using a word or phrase in two different senses within a single argument.

(18) Pseudoquestions: Asking an unanswerable or loaded question or a question based on a false assumption or so many questions that they cannot be answered within the allocated time or space.

(19) Appeal to Tradition: The advocate maintains that we should keep the current policy because it has always been that way.

(20) False Dilemma: Arguing that there are only two choices/solutions to a problem, one wrong and the other right, when there are more than two possible choices.

(21) Irrelevant Reason/Non Sequitur: Cases other than those itemized above where the facts or reasoning offered as proof simply are irrelevant to the claim.

(22) Fallacies involving Statistics: Either the statistics are unknowable or they are misinterpreted.

(23) No fallacies because no argument is attempted.

(24) Emotional Slanting.

(25) Argument attempted but incomplete or insufficient by virtue of missing grounds, unsubstantiated grounds, or missing warrant, but not specified above in a separate category.

(26) No fallacy.

Source: Adapted from Toulmin, Ricke, and Janik (1984); Kahane (1992); and Freeley (1993).

TABLE A.5
Idaho Anti-Gay Initiative Campaign
Campaign Phase and Side Taken on Initiative by Letter Writers

Siding on Initiative	Phase 1 1/1 - 3/4 1993	Phase 2 3/18 - 11/3 1993	Phase 3 11/4 - 6/1 1993/94	Phase 4 7/1 - 11/1 1994	n
Pro	2	10	20	32	64
Anti	10	11	44	44	109
Neutral/Can't Tell	80	71	57	25	233
Total	92	92	121	101	406

Source: Authors' (McCorkle and Most) Computation.

TABLE A.6
Idaho Anti-Gay Intitiative Campaign
Theme in Letter and Attitude Toward Homosexuality by Percentage of Theme Usage by Attitude

	Negative		Favor		Tolerant		Neutral/ Can't Tell		Total
	%	No.	%	No.	%	No.	%	No.	
Political Agenda/ Special Rights	27	39	14	10	17	20	7	6	75[1]
Pedophilia	32	46	19	14	5	6	4	3	69
Sinful Moral State	37	53	9	7	1	1	1	1	62
Legality of the Initiative	2	3	4	3	13	4	16	13	23
Negative Economic Effects	5	7	12	9	18	22	30	25	63
General Nondiscrimination	3	4	64	47	67	80	16	13	144
General Prodiscrimination	22	32	4	3	3	4	5	4	43
Refutation	12	18	35	26	23	27	23	19	90

[1]Of the "n" using this theme, what percentage had each attitude (negative, favorable, tolerant, or neutral/can't tell) toward homosexuality?

Source: Authors' (McCorkle and Most) computation.

TABLE A.7

Idaho Anti-Gay Initiative Themes in Letter and Phase of the Initiative Campaign

	Phase 1 1/1 - 3/4 1993		Phase 2 3/18 - 11/3 1993		Phase 3 11/4 - 6/1 1993/4		Phase 4 7/1 - 11/1 1994		
	%	No.	%	No.	%	No.	%	No.	Total
Military	27	73*	10	27	0	0	0	0	37
Genetic/Choice	14	33	11	26	10	23	8	19	43
Special Rights	15	21	14	20	24	34	18	25	71
Pedophilia	14	20	18	26	11	16	26	38	69
Sinful Morality	13	22	18	30	14	23	15	25	60
Legality	3	14	1	5	9	41	9	41	22
Economic Effect	3	5	5	9	27	47	22	39	57
Antidiscrimination	27	19	29	21	53	38	30	22	139
Prodiscrimination	10	24	5	12	13	32	13	24	41
Refutation	16	18	23	26	28	32	21	32	88
Other-Religion	1	25	3	20	4	27	7	47	15
Other	5	19	3	12	8	31	10	38	26
No Theme	1	25	1	25	2	50	0	0	4
Total %	149		141		203		179		672

*Percentage of usage of the theme across phases.

Source: Authors' (McCorkle and Most) computation.

TABLE A.8
Public Evaluations of Groups in America

	Mean Score	% Saying Zero	% Saying 100
The Poor	70.5	0.1	14.5
The Military	70.0	0.7	14.5
The Police	69.4	1.2	11.9
Environmentalists	67.7	0.8	11.8
Blacks	65.2	0.9	11.9
Catholics	65.0	0.8	10.7
The Women's Movement	62.1	2.2	9.3
Hispanics	61.1	1.0	6.9
Conservatives	55.0	1.1	3.1
Big Business	54.9	2.1	3.5
Fundamentalists	54.9	3.3	8.4
Labor Unions	53.8	4.6	5.6
Congress	51.1	2.4	2.0
Liberals	50.1	3.7	2.0
People on Welfare	51.1	3.5	2.3
Gays and Lesbians	37.8	22.7	2.0
Illegal Immigrants	36.1	15.4	1.1

Note: Valid data only, nonresponses excluded.

Source: American National Election Study, Survey Research Center, University of Michigan.

TABLE A.9
Trends in Opinion over Course of Campaigns: California and Idaho

	Date	Yes	No	Undc/Drop.[†]
California Proposition 6, 1978				
	August 20	61	31	9
	September 20	47	41	12
	October 31	37	58	6
Actual Vote		41	59	5
California Proposition 64, 1986				
	July	31	56	12
	September 24	31	49	20
	October 30	21	58	21*
Actual Vote		29	71	7
Idaho Amendment 1, 1994				
	November 1993[a]	26	54	20*
	May 1994[b]	37	48	15
	October 1994[c]	34	44	21
Actual Vote		49	51	3

[†]Dropoff is the difference between election turnout and the proportion of voters marking the initiative question.
*Only asked of those responding they had heard of the intitiative.

Sources: California Field Polls 8607, 8606, 8605; Magleby, 1984, p. 214.
[a]Boise State University Survey Research Center.
[b]Smith and Andrus.
[c]Political Media Research/KTVB-TV/KHQ-TV/*Spokesman Review*.

TABLE A.10
Probit Estimates of Support of Initiatives

	California Proposition 64 October 30, 1986	California Proposition 102 Fall 1988	Colorado Amendment 2 November 1992
Education	-.28** (.06)	-.19** (.04)	-.36** (.10)
Income	-.06 (.04)	-.04 (.03)	.13 (.09)
Age	.005 (.007)	.03** (.006)	.09 (.09)
Black	-.85 (.60)	.19 (.43)	.25 (1.52)
Gender	.11 (.25)	.56** (.19)	-.35 (.28)
Liberal	-.32 (.41)	-.53** (.24)	-.46 (.36)
GOP	-.03 (.27)	-.04 (.21)	1.06** (.34)
Economy Bad	-.01 (.41)	—	-.16 (.32)
English Only	1.20** (.31)	—	—
Born Again	.82** (.27)	.45* (.23)	—
Awareness	-.25* (.13)	—	-.85** (.30)
Abortion Concerns	—	—	.88** (.30)
Values Concerns	—	—	.52 (1.22)
Identify w/ G/L	—	.54** (.14)	
Constant	-.41	-0.88	1.17
Number of Cases	392	704	277
Model Chi-Square	66.3**	105.7**	54.5**
% Correct	75.0	76.7	67.9

**Significant at p < .01
*Significant at p < .05

Source: Authors' (Donovan and Bowler) computation.

TABLE A.11
Statewide Votes on Anti-Gay Initiatives

	Yes	No
Colorado (1992)	2,003,375	1,597,166
Idaho (1994)	202,681	205,754
Maine (1995)	193,938	221,562
Oregon (1994)	592,746	630,623

Sources: *Colorado*: State Colorado Abstract of Votes Cast, 1992, Colorado Department of State. *Idaho*: Office of Secretary of State. *Oregon*: Oregon State Elections Department. *Maine*: Office of Secretary of State, Division of Corporations and Elections.

TABLE A.12

Partial Regression Coefficients of Selected Independent Variables upon the Percent Yes Vote on Anti-Gay Initiatives (the dependent variable)

Variables	B	Beta	T
Age	.1555	.0558	.722
Education	-.3166	-.2699	-3.221**
Income	3.6898	.1416	2.187*
Percent LDS in county	-27.0524	-.5443	-6.070**
Percent Protestant in county	15.0987	.0831	1.200
Percent families in poverty	.9450	.4152	5.429**
Percent living in urban area	.0404	.1213	1.877
Clinton vote 1992	-65.7249	-.6318	-7.855**

*Significant at $p < .05$
**Significant at $p < .001$

Source: Authors' (Witt and Alm) computation.

Appendix B: Text of Anti-Gay Initiatives

AMENDMENT TWO
No Protected Status Based on Homosexual, Lesbian, or Bisexual Orientation. Colorado, 1992

Neither the State of Colorado, through any of its branches or departments, nor any of its agencies, political subdivisions, municipalities or school districts, shall enact, adopt, or enforce any statute, regulation, ordinances or policy whereby homosexual, lesbian or bisexual orientation, conduct, practice or relationships shall constitute or otherwise be the basis of, or entitle any person or class of persons to have or claim, any minority status, quota preferences, protected status or claim of discrimination.

This section of the Constitution shall be in all respects self-executing.

MEASURE NINE
Amends Constitution. Government Cannot Facilitate, Must Discourage Homosexuality, Other "Behaviors." Oregon, 1992

Amends Oregon Constitution. All governments in Oregon may not use their monies or properties to promote, encourage, or facilitate homosexuality, pedophilia, sadism, or masochism. All levels of government, including public educational systems, must assist in setting a standard for Oregon's youth which recognizes that these "behaviors" are "abnormal, wrong, unnatural, and perverse," and that they are to be discouraged and avoided. State may not recognize this conduct under sexual orientation or sexual preference levels, or through quotas, minority status, affirmative action, or similar concepts.

MEASURE THIRTEEN
Amends Constitution: Governments Cannot Approve, Create Classifications Based on, Homosexuality. Oregon, 1994

Amends Oregon Constitution: Governments cannot: Create classifications based on homosexuality; Advise or teach children, students, employees that homosexuality equates legally or socially with race, other protected classifications; Spend public funds in manner promoting or expressing approval of homosexuality; Grant spousal benefits, marital status based on homsexuality; Deny constitutional rights, services due under existing statutes. Measure nonetheless allows adult library books addressing homosexuality with adult-only access. Public employees' private lawful sexual behaviors may be cause for personnel action, if those behaviors disrupt workplace.

PROPOSITION ONE
An Act Establishing State Policies Regarding Homosexuality. Idaho, 1994

Be it enacted by the people of the State of Idaho:

Section 67–8001. Purpose of Act. The provision of Title 67, Chapter 80 of the Idaho Code are enacted by the people of the State of Idaho in recognition that homosexuality shall not form the basis for the granting of minority status. This chapter is promulgated in furtherance of the provisions of Article 3, Section 24 of the Constitution of the State of Idaho.

Section 67–8002. Special Rights for persons who engage in homosexual behavior prohibited. No agency, department or political subdivision of the State of Idaho shall enact or adopt any law, rule, policy, or agreement which has the purpose or effect of granting minority status to persons who engage in homosexual behavior, solely on the basis of such behavior; therefore, affirmative action, quota preferences, and special classifications such as "sexual orientation" or similar designations shall not be established on the basis of homosexuality. All private persons shall be guaranteed equal protection of the law in the full and free exercise of all rights enumerated and guaranteed by the U.S. Constitution, the Constitution of the State of Idaho and federal and state law. All existing civil rights protections based on race, color, religion, gender, age, or national origin are reaffirmed, and public services shall be available to all persons on an equal basis.

Section 67–8003. Extension of legal institution of marriage to domestic partnerships based on homosexual behavior prohibited. Same-sex marriages and domestic partnerships are hereby declared to be against public policy and shall not be legally recognized in any manner by any agency, department, or political subdivision of the State of Idaho.

Section 67–8004. Public Schools. No employee, representative, or agent of any public elementary or secondary school shall, in connection with school activities, promote, sanction, or endorse homosexuality as a healthy, approved or acceptable behavior. Subject to the provisions of federal law, any discussion of homosexuality within such schools shall be age-appropriate as defined and authorized by the local school board of trustees. Counseling of public school students regarding such students sexual identity shall conform in the foregoing.

Section 67–8005. Expenditure of public funds. No agency, department or political subdivision of the State of Idaho shall expend public funds in a manner that has the purpose or effect of promoting, making acceptable, or expressing approval of homosexuality. This section shall not prohibit government from providing positive guidance toward persons experiencing difficulty with sexual identity. This section shall not limit the availability in public libraries of books and materials written for adults which address homosexuality, provided access to such materials is limited to adults and meets local standards as established through the normal library review process.

Section 67–8006. Employment factors. With regard to public employees, no agency, department or political subdivision of the State of Idaho shall forbid generally the consideration of private sexual behaviors as non-job factors, provided that compliance with Title 67, Chapter 80, Idaho Code is maintained, and that such factors do not disrupt the work place.

Section 67–8007. Severability. The people intended that if any part of this enactment be found unconstitutional, the remaining parts shall survive in full force and effect. This section shall be all parts self-executing.

QUESTION ONE
Citizen Initiative (on Limiting Protected Classifications).
Maine, 1995

Do you favor the changes in Maine law limiting protected classifications, in future state and local laws to race, color, sex, physical or mental disability, religion, age, ancestry, national origin, familial status, and marital status, and repealing existing laws which expand these classifications as proposed by citizen petition?

Bibliography

ACLU v. EchoHawk, 124 Idaho 147, 857 P.2d 626 (1993).

Adam, B. D. (1987). *The rise of a gay and lesbian movement*. Boston: Twayne.

Adams, W. E., Jr. (1994). Pre-Election anti-gay ballot initiative challenges. *Ohio State Law Journal, 55*, 583–647.

Adorno, T. W., Frenkel-Brunswick, E., Levinson, D. J., & Sanford, R. N. (1950). *The authoritarian personality*. New York: Harper.

AFL-CIO members vote against supporting anti-gay initiative. (1993, June 17). *The Idaho Statesman*, p. C3.

AG candidate will introduce anti-gay bill. (1993, December 15). *The Post Register*, p. 83.

Al-Enad, A. H. (1991). Counting items versus measuring space in content analysis. *Journalism Quarterly, 68* (4), 657–662.

Altman, D. (1987). What price gay nationalism. In M. Thompson (Ed.), *Gay spirit: Myth and meaning* (pp. 18–19). New York: St. Martin's Press.

American national election study. (1992). Survey Research Center, University of Michigan.

Anti-gay manual terms homosexuals "spawn of the devil." (1994, July 21). *The Idaho Statesman*, p. C4.

Arbanas, M. (1993a, January 19). Andrus: Keep hate out of Idaho. *The Idaho Statesman*, p. A1.

Arbanas, M. (1993b, March 6). Gay agenda: Civil rights, funds for AIDS research. *Idaho Statesman*, p. A4.

Askew, B. (1993, December 6). I repeat: Pedophiles would be protected. *Springfield News-Leader*, p. A6.

Asseo, L. (1996, May 20). High court dumps anti-gay law. *The Oregonian*, p. A1.

Attorney General's Office State of Idaho. (1993, November 3). Opinion No. 93–11 119. (1993).

Attorney General's Office State of Idaho. (1995, February 22). *Attorney general's position regarding Colorado Amicus Brief* [Press Release].

Bailey, J. (1993a, December 10). State lawmaker plans anti-gay measure. *The Idaho Statesman*, p. A1.

Bailey, J. (1993b, December 12). "Maverick" senator pushes for debate on anti-gay initiative. *The Idaho Statesman*, p. A1.

Bailey, J. (1993c, December 16). Lance calls for gay debate. *The Idaho Statesman*, pp. A1, A12.

Banducci, S., & Karp, J. (1993, March 10–12). *Campaigns, information and public support for term limits*. Paper presented at the Western Political Science Association meeting Albuquerque, NM.

Bates, T. (1996, May 20). Mabon: Fight will continue. *The Oregonian*, p. A1.

Bawer, B. (1993). *A place at the table: The gay individual in American society*. New York: Simon and Schuster.

Beck, C. (1994, February 6). Council's vote for bias bill violated oath. *Springfield News-Leader*, p. B7.

Bell, D., Jr. (1978). The referendum: Direct democracy's barrier to racial equality. *Washington Law Review*, *54*, pp. 1–29.

Bellah, Robert N. (1975). *The Broken Covenant: American Civil Religion in a Time of Trial*. New York: Seabury.

Bennett, W. L., & Edelman, M. (1985, Autumn). Toward a new political narrative. *Journal of Communication*, *35*, 158.

Berke, R. (1994, September 21). Survey finds voters in U.S. rootless and self-absorbed. *New York Times*, p. A21.

Bernt, J. P., & Greenwald, M. S. (1992). Differing views of senior editors and gay/lesbian journalists regarding newspaper coverage of the gay and lesbian community. *Newspaper Research Journal*, *13/14* (3/1), 99–110.

Birch, E. (1996, May 20). Statement. Human Rights Campaign.

Birnbaum, J. H. (1995, May 15). The gospel according to Ralph. *Time*, pp. 28–35.

Blank, R. H. (1978). *Regional diversity of political values: Idaho political cultures*. Washington, DC: University Press of America.

Blumenthal, S. (1994, July 18). Christian soldiers. *New Yorker*, pp. 31–37.

Blunt, G. D. (1993, November). Time for traditional values adherents to stand up. *Kansas City Christian*, p. 4.

Boeyink, D. E. (1992/93). Analyzing newspaper editorials: Are the arguments consistent? *Newspaper Research Journal*, *13/14* (3/1), 28–39.

Booth, M. (1993a, February 22). Anti-gay rights petitions on rise. *Denver Post*, p. 1A.

Booth, M. (1993b, November). Plans made early for court challenge to anti-gay rights laws. *Denver Post*.

Bork, R. H., & Duncan, R. F. (1995). *Brief of Amici Curiae states in support of a petition for Writ of Certiorari, Evans v. Romer*, Supreme Court Docket 94–1039.

Both sides get ready for another fight. (1993, October 26). *Springfield News-Leader*, p. B1.

Bourdieu, P. (1991). *Language and symbolic power* (J. B. Thompson, Trans.). Oxford, Eng.: Polity Press.

Bourdieu, P. (1994). Structures, habitus, power: Basis for a theory of symbolic power. In N. B. Dirks, G. Eley, & S. B. Ortner (Eds.), *Culture/Power/History: A reader in contemporary social theory* (pp. 155–199). Princeton, NJ: Princeton University Press.

Bowers v. Hardwick, 478 U.S. 186 (1986).

Bowker, J. K. (1993). Traditional values: Argument fields and serial argument of the YES on 9 campaign. In R. E. McKerrow (Ed.), *Argument and the postmodern challenge* (pp. 423–438). Speech Communication Association.

Bowler, S., & Donovan, T. (1994a). Economic conditions and voting on ballot propositions. *American Politics Quarterly, 22,* 27–40.

Bowler, S., & Donovan, T. (1994b). Information and opinion change on ballot propositions. *Political Behavior,* 411–435.

Bowler, S., & Donovan, T. (1994c, September). *Self-interest and voting on ballot propositions.* Paper presented at the American Political Science Association meeting, New York, NY.

Boxall, B. (1994, June 9). Anti-gay rights measures ignite aggressive battles in seven states. *Los Angeles Times,* p. A5.

Bradley, C. (1994, July 13). Goldwater opposes anti-gay proposals. *The Idaho Statesman,* p. C1.

Bradley, M. B., Green, N. M., Jr., Jones, D. E., Lynn, M., & McNeil, L. (1992). *Churches and church membership in the United States 1990.* Atlanta, GA: Glenmary Research Center.

Bradley, R. (1992). The abnormal affair of *The normal heart. Text and Performance Quarterly, 12,* 362–371.

Brandt, E. (1996, July 26). ICA proponent misstates court's opinion on Colorado initiative. *The Idaho Statesman,* p. A8.

Branham, R., & Pearce, W. B. (1987). A contract for civility: Edward Kennedy's Lynchburg address. *Quarterly Journal of Speech, 73,* 424–443.

Bray, R. (1994, May 19). Magic messages and strong movements. *Gay & Lesbian Times,* p. 32.

Brockriede, W. (1990). Where is argument? In R. Trapp & J. Schuetz (Eds.), *Perspectives on argumentation* (p. 4). Prospect Heights, IL: Waveland.

Brogan, P. (1993, January 3). With an ally in the White House, gay activists hope to end the military ban on homosexuals in 1993. *The Idaho Statesman,* p. F1.

Bronski, M. (1984). *Culture clash: The making of gay sensibility.* Boston: South End Press.

Brook, J. (1996, May 28). Colorado gay life thrives where ballot fight began. *New York Times,* [internet version].

Brooks, P. (1984). *Reading for the plot.* New York: Alfred A. Knopf.

Brown, F. (1993, December 15). Poll: Public sends mixed messages. *Denver Post,* p. A14.

Brown, K. M. (1994). Fundamentalism and the control of women. In J. S. Hawley (Ed.), *Fundamentalism and gender* (pp. 175–201). New York: Oxford University Press.

Brown, W. S. (1982). Attention and the rhetoric of social intervention. *Quarterly Journal of Speech, 68,* 17–27.

Browning, F. (1993). *The culture of desire: Paradox and perversity in gay lives today.* New York: Crown.

Bruce, S. (1988). *The rise and fall of the new Christian right*. New York: Oxford University Press.

Bruce, S., Kivisto, P., & Swatos, W. H. (Eds.). (1995). *The rapture of politics*. New Brunswick, NJ: Transaction Publishers.

Brummett, B. (1981). Ideologies in two gay rights controversies. In J. W. Chesebro (Ed.), *Gayspeak: Gay male and lesbian communication* (pp. 291–302). New York: Pilgrim Press.

Bryant, A. (1977). *The Anita Bryant story: The survival of our nation's families and the threat of militant homosexuality*. Old Tappan, NJ: Fleming H. Revell.

Buell, E. H. (1975). Eccentrics or gladiators? People who write about politics in letters-to-the-editor. *Social Science Quarterly, 53* (3), 440–449.

Cagan, L. (1993). Community organizing and the religious right: Lessons from Oregon's measure 9 campaign. *Radical America, 24* (4), 68–69, 75.

Cannon, L. (1978, October 27). After low-key campaign, comeback is seen for gay rights. *Washington Post*, p. A5.

Cantor, D. (1994). *The religious right: The assault on tolerance and pluralism in America*. New York: Anti-Defamation League.

Capps, W. H. (1990). *The new religious right: Piety, patriotism and politics*. Columbia, SC: University of South Carolina Press.

Carmines, E., & Stimson, J. (1980). The two faces of issue voting. *American Political Science Review, 74*, 78–91.

Cassala, D. (1993, January 28). Ban on gays will fall, Aspin says. *The Idaho Statesman*, p. A1.

Catholic leaders blast Proposition Six (1978, October 12). *Oakland Tribune*.

Chaisson, L. E. (1991). The Japanese-American encampment: An editorial analysis of twenty-seven west coast newspapers. *Newspaper Research Journal, 12* (2), 92–107.

Chatman, S. (1979). *Story and discourse, narrative structure in fiction and film*. Ithaca, NY: Cornell University Press.

Chauncey, G. (1994). *Gay New York: Gender, urban culture, and the making of the gay male world, 1890–1940*. New York: Basic Books.

Chinn, S., & Franklin, K. (1992). "I am what I am" (or am I): The making and unmaking of lesbian and gay identity in *High tech gays. Discourse, 15* (1), 11–26.

Christian Coalition. (1995). *Contract with the American family*. Nashville, TN: Moorings.

Church leaders unite to oppose Proposition One. (1994, September 10). *The Idaho Statesman*, p. C1.

Citizens Against Rent Control v. City of Berkeley, 454 U.S. 290, 102 S. Ct. 434 (1981).

Citrin, J., Reingold, B., Walters, E., & Green, D. P. (1990). The "official English" movement and the symbolic politics of language in the United States. *Western Political Quarterly, 43*, 535–560.

City Council. (1993). An ordinance [Document #381–Bill 93–277]. Springfield, MO: City of Springfield.

City employees in Troy protected from sex-orientation discrimination. (1994, January 19). *The Idaho Statesman*, p. C2.

Clark, K. (1994, March 11). Onward Christian soldiers I: African American churches, the theocratic right. *News-Telegraph*, p. 12.

Clergy announce opposition to ICA initiative. (1994, June 22). *The Idaho Statesman*, p. C3.

Cohan, A. S. (1992). Obstacles to equality: Government responses to the gay rights movement in the United States. In W. R. Dynes & S. Donaldson (Eds.), *Homosexuality and government, politics, and prisons* (pp. 17–34). New York: Garland.

Coles, M. (1996, May 20). ACLU applauds Supreme Court decision striking down Colorado's anti-gay Amendment Two. News release of the American Civil Liberties Union.

Colorado darkens as stars fall on Sun Valley. (1993, January 3). *The Idaho Statesman*, p. C3.

Conason, J. (1992, April 27). The religious right's quiet revival. *Nation*, pp. 542, 553–559.

Condit, C. M. (1987). Crafting virtue: The rhetorical construction of public morality. *Quarterly Journal of Speech, 73*, 79–97.

Condit, C. M. (1990). *Decoding abortion rhetoric: Communicating social change*. Urbana: University of Illinois Press.

Condit, C. M., & Lucaites, J. L. (1993). *Crafting equality: America's Anglo-African word*. Chicago: University of Chicago Press.

Conrad, C. (1983). The rhetoric of the moral majority: An analysis of romantic form. *Quarterly Journal of Speech, 69*, 159–170.

Converse, P. (1962). Information flow and the stability of partisan attitudes. *Public Opinion Quarterly, 26*, 578–599.

Cooper, M. (1992, October 13). Queer baiting in the culture war. *Village Voice*, pp. 29–36.

Corrigan, D. M. (1990). Value coding consensus in front page news leads. *Journalism Quarterly, 67* (4), 653–662.

Cottonwood. (1994, October 13). *The Idaho Statesman*, p. B2.

Crapo says reports didn't reflect completely his stand on initiative. (1994, June 18). *The Idaho Statesman*, p. C4.

Crawford, A. (1980). *Thunder on the right*. New York: Pantheon.

Cromartie, M. J. (Ed.). (1992). *The religious new right in American politics*. Washington, DC: Ethics and Public Policy Center.

Cromartie, M. J. (Ed.). (1993). *No longer exiles: The religious new right in American politics*. Washington, DC: Ethics and Public Policy Center.

Cromartie, M. J. (Ed.). (1994). *Disciples and democracy: Religious conservatives and the future of American politics*. Washington, DC: Ethics and Public Policy Center.

Cronin, T. (1989). *Direct democracy*. Cambridge, MA: Harvard University Press.

Cruickshank, M. (1992). *The gay and lesbian liberation movement*. New York: Routledge, Chapman & Hall.

Dannemeyer, W. (1989). *Shadow in the land: Homosexuality in America*. San Francisco: Ignatius.

D'Antonio, M. (1989). *Fall from grace: The failed crusade of the Christian right*. New York: Farrar, Straus.

Davies, C. (1982). Sexual taboos and social boundaries. *American Journal of Sociology, 87* (5), 1032–1063.

Dawidoff, D. (1994). Kill a queer for Christ. In M. Thompson (Ed.), *Long road to freedom: The advocate history of the gay and lesbian movement* (pp. 145–146). New York: St. Martin's Press.

Debate between Nelson Parnell and Paul Summers. (1994, January 24). *Springfield Telecable*.

Dejowski, E. F. (1992). Public endorsement of restrictions on three aspects of free expression by homosexuals *Journal of Homosexuality, 23*, 1–18.

Delgado, R., & Stefancic, J. (1994). Imposition. *William and Mary Law Review, 35*, 1026.

Delson, S. (1986, September 5). Proposition Sixty-four. *Hayward Daily Review*.

D'Emilio, J. (1992). *Making trouble: Essays on gay history, politics, and the university*. New York: Routledge.

DeParle, J. (1996, July 14). A fundamental problem. *The New York Times Magazine*, pp. 18–25.

deParrie v. Keisling, 318 OR. 62, 862 P.2d 494 (1993).

Diamond, S. (1989). *Spiritual warfare: The politics of the Christian right*. Boston: South End Press.

Diamond, S. (1995). *Roads to dominion: Right-wing movements and political power in the United States*. New York: Guilford Press.

Dobson, J. C. (1994). Letter circulated by Idaho Family Forum.

Dobson, J., & Bauer, G. L. (1990). *Children at risk: The battle for the hearts and minds of our kids*. Dallas, TX: Word Publishers.

Dobson, J., & Hindson, E. (1988). *The seduction of power*. Old Tappan, NJ: Fleming H. Revell.

"Don't sign on" group changes name. (1994, August 3). *The Idaho Statesman*, p. C3.

Douglass, D. (1993). Public moral argument and the narrative paradigm: An analysis of the OCA's "no special rights" campaign. In R. E. McKerrow (Ed.), *Argument and the postmodern challenge* (pp. 405–411). Speech Communication Association.

D'Souza, D. (1984). *Falwell: Before the millennium*. Chicago: Regnery Gateway.

Eberly, D. (1992). Homophobia, censorship, and the arts. In W. J. Blumenfeld (Ed.), *Homophobia: How we all pay the price* (pp. 205–216). Boston: Beacon Press.

Eckart, K. (1993a, January 24). Anti-special rights leader distances plan from Oregon's. *The Idaho Statesman*, p. A1.

Eckart, K. (1993b, January 24). On an anti-special rights mission. *The Idaho Statesman*, p. A4.

Eckart, K. (1993c, January 30). Clergy: Gays will suffer. *The Idaho Statesman*, p. C1.

Eckart, K. (1993d, February 10). Gay rights group gets a leader. *The Idaho Statesman*, p. A1.

Eckart, K. (1993e, February 10). Gays, lesbians encounter discrimination—and it's legal. *The Idaho Statesman*, p. A8.

Eckart, K. (1993f, February 27). Group plans "pro-active" stance. *The Idaho Statesman*, p. C2.

Eckart, K. (1993g, February 27). ICA leader: Initiative would ban advocating homosexuality in school. *The Idaho Statesman*, p. A1.

Eckart, K. (1993h, March 7). Is it a national agenda? *The Idaho Statesman*, pp. A1, A10.

Eckart, K. (1993i, March 19). EchoHawk: Initiative flawed. *The Idaho Statesman*, p. A1.

Eckart, K. (1993j, April 9). Group takes lead to battle anti-gay initiative. *The Idaho Statesman*, p. C2.

Eckart, K. (1993k, April 9). New initiative bans same-sex marriages. *The Idaho Statesman*, p. D1.

Eckart, K. (1991, April 22). Commissioner Glenn backs anti-gay initiative. *The Idaho Statesman*, p. A1.

Eckart, K. (1993m, April 22). Walton cheers Glenn for backing initiative. *The Idaho Statesman*, p. A12.

Eckart, K. (1993n, April 23). Anti-gay initiative gets name. *The Idaho Statesman*, p. C1.

Eckart, K. (1993o, May 6). Poll: 40 percent don't know about initiative. *The Idaho Statesman*, p. A1.

Eckart, K. (1993p, May 16). Rallies launch ICA petition drive. *The Idaho Statesman*, p. A1.

Eckart, K. (1993q, May 16). Supporters, opponents of ICA turn out for rally. *The Idaho Statesman*, p. C1.

Eckart, K. (1993r, May 27). Foes begin drive against anti-gay initiative. *The Idaho Statesman*, p. A1.

Eckart, K. (1993s, May 27). Foes hold confidence that initiative will fail. *The Idaho Statesman*, p. A4.

Eckart, K. (1993t, July 6). ICA members have variety of goals. *The Idaho Statesman*, p. A6.

Eckart, K. (1993u, July 6). Initiative supporters fight "special rights." *The Idaho Statesman*, pp. A1, A6.

Eckart, K. (1993v, August 29). Rights group takes on ICA. *The Idaho Statesman*, pp. C1, C2.

Eckart, K. (1993w, September 12). ICA tops halfway mark in signature drive. *The Idaho Statesman*, pp. C1, C4.

Eckart, K. (1993x, November 3). ICA calls ruling "road bump"; foes see precedent. *The Idaho Statesman*, p. A11.

Eckart, K. (1993y, November 4). EchoHawk: Initiative denies rights. *The Idaho Statesman*, p. C1.

Eckart, K. (1993z, November 15). Anti-gay see windfall of support. *The Idaho Statesman*, pp. A1, A3.

Eckart, K. (1994a, January 21). Petition foe blasts Glenn for violent terminology. *The Idaho Statesman*, p. C1.

Eckart, K. (1994b, April 16). In Lewiston, they'd rather talk about fish than the ICA. *The Idaho Statesman*, pp. A1, A2.

Eckart, K. (1994c, May 10). ICA sees Idaho Falls as fertile ground. *The Idaho Statesman*, pp. A1, A5.

Eckart, K. (1994d, July 8). Idaho Catholic bishop says church will oppose anti-gay initiative. *The Idaho Statesman*, p. A1.

Eckart, K., & Arbanas, M. (1993, March 19). Echohawk's opinion puts initiative factions on guard. *The Idaho Statesman*, p. A4.

Edelman, L. (1994). *Homographesis: Essays in gay literary and cultural theory*. New York: Routledge.

Edelman, M. (1964). *The symbolic use of politics*. Urbana, IL: University of Illinois Press.

Editors. (1992, March 30). The other minority. *New Republic*, 7.

Editors. (1993). Introduction. *Radical America, 24* (4), 3.

Editors. (1994, November 14). Notebook. *New Republic*, 8.

Ehrensaft, D., & Milkman, R. (1979). Sexuality and the state: The Briggs initiative and beyond. *Socialist Review, 9* (3) 55–72.

Eisenberg, A. M., & Ilardo, J. A. (1980). *Argument*. Englewood Cliffs, NJ: Prentice Hall.

Etlinger, C. (1993, June 19). Republican hopeful supports initiative. *The Idaho Statesman*, p. C1.

Etlinger, C. (1994, January 28). Idahoans against anti-gay initiative but favor 1 percent revision, survey shows. *The Idaho Statesman*, pp. A1, A8.

Evans v. Romer, 854 P.2d 1270 (Colo. 1993).

Evans v. Romer, 882 P.2d 1335 (Colo. 1994).

Ex-Falwell ghostwriter to give free talk. (1994, October 6). *The Idaho Statesman*, p. B3.

Faber, J. M. (1996). *Government interference, taxpayer expense and constitutionality: The degaying of Idaho's anti-gay initiative*. Paper presented at the International Communication Association meeting, Chicago, Illinois.

Falwell, J. (1980). *Listen America!* New York: Bantam Books.

Fielding, I. (1993). Examining the military's anti-homosexual policy as value argument. In R. E. McKerrow (Ed.), *Argument and the postmodern challenge* (pp. 429–436). Speech Communication Association.

Fight the Right Project Staff. (1993). In S. C. Gregory & S. Nakagawa (Eds.), *Fight the right action kit* (pp. 69–112). Washington, DC: National Gay & Lesbian Task Force.

Fight the Right Project Staff. (1994). *The record on gay-related referenda questions*. Washington, DC: National Gay & Lesbian Task Force.

First National Bank of Boston v. Bellotti, 435 U.S. 765 (1978).

Fischli, R. D. (1981). Religious fundamentalism and the democratic process. In J. W. Chesebro (Ed.), *Gayspeak: Gay male & lesbian communication* (pp. 303–313). New York: Pilgrim Press.

Fisher, W. F. (1987). *Human communication as narration: Toward a philosophy of reason, value, and action*. Columbia, SC: University of South Carolina Press.

Fitzgerald, F. (1981, May 18). A disciplined, charging army. *New Yorker*, pp. 53–141.

Flagg, M. (1993, February 4). Arts groups oppose limits on rights protection. *The Idaho Statesman*, p. D1.

Flagg, M. (1994a, January 21). Julian Bond will speak tonight on need to work for civil rights. *The Idaho Statesman*, p. C2.

Flagg, M. (1994b, March 24). In Emmett, it's not a topic for the coffee shops yet. *The Idaho Statesman*, pp. A1, A4.

Flagg, M. (1994c, April 24). Boise lesbian couple casts aside privacy to battle the ICA. *The Idaho Statesman*, pp. A1, A2.

Flagg, M. (1994d, May 23). Initiative forces Idaho to ponder "gay agenda." *The Idaho Statesman*, p. A1.

Flagg, M. (1994e, June 8). Gays: Discrimination against homosexuals does exist in Idaho. *The Idaho Statesman*, pp. A1, A9.

Flagg, M. (1994f, June 10). Librarians set tab for ICA compliance. *The Idaho States-man*, p. C1.

Flagg, M. (1994g, June 10). One hundred protest gay parade permit. *The Idaho States-man*, p. C1.

Flagg, M. (1994h, June 12). Anti-gays express opinion at rally. *The Idaho Statesman*, p. A12.

Flagg, M. (1994i, June 12). 1,167 turn out for gay parade. *The Idaho Statesman*, p. A1.

Flagg, M. (1994j, June 14). Conservatives in Meridian jump on ICA bandwagon. *The Idaho Statesman*, pp. A1, A8.

Flagg, M. (1994k, June 29). ICA, term limits initiatives head for ballot. *The Idaho Statesman*, p. A1.

Flagg, M. (1994l, July 2). ICA's foes beat it to revealing anti-gay proposal makes ballot. *The Idaho Statesman*, p. C2.

Flagg, M. (1994m, July 7). Anti-gay initiative heads for ballot. *The Idaho Statesman*, p. C1.

Flagg, M. (1994n, July 19). Craig: Anti-gay initiative isn't needed in Idaho. *The Idaho Statesman*, p. A1.

Flagg, M. (1994o, July 30). ICA names new executive director. *The Idaho Statesman*, p. C2.

Flagg, M. (1994p, August 3). New ICA head did time for cocaine sales. *The Idaho Statesman*, p. A1.

Flagg, M. (1994q, September 8). Eight ministers denounce Proposition One. *The Idaho Statesman*, p. C1.

Flagg, M. (1994r, September 8). "I'm not the same person I was then." *The Idaho Statesman*, pp. A1, A12.

Flagg, M. (1994s, October 1). Fifty-six Idaho clergy back anti-gay initiative. *The Idaho Statesman*, p. B1.

Flagg, M. (1994t, October 1). Proposition One survey: 59 percent still undecided. *The Idaho Statesman*, p. B1.

Flagg, M. (1994u, October 12). Court rules against Colorado's anti-gay laws. *The Idaho Statesman*, p. A1.

Flagg, M. (1994v, October 15). Controversial researcher to speak in Boise. *The Idaho Statesman*, p. B1.

Flagg, M. (1994w, October 17). Affirmative action hard to come by. *The Idaho States-man*, pp. A1, A4.

Flagg, M. (1994x, October 20). Proposition One ads to hit the airwaves. *The Idaho Statesman*, p. B1.

Flagg, M. (1994y, November 6). Proposition One foes rally to get out the vote. *The Idaho Statesman*, p. B1.

Flagg, M. (1994z, November 8). Senior voters may have been misled on Proposition One, clerk says. *The Idaho Statesman*, p. B1.

Flagg, M. (1994aa, November 10). Anti-gay initiative narrowly fails: But both sides declare victory. *The Idaho Statesman*, pp. A1, A16.

Flagg, M. (1995, June 24). New anti-gay initiative introduced. *The Idaho Statesman*, p. 3A.

Foes outspend backers of measures. (1992, December 4). *The Oregonian*, p. F1.

For the record measure 9. (1992, November 1). *The Oregonian*, p. B5.

Foster, D. (1993, May 16). Anti-gay activist's strategy focuses on children. *The Idaho Statesman*, p. C6.

Fountaine, C. (1988). Lousy lawmaking: Questioning the desirability and constitutionality of legislating by initiative. *Southern California Law Review, 61*, 733–776.

Four hundred rally to defeat anti-gay initiative. (1994, September 9). *The Idaho Statesman*, p. C1.

Fowler, R. B., & Hertzke, A. D. (1995). *Religion and politics in America*. Boulder, CO: Westview Press.

Freeley, A. (1993). *Argumentation and debate*. Belmont, CA: Wadsworth.

Fuss, D. (1991). Inside/out. In D. Fuss (Ed.), *Inside/out: Lesbian theories, gay theories* (pp. 1–10). New York: Routledge.

Gallagher, D. (1994, September 11). Boycotts could follow passage of Proposition One. *The Idaho Statesman*, p. C14.

Gallagher, J. (1994a, July 12). Pride and prejudice. *Advocate*, pp. 38–39.

Gallagher, J. (1994b). The rise of fascism in America. In M. Thompson (Ed.), *Long road to freedom: The advocate history of the gay and lesbian movement* (p. 396). New York: St. Martin's Press.

Galvin, T. (1993, October 23). Local initiatives send signals on national trends. *CQ Weekly Report, 51*, pp. 2853–2932.

Garber, A. (1993, June 13). 550 rally for gay freedom. *The Idaho Statesman*, p. C1.

Gay freedom efforts compared to civil rights movement. (1994, January 21). *The Post Register*, p. B1.

Gay rights, special rights. (1993). [Videotape]. Jeremiah Films.

Gerassi, J. (1966). *The boys of Boise: Furor, vice and folly in an American city*. New York: Macmillan.

Getting God's kingdom into politics. (1980, September 19). *Christianity Today*, p. 10.

Gibson, J. L., & Tedin, K. L. (1988). The etiology of intolerance of homosexual politics. *Social Science Quarterly, 69*, 587–604.

Gillming, K. E. (1993, December 16). All have right to expression. *Springfield News-Leader*, p. A7.

Gitlin, T. (1980). *The whole world is watching: Mass media in the making and unmaking of the new left*. Berkeley: University of California Press.

Glazer, N. (1987). Fundamentalists: A defensive offensive. In R. J. Neuhaus & M. J. Cromartie (Eds.), *Piety and politics: Evangelicals and fundamentalists confront the world*. Washington, DC: Ethics and Public Policy Center.

Glenn issues apology for comments. (1994, January 22). *The Idaho Statesman*, p. C2.

Goggin, M. L. (1993). Introduction: A new framework for understanding the new politics of abortion. In M. L. Goggin (Ed.), *Understanding the new politics of abortion*. Newbury Park, CA: Sage.

Goldberg, S. (1993). Civil rights, special rights, and our rights. In S. C. Gregory & S. Nakagawa (Eds.), *Fight the right action kit* (pp. 63–65). Washington, DC: National Gay and Lesbian Task Force.

GOP bypasses anti-gay effort. (1993, April 25). *The Idaho Statesman*, p. C1.

Governor hopeful Eastland backs anti-gay initiative. (1994, February 12). *The Idaho Statesman*, p. C4.

Green, J. C. (1995a). The Christian right and the 1994 elections: An overview. In M. J. Rozell and C. Wilcox (Eds.), *God at the grassroots: The Christian right in the 1994 elections* (pp. 1–18). Lanham, MD: Rowan and Littlefield.

Green, J. C. (1995b, March). The Christian right and the 1994 elections: A view from the states. Political Science: *Political Science and Politics*, pp. 5–8.

Green, J. C., Guth, J. L., Kellstedt, L. A., & Smidt, C. E. (1995, July 5–12). Evangelical realignment: The political power of the Christian right. *Christian Century*, pp. 676–679.

Greenberg, D. F. (1988). *The construction of homosexuality*. Chicago: University of Chicago Press.

Greenhouse, L. (1995, February 21). High court to rule on Colorado law barring protection of homosexuals against bias. *New York Times*, p. A4.

Grey, T. (1986, November 1). AIDS proposition losing ground. *Sacramento Bee*.

Gross, L. (1991). Out of the mainstream: Sexual minorities and the media. *Journal of Homosexuality, 21* (1/2), 19–46.

Grossman, J. B., & Levin, D. (1995). Majority rule/minority rights. In S. Lipset (Ed.), *Encyclopedia of democracy*. Washington, D.C.: Congressional Quarterly Press.

Gusfield, J. R. (1963). *Symbolic crusade: Status politics and the American temperance movement*. Urbana, IL: University of Illinois Press.

Guth, J. L. (1983). The new Christian right. In R. C. Liebman & R. Wuthnow (Eds.), *The new Christian right: Mobilization and legitimation*. New York: Aldine.

Guth, J., Green, J., Kellstedt, L., & Smidt, C. (1993, February 17). God's own party: Evangelicals and republicans in the 1992 election. *Christian Century*, pp. 172–176.

Habermas. J. (1981). *The theory of communicative action: Reason and the rationalization of society* (T. McCarthy, Trans.). Boston: Beacon Press.

Hadden, J. K., & Shupe, A. (1988). *Televangelism: Power and politics on God's frontier*. New York: Henry Holt.

Haeberle, E. J. (1989). Swastika, pink triangle, and yellow star: The destruction of sexology and the persecution of homosexuals in Nazi Germany. In M. B. Duberman, M. Vicinus, & G. Chauncey (Eds.), *Hidden from history: Reclaiming the gay and lesbian past* (pp. 365–378). New York: New American Library.

Haider-Markel, D. P., & Meier, K. J. (1996, May). The politics of gay and lesbian rights: Expanding the scope of the conflict. *Journal of Politics, 58*, p. 332–349.

Hall, S. (1993). Deviance, politics, and the media. In H. Abelove, M. A. Barale, & D. M. Halperin (Eds.), *The lesbian and gay studies reader* (pp. 62–90). New York: Routledge.

Halley, J. E. (1991). Misreading sodomy: A critique of the classification of "homosexuals" in federal equal protection law. In J. Epstein (Ed.), *Body guards: The cultural politics of gender ambiguity* (pp. 351–377). New York: Routledge.

Halperin, D. M. (1990). *One hundred years of homosexuality: And other essays on Greek love*. New York: Routledge.

Hardisty, J. (1993, March). Constructing homophobia: Colorado's right-wing attack on homosexuals. *The Public Eye*, 1–10.

Hastings, D. (1986, October 15). Polls: Most still undecided on Proposition Sixty-four. *Los Angeles Herald Examiner*.

Hate crime ordinance clears council on 7–2 vote. (1993, October 5). *Springfield News-Leader*, p. A1.

Hawley, J. S., & Proudfoot, W. (1994). Introduction. In J. S. Hawley (Ed.), *Fundamentalism and gender* (pp. 3–44). New York: Oxford University Press.

Heinz, D. (1983). The struggle to define America. In R. C. Leibman & R. Wuthnow (Eds.), *The new Christian right: Mobilization and legitimation* (pp. 133–148). New York: Aldine.

Herman, D. (1994). *Rights of passage: Struggle for lesbian and gay legal equality*. Toronto: University of Toronto Press.

Hertzke, A. (1993). *Echoes of discontent: Jesse Jackson, Pat Robertson, and the resurgence of populism*. Washington, DC: Congressional Quarterly Press.

Hibbard, S. G. (1994). *The right response: A survey of voters attitudes about gay-related questions*. Washington, DC: National Gay & Lesbian Task Force.

High court accepts anti-gay initiative titles. (1993, August 4). *The Idaho Statesman*, p. C3.

Hill, D. B. (1981). Letter opinion on ERA: A test of the newspaper bias hypothesis. *Public Opinion Quarterly, 45*, 384–392.

Hills, S. S., & Owen, D. E. (1982). *The new religious political right in America*. Nashville, TN: Abingdon Press.

Himmelstein, J. L. (1983). The new right. In R. C. Leibman & R. Wuthnow (Eds.), *The new Christian right: Mobilization and legitimation* (pp. 13–30). New York: Aldine.

Himmelstein, J. L. (1990). *To the right: The transformation of American conservatism*. Berkeley, CA: University of California Press.

Holsti, O. (1969). *Content analysis for the social sciences and humanities*. Reading, MA: Addison-Wesley.

Homosexual teachers the issue in Proposition Six. (1978, October 15). *San Jose Mercury News*.

Homosexuality in the schools. (1994). Salem, OR: Yes on 13 Committee.

Homosexuality, the classroom and your children. (1992). [Broadsheet]. Salem, OR: The Oregon Citizens Alliance.

Hunter, J. D. (1983a). *American evangelicalism: Conservative religion and the quandry of modernity*. New Brunswick, NJ: Rutgers University Press.

Hunter, J. D. (1983b). The liberal reaction. In R. C. Liebman & R. Wuthnow (Eds.), *The new Christian right: Mobilization and legitimation* (pp. 149–163). New York: Aldine.

Hunter, J. D. (1987). *Evangelicalism: The coming generation*. Chicago: University of Chicago Press.

Hunter, J. D. (1991). *Culture wars: The struggle to define America*. New York: Basic Books.

Hunter, J. D. (1994). *Before the shooting begins: Searching for democracy in America's culture war*. New York: Free Press.

Hunter, N. D., Michaelson, S. E., & Stoddard, T. B. (1992). *The rights of lesbians and gay men*. Carbondale, IL: Southern Illinois University Press.

Hynds, E. C. (1992). Editorial page editors discuss use of letters. *Newspaper Research Journal, 13* (1 & 2), 124–136.

ICA endorses thirty-six GOP candidates. (1994, May 2). *The Idaho Statesman*, p. C1.

ICA initiative draws fire. (1994, July 6). *Idaho Press-Tribune*, p. 4A.

ICA leadership manual. (n.d.). Boise, ID: Idaho Citizens Alliance.

ICA's anti-gay initiative brings tourism worries. (1993, May 8). *The Idaho Statesman*, p. C5.

Idaho Citizens Alliance Statement of Principles, Revision 3 (1993, February 3).

Idaho Code, Title 18, §6605.

Idaho Public Policy Survey. (1995, May). Survey Research Center, Boise State University.

Idaho resorts worry about anti-gay proposals. (1993, January 13). *The Idaho Statesman*, p. C3

Impact statement number 1: The OCA's ballot measure 9. (1992). Portland, OR: No On 9 Committee.

Initiative foes say it's a waste of money. (1993, November 5). *Lewiston Morning Tribune*, p. 4C.

Jacobs, J. (1978, October 3). Briggs' wild rumors. *San Francisco Examiner*.

Jacoby, W. (1994). Public attitudes toward government spending. *American Journal of Political Science, 38*, 336–493.

Jamieson, K. H. (1992). *Dirty politics: Deception, distortion, and democracy*. New York: Oxford University Press.

Jelen, T. G. (1991). *The political mobilization of religious belief*. Westport, CT: Praeger.

Jorstad, E. (1970). *The politics of doomsday: Fundamentalists of the far right*. Nashville, TN: Abingdon Press.

Jorstad, E. (1981). *The politics of moralism*. Minneapolis, MN: Augsburg.

Judis, J. B. (1994, September 12). Crosses to bear. *New Republic*, 21–25.

Kahane, H. (1992). *Logic and contempory rhetoric* (6th ed.). Belmont, CA: Wadsworth.

Kane, R. (1993). Soundbites: Articulate responses to homophobic lies and rhetoric. In S. C. Gregory & S. Nakagawa (Eds.), *Fight the right action kit* (pp. 75–76). Washington, DC: National Gay & Lesbian Task Force.

Karp, J. (November 1994). *Political awareness, elite leadership and mass opinion in initiative campaigns*. Paper presented at the Pacific Northwest Political Science Association meeting, Portland, OR.

Kazin, M. (1995). *The populist persuasion*. New York: Basic Books.

Kehler, D., & Stern, R. M. (1994). Initiatives in the 1980s and 1990s. *The book of the states 1994–95*. Lexington, KY: The Council of State Governments.

Kellstedt, L. A., & Green, J. C. (1993). Knowing God's many people: Denominational preference and political behavior. In D. C. Leege & L. A. Kellstedt (Eds.), *Rediscovering the religious factor in American politics*. Armonk, NY: M. E. Sharpe.

Kellstedt, L. A., Green, J. C., Guth, J. L., & Smidt, C. E. (1994). Religious voting blocs in the 1992 election: The year of the evangelical? *Sociology of Religion, 55*, 307–326.

Kelly Walton dares ACLU to sue over initiative's constitutionality. (1994, July 6). *The Idaho Statesman*, p. C2.

Key, V. O. (1961). *Public opinion and American democracy*. New York: Alfred A. Knopf.

Kilpatrick, J. J. (1996, July 26). Overturning Colorado law on homosexuality was court's "worst" of '96. *The Oregonian*, p. C11.

Kirk, M., & Madsen, H. (1989). *After the ball: How America will conquer its fear and hatred of gays in the 90s*. New York: Doubleday.

Kivisto, P. (1995). The rise or fall of the Christian right? Conflicting reports from the frontline. In S. Bruce, P. Kivisto, & W. H. Swatos (Eds.), *The rapture of politics*. New Brunswick, NJ: Transaction.

Klatch, R. (1987). *Women of the new right*. Philadelphia: Temple University Press.

KOZK. (1993, November 11). Debate on bias crime ordinance.

KOZK. (1994, January 31). Debate on bias crime ordinance.

KSMU. (1994, February 7). Debate on bias crime ordinance.

Ladd, E. C. (1995, Spring). The 1994 congressional elections: The post industrial realignment continues. *Political Science Quarterly*, 1–23.

LaHaye, T. (1978). *The unhappy gays: What everyone should know about homosexuality*. Wheaton, IL: Tyndale.

LaHaye, T. (1982). *The battle for the family*. Old Tappan, NJ: Fleming H. Revell.

Lake, R. A. (1984). Order and disorder in anti-abortion rhetoric: A logological view. *Quarterly Journal of Speech, 70*, 425–433.

Lake Research Inc. (1995). Nationwide poll, May.

LaMay, C. (1993, April 10). Initiative doesn't please critics. *The Idaho Statesman*, p. 6A.

Lambkin, D. P., & Morneau, R. H. (1988). How police are viewed in editorials and letters to the editor: An analysis of themes. *Journal of Police Science and Administration, 16* (3), 195–197.

Larocco: Anti-gay initiative would burden Idaho with expense, divisiveness. (1993, December 7). *The Idaho Statesman*, p. C2.

Lawson, K. A. (1992a, October 5). A republican God. *Christianity Today*.

Lawson, K. A. (1992b, July 20). The new face(s) of the religious right. *Christianity Today*.

Legge, J. (1983). The determinants of attitudes toward abortion in the American electorate. *Western Political Quarterly, 36*, 479–490.

Le Guin, U. K. (1989). Some thoughts on narrative. In *Dancing at the edge of the world* (pp. 37–45). New York: Harper and Row.

Lesher, D. (1994, April 24). Dannemeyer sees senate bid as spiritual quest. *Los Angeles Times* (Orange Co. Edition), pp. A1, A36–A37.

Lewis-Beck, M. S. (1980). *Applied regression: An introduction*. Newbury Park, CA: Sage.

Licata, S. J. (1981). The homosexual rights movement in the United States: A traditionally overlooked area of American history. In S. J. Licata & R. P. Peterson (Eds.), *Historical perspectives on homosexuality* (pp. 161–189). New York: Haworth Press.

Liebman, R. C. (1983a). The making of the new Christian right. In R. C. Liebman & R. Wuthnow (Eds.), *The new Christian right: Mobilization and legitimation* (pp. 229–238). New York: Aldine.

Liebman, R. C. (1983b). Mobilizing the moral majority. In R. C. Liebman & R. Wuthnow (Eds.), *The new Christian right: Mobilization and legitimation* (pp. 49–73). New York: Aldine.

Liechtiling, G., Mazzochi, J., & Gardiner, S. (1993). *The covert crusade: The Christian right and politics in the West*. Portland, OR: Western States Center.

Lienesch, M. (1982). Right-wing religion: Christian conservation as a political movement. *Political Science Quarterly, 97*, 403–425.

Lienesch, M. (1993). *Redeeming America: Piety and politics in the new Christian right*. Chapel Hill, NC: University of North Carolina Press.

Linde, H. A. (1993). When initiative lawmaking is not "republican" government: The campaign against homosexuality. *Oregon Law Review 72*, 19–45.

Lipset, S. M. (1963). *Political man* (Chapter 4). Two Harbors, MI: Anchor Books.

Lipset, S., & Raab, E. (1970). *The politics of unreason*. New York: Harper and Row.

Lowery, D., & Sigelman, L. (1981). Understanding the tax revolt: Eight explanations. *American Political Science Review, 75*, 963–974.

Lowi, T. J., & Ginsberg, B. (1996). *American government: Freedom and power*. New York: W. W. Norton.

Lunch, W. M. (1995). Oregon: Identity and politics in the northwest. In M. J. Rozell & C. Wilcox (Eds.), *God at the grassroots: The Christian right in the 1994 elections*. Lanham, MD: Rowan and Littlefield.

Lupia, A. (1994). Shortcuts versus encyclopedias: Information and voting behavior in California insurance reform elections. *American Political Science Review, 88*, 63–76.

Mabon v. Keisling, 856 P.2d 1023 at 1026 (1993).

Maddox, G. (1989). Constitution. In T. Ball, J. Farr, & R. L. Hanson (Eds.), *Political innovation and conceptual change* (pp. 51, 59). Cambridge, Eng.: Cambridge University Press.

Madison, James. (1949). The Federalist no. 10. In H. S. Commager (Ed.), *Selections from the Federalist Hamilton, Madison, Jay*. Arlington Heights, IL: Harlon Davidson.

Magleby, D. B. (1984). *Direct legislation: Voting on ballot propositions in the United States*. Baltimore: Johns Hopkins University Press.

Magleby, D. B. (1995). Let the voters decide? An assessment of the initiative and the referendum process. *University of Colorado Law Review, 66* 13–46.

Mansbridge, J. J. (1986). *Why we lost the ERA*. Chicago: University of Chicago Press.

Marcossan, S. (1995). The "special rights" canard in the debate over lesbian and gay civil rights. *Notre Dame Journal of Law, Ethics and Public Policy, 9*, pp. 137–183.

Marcus, E. (1992). *Making history: The struggle for gay and lesbian equal rights, 1945–1990*. New York: HarperCollins.

Marsden, G. M. (1980). *Fundamentalism and American culture*. New York: Oxford University Press.

Marty, M. E. (1970). *Righteous empire: The Protestant experience in America*. New York: Dial Press.

Marty, M. E. (1984). Fundamentalism as a social phenomenon. In G. Marsden (Ed.), *Evangelicalism and modern America* (pp. 56–68). Grand Rapids, MI: Eerdmans.

Marty, M. E., & Appleby, S. (1993). Introduction: A sacred cosmos, scandalous code, defiant society. In M. E. Marty & S. Appleby (Eds.), *Fundamentalisms and society: Reclaiming the sciences, the family, and education* (pp. 1–19). Chicago: University of Chicago Press.

Mason, T. L. (1994). *Governing Oregon*. Dubuque, IA: Kendall/Hunt.

Massachusetts General Laws Annotated, Chapter 151B, §4 (Supp. 1993).

Mathews, D. G., & DeHart, J. S. (1990). *Sex, gender, and the politics of ERA: A state and the nation*. New York: Oxford University Press.

Mayer, A. J. (1980, September 15). A tide of born-again politics. *Newsweek*, 28–36.

Mayer, W. G. (1992). *The changing American mind*. Ann Arbor, MI: University of Michigan Press.

Mayhead, M. (1993). It will happen: Causal argumentation in Oregon's ballot measure 9 controversy. In R. E. McKerrow (Ed.), *Argument and the postmodern challenge* (pp. 419–422). Speech Communication Association.

McCloskey, H. (1964). Consensus and ideology in American politics. *American Political Science Review, 58,* 361–382.

McCloskey, H., & Brill, A. (1983). *Dimensions of tolerance*. New York: Russell Sage.

McCorkle, S., & Mills, J. (1992). Rowboat in a hurricane: Metaphors of interpersonal conflict management. *Communication Reports, 5* (2), 57–66.

McGrath, T. (1994, February 6). Gay rights, special rights. *Springfield News-Leader,* p. A3.

Measure 9 reveals deep splits among Oregon voters. (1992, November 5). *The Oregonian,* p. A1.

Medhurst, M. J. (1982). The first amendment versus human rights: A case study in community sentiment and argument from definition. *Western Journal of Speech Communication, 46,* 1–19.

Media explodes in anti-OCA hysteria. (1991, June/July). *The Oregon Alliance,* pp. 1, 3.

Meehan, B. T. (1992, November 29). Oregon's initiative system under fire. *The Oregonian,* p. D1.

Meyer v. Grant, 486 U.S. 414, 108 S. Ct. 1886 (1988).

Mieli, M. (1980). *Homosexuality and liberation* (D. Fernback, Trans.). London: Gay Men's Press.

Milbraith, L., & Goal, M. L. (1977). *Political participation* (2nd ed.). Chicago: Rand McNally.

Miller, D. (n.d.). Group plans drive to restrict gay rights. *The Idaho Statesman,* p. B1.

Miller, D. (1993, October 2). Anti-gay group pushes "war of values." *The Idaho Statesman,* p. A1.

Miller, M. J. (1994, November). *The religious right and the gay community: What fundamentalism says to non-traditionalism*. Paper presented at the meeting of the Speech Communication Association, New Orleans, LA.

Minnesota Statutes §363.01 (Supp. 1993).

Moen, M. C. (1989). *The Christian right and Congress*. Tuscaloosa, AL: University of Alabama Press.

Moen, M. C. (1992a). The Christian right in the United States. In M. C. Moen & L. S. Gustafson (Eds.), *The religious challenge to the state* (pp. 75–101). Philadelphia: Temple University Press.

Moen, M. (1992b). *The transformation of the Christian right*. Tuscaloosa, AL: University of Alabama Press.

Moen, M. C., & Gustafson, L. S. (Eds.). (1992). *The religious challenge to the state*. Philadelphia: Temple University Press.

Mohr, R. D. (1988). *Gays/justice: A study of ethics, society, and the law*. New York: Columbia University Press.

Mohr, R. D. (1994, March 11). Special rights, equal rights, gay rights. *News-Telegraph,* p. 13.

Molotoch, H. (1979). Media and movements. In M. N. Zald, & J. D. McCarthy (Eds.), *The dynamics of social movements: Resource mobilization, social control, and tactics* (pp. 71–93). Cambridge, MA: Winthrop Publishers.

Moon, J. D. (1993). *Constructing community: Moral pluralism and tragic conflicts*. Princeton, NJ: Princeton University Press.

Morello, J. T. (1991). "Who won?": A critical examination of newspaper editorials evaluating nationally televised presidential debates. *Argumentation and Advocacy, 27* (3), 114–125.

Nava, M., & Dawidoff, R. (1994). *Why gay rights matter to America*. New York: St. Martin's Press.

Netzhammer, E. C. (1994, November). *Radical rhetoric and the construction of homosexuality: The gay agenda and gay rights, special rights*. Paper presented at the meeting of the Speech Communication Association, New Orleans, LA.

Neuhaus, R. J. (1984). *The naked public square: Religion and democracy in America*. Grand Rapids, MI: Eerdnans.

Neuhaus, R. J., & Cromartie, M. J., (Eds.). (1987). *Piety and politics: Evangelicals and fundamentalists confront the world*. Washington, DC: Ethics and Public Policy Center.

No on One. (1994). [Television advertisement].

No special rights. (1992). [video tape]. Salem, OR: No Special Rights Committee.

Norton, R. (1992). *Mother Clap's molly house: The gay subculture in England, 1700–1830*. London: Gay Men's Press.

Norusis, M. (1993). *SPSS for Windows: Base system users' guide (Release 6.0)*. Chicago: SPSS, Inc.

Note. (1993). Constitutional limits on anti-gay rights initiatives. *Harvard Law Review, 106*, 1905–1925.

Oberschall, A. (1993). *Social movements: Ideologies, interests, and identities*. New Brunswick, NJ: Transaction.

OCA banking on its grass-roots network. (1992, October 9). *The Oregonian*, p. D4.

OCA family business listing. (1992, June/July). *The Oregon Alliance*, p. 5.

Ogintz, E. (1980, January 13). Evangelicals seek political clout. *Chicago Tribune*, p. 5.

Oldfield, A. (1990). *Citizenship and community: Civic republicanism and the modern world*. London: Routledge.

Olson, K. M., & Goodnight, G. T. (1994). Entanglements of consumption, cruelty, privacy, and fashion: The social controversy over fur. *Quarterly Journal of Speech, 80*, 249–276.

Opponents fire accusations in Proposition One debate. (1994, October 2). *The Idaho Statesman*, p. B3.

Our view: A few New Year's Day resolutions. (1994, January 1). *The Idaho Statesman*, p. A11.

Our view: Future of Idaho demands a no vote on Proposition One. (1994, July 9). *The Idaho Statesman*, p. A11.

Page, B., & Shapiro, R. (1992). *The rational public*. Chicago: University of Chicago Press.

Palmer, S. A. (1993). Abnormal, wrong, unnatural, and perverse: A critical study of the Oregon Citizens Alliance targeted tabloids. In R. E. McKerrow (Ed.), *Argument and the postmodern challenge* (pp. 412–418). Speech Communication Association.

Parks, J. C. (1981). Referendum campaigns versus gay rights. In J. W. Chesebro (Ed.), *Gayspeak: Gay male & lesbian communication* (pp. 286–290). New York: Pilgrim Press.

Paull, B. (1993, January 28). Churches: Don't limit rights. *The Idaho Statesman*, p. C1.

Paulson, J. (1993, December 16). Canby city council sadly accepts recall. *The Oregonian*, p. E4.

Pearce, W. B., Littlejohn, S. W., & Alexander, A. (1987). The new Christian right and the humanist response: A reciprocated diatribe. *Communication Quarterly*, *35*, 171–192.

People for the American Way. (1994). *The religious right—then and now.* [Videotape].

People of Faith Against Bigotry. (1992). *Why we oppose ballot measure 9: A Christian perspective.* Portland, OR: People of Faith Against Bigotry.

Persinos, J. F. (1994, September). Has the Christian right taken over the Republican party? *Campaigns and Elections*, pp. 21–24.

Peters, B. (1994, October 20). Initiative isn't unconstitutional. *The Idaho Statesman*.

Peterson, A. (1993, June 14). Candlelight vigil stresses equality. *The Idaho Statesman*, p. C1.

Plant, R. (1986). *The pink triangle: The Nazi war against homosexuals.* New York: Holt.

Plessy v. Ferguson, 163 U.S. 537 (1896).

Poll showing growing shift in opinion against Proposition Six (1978, October 5). *Oakland Tribune*.

Poll shows anti-gay initiative gaining over opponents. (1993, June 27). *The Idaho Statesman*, p. C2.

Poll shows two initiative face close votes. (1994, March 13). *The Idaho Statesman*, p. C7.

Popkey, D. (1993a, January 14). Gay law may hit tourism. *The Idaho Statesman*, p. C5.

Popkey, D. (1993b, January 14). Idaho group pushes for anti-gay law. *The Idaho Statesman*, pp. C1, C5.

Popkey, D. (1993c, May 15). GOP leader: ICA initiative not needed. *The Idaho Statesman*, p. C1.

Popkey, D. (1993d, July 22). National GOP chair: Idaho's anti-gay plan unnecessary. *The Idaho Statesman*, p. C3.

Pratte, T. (1993). A comparative study of attitudes toward homosexuality: 1986 and 1991. *Journal of Homosexuality*, *26*, 77–93.

Price, C. M. (1988, November). Initiative campaigns: Afloat on a sea of cash. *California Journal*, 481–486.

Prichard, R. (1994a, April 28). Larry Eastland: I'm no Democrat lite. *The Idaho Statesman*, p. A1.

Prichard, R. (1994b, June 22). Crapo won't back anti-gay initiative. *The Idaho Statesman*, p. C1.

Prichard, R. (1994c, July 7). No 1 percent initiative on November ballot, but the ICA will be. *The Idaho Statesman*, p. A1.

Pritchard, D., & and Berkowitz, D. (1991). How readers' letters may influence editors and news emphasis: A content analysis of ten newspapers, 1948–1978. *Journalism Quarterly*, *68* (3), 388–395.

Pronk, P. (1993). *Against nature?: Types of moral argumentation regarding homosexuality.* Grand Rapids, MI: Eerdmans.

Pursley, S. (1995, January 23). With the lesbian avengers in Idaho. *The Nation, 260*, 94.

Ramirez, P. (1978, October 12). Scuffling marks Proposition Six debate. *San Francisco Examiner*.

Redwing, D. (1994, December 5). Interviewed by R. Smith.

Reed, R. (1993, Summer). Casting a wider net: Religious conservatives move beyond abortion and homosexuality. *Policy Review*, pp. 31–35.

Reed, R. (1994a). *Politically incorrect: The emerging faith factors in American politics*. Dallas, TX: Word Publishing.

Reed, R. (1994b). What do religious conservatives really want? In Michael J. Cromartie, (Ed.), *Disciples and democracy*. Washington, DC: Ethics and Public Policy Center.

Reed, R. (1996). *Active faith: How Christians are changing the soul of American politics*. New York: Simon and Schuster.

Regents of the University of California v. Bakke, 438 U.S. 265 (1979).

Reichley, A. J. (1987). The evangelical and fundamentalist revolt. In R. J. Neuhaus & M. Cromartie (Eds.), *Piety and politics: Evangelicals and fundamentalists confront the world* (pp. 69–95). Lanham, MD: University Press of America.

Reichley, J. (1985). *Religion in American public life*. Washington, DC: Brookings Institution.

Ribuffo, L. P. (1985). *The old Christian right: The Protestant far right from the great depression to the cold war*. Philadelphia: Temple University Press.

Richards, A. (1986, September 2). Forces line up against Proposition Sixty-Four. *Riverside Press Enterprise*.

Richert, K. (1994, January 20). Gay rights debate heats up at ISU forum. *The Post Register*, p. A1.

Riffe, D., Aust, C. F., & Lacy, S. R. (1993). The effectiveness of random, consecutive day and constructed week sampling in newspaper content analysis. *Journalism Quarterly*, *70* (1), 133–139.

Riggle, E. D., & Ellis, A. L. (1994). Political tolerance of homosexuals: The role of group attitudes and legal principles. *Journal of Homosexuality*, *26*, 135–147.

Roberts, B. (1994a, July 2). Pending vote on anti-gay initiative divides Christians. *The Idaho Statesman*, p. D1.

Roberts, B. (1994b, November 3). Presbyterians vote "no on one." *The Idaho Statesman*, p. B3.

Romer v. Evans, __U.S. __, 116 S.Ct. 1620 (1996).

Roof, W. C., & McKinney, W. (1987). *American mainline religion its changing shape and future*. New Brunswick, NJ: Rutgers University Press.

Rottman, L. (1991, August). The battle of *The normal heart*. *Academe*, 30–35.

Rozell, M. J., & Wilcox, C. (Eds.). (1995). *God at the grassroots: The Christian right in the 1994 elections* (pp. 253–264). Lanham, MD: Rowan and Littlefield.

Rubenstein S. (1992, December 18). Poll finds opposition to anti-gay move. *The Oregonian*, p. E1.

Rubenstein, S. (1993a, September 22). Anti-gay-rights measures win handily. *The Oregonian*, p. C1.

Rubenstein, S. (1993b, December 2). OCA launches effort to pass new initiative. *The Oregonian*, p. D1.

Rubenstein, S. (1993c, December 11). The issue that just won't go away in Canby. *The Oregonian*, p. D2.

Rubin, G. S. (1993). Thinking sex: Notes for a radical theory of the politics of sexuality. In H. Abelove, M. A. Barale, & D. M. Halperin (Eds.), *The lesbian and gay studies reader.* (pp. 3–44). New York: Routledge.

Rueda, E. (1982). *The homosexual network: Private lives and public policy.* Old Greenwich, CT: Devin Adair.

Ruse, M. (1988). *Homosexuality: A philosophical inquiry.* London: Blackwell.

Russo, V. (1987). *The celluloid closet: Homosexuality in the movies* (Rev. ed.). New York: Harper and Row.

Sandel, M. (1984). Introduction. *Liberalism and its critics.* New York: New York University Press.

Sanger, K. L. (1994, November). *The religious right and the illusion of moderation: "Gay rights, special rights: Inside the homosexual agenda."* Paper presented at the meeting of the Speech Communication Association, New Orleans, LA.

Sarasohn, D. (1994, December 4). *The Oregonian*, p. E2.

Schacter, J. S. (1994). The gay civil rights debate in the states. *Harvard Civil Rights-Civil Liberties Law Review, 29*, 283–317.

Schacter, J. S. (1995, October). The pursuit of popular intent. *Yale Law Journal, 105*, 107–176.

Schaeffer, F. A. (1982). *A Christian manifesto.* Westchester, MA: Crossways Books.

Schneider, W., & Lewis, I. A. (1984). The straight story on homosexuality and gay rights. *Public Opinion, 7*, 16–20, 59–60.

Sears, D. (1993). Symbolic politics: A socio-psychological theory. In S. Iyengar & W. J. McGuire (Eds.), *Explorations in political psychology.* Durham, NC: Duke University Press.

Sears, D., & Funk, C. (1990). Self-interest in American's political opinions. In J. Mansbridge (Ed.), *Beyond self-interest.* Chicago: University of Chicago Press.

Sears, D., Lau, R., Tyler, T. R., & Allen, H. (1980). Self-interest versus symbolic politics in policy attitudes and presidential voting. *American Political Science Review, 74*, 139–151.

Sears, D. C., Hensler, C., & Speer, L. (1979). Whites opposition to "busing": Self-interest or symbolic politics? *American Political Science Review, 73*, 369–384.

Secretary of State refuses ICA's voter pamphlet rebuttal statement. (1994, August 12). *The Idaho Statesman*, p. C3.

Shilts, R. (1982). *The mayor of Castro Street: The life and times of Harvey Milk.* New York: St. Martin's Press.

Shilts, R. (1986, June 25). AIDS initiative to qualify. *San Francisco Chronicle.*

Sides urge calm, warn of health threat. (1994, October 17). *The Idaho Statesman*, p. B1.

Siegel, P. (1991). Lesbian and gay rights as a free speech issue: A review of relevant caselaw. *Journal of Homosexuality, 21* (1–2), 203–259.

Sigelman, L., & Walkosz, B. J. (1992). Letters to the editor as a public opinion thermometer: The Martin Luther King holiday vote in Arizona. *Social Science Quarterly, 73* (4), 938–946.

Simpson: Leave gay rights issue alone in legislature. (1993, December 18). *The Idaho Statesman*, p. C2.

Sixty-six evangelical ministers declare support for the ICA. (1994, August 27). *The Idaho Statesman*, p. A1.

Slagle, R. A. (1995). In defense of queer nation: From identity politics to politics of difference. *Western Journal of Communication, 59* (2), 85–102.

Smidt, C. E. (Ed.). (1988). *Contemporary evangelical political involvement.* Lanham, MD: University Press of America.

Sniderman, P., Brody, R., & Tetlock, P. (1991). *Reasoning and choice.* Cambridge, Eng.: Cambridge University Press.

Sonner, S. (1994, November 3). Civil rights leaders decry three anti-gay initiatives. *The Idaho Statesman,* p. A9.

Springer, L. J. (1994, December 29). Oregon has had enough chances to vote in anti-homosexual measures [Letter to the editor]. *The Oregonian,* p. C8.

Springfield Area Chamber of Commerce. (1994). *Pockets facts.* Springfield, MO: Springfield Area Chamber of Commerce.

Steinfels, P. (1989, June 12). Moral majority to dissolve; says mission accomplished. *New York Times,* p. A12.

Stouffer, S. (1955). *Communism, conformity and civil liberties.* Gloucester, MA: Peter Smith.

Students cheer at Andrus' initiative stance. (1993, May 6). *The Idaho Statesman,* p. C3.

Students pass measure 9, elect Perot. (1992, October 30). *The Oregonian,* p. C1.

Sullivan, J. J., Pierson, J., & Marcus, G. E. (1979). An alternative conceptualization of political tolerance: Illusory increases 1950s–1970s. *American Political Science Review, 73,* 781–810.

Summers, P. (1993, November 29). Homosexuals not productive to society. *Springfield News-Leader,* p. A7.

Summers, P. (1994, February). Springfield's bias crime ordinance: Con. *Bear Review,* pp. 1, 7.

Suo, S. (1994, December 16). *The Oregonian,* p. A1.

Supporters fight back. (1994, January 28). *Springfield News-Leader,* p. A1.

Survey: Nine of 105 lawmakers support anti-gay initiative. (1993, December 22). *The Idaho Statesman,* p. C2.

Tarbox, J. J. (1995, November). *Ballot initiatives and the communication perspective.* Paper presented at the Speech Communication Association Annual Meeting, San Antonio, TX.

Taylor, B. C. (1994, November). *The gay agenda: Notes toward a critique of homophobic realism.* Paper presented at the meeting of the Speech Communication Association, New Orleans, LA.

Tedin, K. (1994). Self-interest, symbolic values, and the financial equalization of the public schools. *Journal of Politics, 56,* 628–649.

Testimony to City Council. (1993, September 20). Springfield, MO.

The text. (1993, December 2). *The Oregonian,* p. D8.

Thiemann, R. F. (1996). *Religion in public life: A dilemma for democracy.* Washington, DC: Georgetown University Press.

Thompson, G. (1993, October 17). Hate-filled liberals try to quash democracy. *Springfield News-Leader,* p. B7.

Thompson, M. (1993, January 29). Military chiefs clash with Clinton over gays. *The Idaho Statesman,* p. A3.

Thorne, J. (1994). A pro/con look at Proposition One, in focus on the family. *Idaho citizen special voter guide edition, 4,* no. 10, p. 6.

Threlkeld, M. (1993a, May 15). Library board against the anti-gay initiative. *The Idaho Statesman*, p. C3.

Threlkeld, M. (1993b, September 26). Seminar: Oppose initiative cordially. *The Idaho Statesman*, p. C1.

Tims, D. (1994, October 9). Battle over gay-rights issue rages in Lake County. *The Oregonian*, p. BO4.

Toulmin, S., Rieke, R., & Janik, A. (1984). *An introduction to reasoning*. New York: Macmillan.

Travel group opposes Proposition One. (1994, September 28). *The Idaho Statesman*, p. B5.

Trillhaase, M. (1995, July 22). Lance urges ICA to delay pushing anti-gay proposal. *The Idaho Statesman*, p. B1.

U of I protects gay rights. (1993, May 2). *The Idaho Statesman*, p. C1.

Vanderford, M. L. (1989). Vilification and social movements: A case study of pro-life and pro-choice rhetoric. *Quarterly Journal of Speech, 75*, 166–182.

Van Valkenburgh, J. (1994, October 20). Distinguish fact from fiction. *The Idaho Statesman*.

Vecsey, G. (1980, January 21). Militant television preachers try to weld fundamentalist Christians' political power. *New York Times*, p. A21.

Von Drehle, D., & Edsall, T. B. (1994, August 29–September 4). The religious right returns. *Washington Post National Weekly Edition*, pp. 8–9.

Vote yes on measure 9! (1992). [Pamphlet]. Salem, OR: No Special Rights Committee.

Voters' choice loud, clear. (1994, February 9). *Springfield News-Leader*, p. A1.

Wald, K. D. (1992). *Religion and politics in the United States* (2nd ed.). Washington, DC: Congressional Quarterly Press.

Waldman, A. (1995, December). Why we need a religious left. *Washington Monthly*, pp. 37–43.

Walton, K. (1994, October 23). Proposition One obituary is extremely premature. *The Times News*, p. A9.

Walton shrugs off taxpayers' costs (1993, September 17). *The Idaho Statesman*, p. C2.

Watney, S. (1991). School's out. In D. Fuss (Ed.), *Inside/out: Lesbian theories, gay theories* (pp. 387–401). New York: Routledge.

Weiss, H. J. (1992). Public issues and argumentation structures: An approach to the study of the contents of media agenda-setting. In S. A. Deetz (Ed.), *Communication yearbook 15* (pp. 374–396). Newbury Park, CA: Sage.

Weisskopf, M. (1993, February 1). Energized by pulpit or passion, the public is calling. *Washington Post*, p. A1.

Wells, M. W. (1978). *Anti-Mormonism in Idaho, 1872–92*. Provo, UT: Brigham Young University Press.

Weston, K. (1991). *Families we choose: Lesbians, gays, kinship*. New York: Columbia University Press.

What the "family and child protection act" says. (1995, June 24). *The Idaho Statesman*, p. A10.

White, M. (1994). *Stranger at the gate: To be gay and Christian in America*. New York: Simon and Schuster.

Who's who in the OCA. (1993, June 20). *Sunday Oregonian*.

Why we oppose ballot measure 9: A Christian perspective. (1992). [Pamphlet]. Salem, OR: People of Faith Against Bigotry.

Wickline, M. R. (1994, January 14). Attorney general hopeful slams anti-gay initiative. *Lewiston Morning Tribune.*

Wilcox, C. (1992). *God's warriors: The Christian Right in twentieth-century America.* Baltimore: Johns Hopkins University Press.

Wilcox, C. (1995). Premillennialists at the millennium: Some reflections on the Christian right in the twenty-first century. In S. Bruce (Ed.), *The rapture of politics.* New Brunswick, NJ: Transaction Publishers.

Wilcox, C. (1996). *Onward Christian soldiers?: The religious right in American politics.* Boulder, CO: Westview Press.

Wills, G. (1990). *Under God: Religion and American politics.* New York: Simon and Schuster.

Witt, S. L., & Moncrief, G. (1993). Religion and roll call voting on abortion. In M. L. Goggin (Ed.), *Understanding the new politics of abortion* (pp. 123–133). Newbury Park, CA: Sage.

Wolfinger, R., & Greenstein, F. (1968). The repeal of fair housing in California. *American Political Science Review, 62,* 753–769.

Wonn, S. J. (1996, March 14–16). *We're here, we're queer, so what? Generation X and its attitudes on gay rights issues.* Paper presented at the Western Political Science Association meeting. San Francisco, CA.

Woolsey, D. (1993a, April 4). Teachers to oppose anti-gay initiative. *The Idaho Statesman,* p. A1.

Woolsey, D. (1993b, April 6). Video heats up anti-gay battle. *The Idaho Statesman,* p. C1.

Woolsey, D. (1993c, June 27). Poll shows anti-gay initiative gaining over opponents. *The Idaho Statesman,* p. 2C.

Woolsey, D. (1993d, June 27). Rights agency votes against anti-gay plan. *The Idaho Statesman,* p. A1.

Wuthnow, R. (1983). The political rebirth of American evangelicals. In R. C. Liebman & R. Wuthnow (Eds.), *The new Christian right: Mobilization and legitimation* (pp. 167–185). New York: Aldine.

Wuthnow, R. (1993). *Christianity in the twenty-first century.* New York: Oxford University Press.

Wuthnow, R. (1994). *Producing the sacred: An essay on public religion.* Chicago: University of Illinois Press.

Zaller, J. (1990). Political awareness, elite opinion leadership and the mass survey response. *Social Cognition 8,* 125–53.

Zaller, J. (1992). *The nature and origins of mass opinion.* Cambridge, Eng.: Cambridge University Press.

Zwier, R. (1982). *Born-again politics: The new Christian right in America.* Downers Grove, IL: Inter-Varsity Press.

Index

Abington v. Schempp, 10
Abortion, attitudes about, 119, 121, 132; the Christian Right and, 10, 11, 14, 15; as example of scope of conflict, 5, 6
ACLU, 38, 47–48, 57, 61, 135, 139
ACLU v. EchoHawk, 37, 40, 41
Ada County Human Rights Task Force, 83
Adams, William, 37
Advocate, 58
AIDS, 22, 25, 35, 44, 47, 102, 110; as subject of initiatives, 115, 123 n.7, 124 nn.9, 10, 142
AFL-CIO, 18, 55
Andrus, Cecil, 52, 54, 60
Anti-Gay ballot initiative results: in California, 115, 117; in Colorado, 112, 129–31, 134, 160; in Idaho (1994), 4, 63, 73, 122, 129–31, 160; in Maine, 129–31, 160; in Missouri, 96; in Oregon (1992), 19; in Oregon (1994), 20, 129–31, 160; in Oregon (1996), 21; in Oregon, City/County Ordinances, 19, 20
Anti-Gay ballot initiative spending: in California, 116; in Idaho, 55, 80, 84, 88, 90, 92; in Oregon, 19

Anti-Gay ballot initiative support/opposition demographics, 19, 73, 78, 82, 127
Anti-Gay ballot initiatives in Arizona, 37, 49 n.1, 123 n.1, 136, 142
Anti-Gay ballot initiatives in California (1978), 44, 142; in California (1988) Proposition 102, 117–21; in California (1978) Proposition Six, 110, 114–15; in California (1986) Proposition Sixty-four, 114, 115–21
Anti-Gay ballot initiatives in Colorado, 1, 3, 36, 37, 108, 117–21, 127, 133–39, 142; text of, 196
Anti-Gay ballot initiatives in Florida, 37, 123 n.1, 136
Anti-Gay ballot initiatives in Idaho, 3; in Idaho (1996), 39–40; Proposition One (1994), 1, 33–35, 36–49, 51–94, 108, 114, 116, 136, 142; text of (1994), 166–67
Anti-Gay ballot initiatives in Maine, 1, 3, 37, 49 n.2, 123 n.1; text of, 167
Anti-Gay ballot initiatives in Michigan, 123 n.1, 136
Anti-Gay ballot initiatives in Missouri, 1, 37, 123 n.1

Anti-Gay ballot initiatives in Nevada, 37, 49 n.1, 136, 142
Anti-Gay ballot initiatives in Ohio, 1, 123 n.1
Anti-Gay ballot initiatives in Oregon, 3, 17, 31, 125 n.25, 136, 142; Measure 9 (1992), 18, 24, 25, 36, 44, 49 n.1, 52, 65, 108, 116, 127, 142; Measure 13 (1994), 30, 37, 108, 127, 142; text of Measure, 9, 165; text of Measure 13, 165
Anti-Gay ballot initiatives in Washington, 37, 49 n.1, 108, 123 n.1, 136, 142
Anti-Gay ballot referenda/ordinances, 6 n.4, 96; in Colorado, 37, 134, 136; defined, 3, 6 n.1; in Idaho, 38; in Maine, 108; in Missouri, 3, 95–105; in Oregon, 37, 125 n.25; in Springfield, Missouri, 96
Antonio, Gene, 104

Ballot initiative, defined, 2, 3
Ballot initiative, funding, 4
Ballot initiative, paid signature gatherers, 3, 6, 117
Ballot initiative, process, 1–6, 32, 53, 144–45
Ballot initiative, signature requirements, 3, 144
Ballot initiative, tax policy, 108
Baptists, 7. *See also* Southern Baptists
Barbour, Haley, 56
Batt, Phil, 116
Bauer, Gary, 13, 14, 139
Bayless, Jeffrey, 135
Behavioral vs. genetic cause (of homosexuality), 27, 29, 58, 67, 69, 78, 98
Berain, Jesse, 86
Bergquist, Brian, 52, 57, 58, 60, 61, 81–90
Bias Crime Ordinance. *See* Anti-Gay ballot referenda/ordinances
Birch, Elizabeth, 134, 139
Black, Edwin, 65
Blackfoot, Idaho, 85
Bock, Les, 83
Boise, Idaho, 54, 55, 68, 78, 82, 85, 86

Boise City Arts Commission, 52
Bond, Julian, 42
Booth, Michael, 133
Bork, Robert, 39, 48
Bowers v. Hardwick, 138
Boycott, 51, 60, 85
Bradley, Tom, 115
Breyer, Stephen, 139
Briggs, John, 114
Brown, Fred, 135
Brown, Jerry, 114
Brown, Willie, 115
Bryant, Anita, 99, 102
Buchanan, Pat, 128
Buckley, William F., 19
Bundy, Edgar C., 9
Burgenar, Clair, 115
Burley, Idaho, 85
Bush voters, 125 n.23

Caldwell, Idaho, 86
California, Project 10, 25, 28, 32
Cameron, Paul, 60, 96
Catholics, 59, 128
Cenarusa, Pete, 60
Chase, Dallas, 54
Chenoweth, Helen, 55, 79
Christian Coalition, 116
Christians. *See* Catholics; Church of Jesus Christ of Latter Day Saints; Episcopalians; Evangelical Protestants; Fundamentalists; Nazarenes; Presbyterians; Southern Baptists
Church of Jesus Christ of Latter Day Saints, 60, 92, 123, 128, 129, 131, 132 n.8
Cicero, 34
Citizens Against Rent Control v. Berkeley, 4
Citizens for Decent Standards, 96
Civil rights, 16, 61, 105; of gays, 33–35
Clinton, Bill, 12
Cold War, 9
Cole, Matthew, 139
Colorado, 51, 61, 85, 122; *See also* Anti-Gay ballot initiatives in Colorado
Colorado for Family Values, 133, 135

Colorado Legal Initiatives Project, 133, 135
Colorado Supreme Court, 61
Constitution, Liberal v. Communitarian theory, 34
Contract with America, 13
Contract with the American Family, 13
Couer D'Alene, Idaho, 82, 85
Craig, Larry, 59
Cranston, Alan, 115
Crapo, Michael, 35–36, 116
Curb, Mike, 114

Dannemeyer, William, 22, 115, 117, 120
Delgado, Richard, 43
Democratic party platform, 128
Deukmejian, George, 115
Dinkins, David, 19
Direct democracy, 107
Dobson, James, 13, 14, 34, 45, 48, 100
Don't Sign On PAC, 54, 55, 59, 60, 79
Doolitle, John, 116

Eastland, Larry, 57, 79, 116, 124 n.10
EchoHawk, Larry, 38, 53, 55, 56, 116
Education: associations, 18, 52, 53, 78, 83; as campaign issue, 28–30, 53, 58, 90
Engle v. Vitale, 10
Episcopalians, 52, 56, 128
Equal Rights Amendment, 10, 82, 100, 110
Equality Colorado, 135
Evangelical Protestants, 35, 105, 116, 119, 120; as political force, 7–16, 95; and voting on initiatives, 128, 129, 130, 131 n.3
Evans v. Romer, 39, 135
Evans, Jerry, 86

Fallacy, defined, 67
Falwell, Jerry, 7, 8, 10, 12, 14, 60
Family Research Council, 139
Federal Lesbian & Gay Civil Rights Bill, 32
Feinstien, Diane, 115
First National Bank of Boston v. Bellotti, 4

Focus on the Family, 34, 96, 100
Freedom parade, 46, 55, 58
Fundamentalists, 35

Gay Agenda (video), 53, 64, 92, 131
Gay agenda issue, 57
Gay and Lesbian Alliance Against Defamation, 135
Gay Rights, Special Rights (video), 65, 87
Gays in the Military, 65, 67, 71, 74, 128
Gibson, James, 35
Ginzburg, Ruth Bader, 139
Glazer, Nathan, 11
Glenn, Gary, 53, 57
Godmakers (video), 92
Goldwater, Barry, 59
Greenhouse, Linda, 135
Ground Zero, 136

Hardisty, J., 95
Hargis, Billy James, 9
Harlan, John Marshall, 136
Hawkins, Stan, 56
Heinz, Donald, 14
Hibbits, Tom, 19
Himmelstein, Jerome, 9
Homosexuality, causes, 27
Human Rights Campaign, 134, 139
Hunter, James Davison, 15, 98

Idaho Citizen's Alliance, 6, 35, 36, 38, 39, 42, 44, 45, 46, 48, 52, 53, 57, 58, 59, 61, 116, 131; strategies of in campaign, 77–81, 90–93;
Idaho Commission on the Arts, 52
Idaho Falls, Idaho, 85
Idaho Family Forum, 45, 48, 57
Idaho GOP, 53, 116
Idaho Human Rights Commission, 55
Idaho Library Association, 45
Idaho Republican Party, 53, 116
Idaho Supreme Court, 55, 59
Idaho Women's Network, 83
Idaho for Human Dignity, 52, 54, 60
Indirect democracy, defined, 2
Internal Revenue Service, 10, 14

Jackson, Jessie, 19, 61
Jarvis, Howard, 114
Jelen, Ted, 15
Jews, 128

Kempthorne, Dirk, 116
Kennedy, Anthony, 137, 139
Kilpatrick, James J., 139
King, Coretta Scott, 61
King, Martin Luther, Jr., 42

Lambda Legal Defense and Education
    Fund, 135
Lance, Al, 39
Larouche, Lyndon, 115, 120, 124 n.9
Latter Day Saints. *See* Church of Jesus
    Christ of Latter Day Saints
LeGuin, Ursula, 29
Lewiston, Idaho, 85
Libraries, censorship in, 20, 33, 34, 37,
    38, 39, 43–45; Idaho Association of,
    58–59; Idaho State Board of, 54; ma-
    terial addressing homosexuality in,
    40, 111, 146
Lupia, A., 113

Mabon, Lon, 19, 22, 27, 51, 54, 81,
    139
Mabon v. Keisling, 40
Madison, James, 5
Mansfield, Dennis, 61
Marcossan, Samuel, 42
McIntire, Carl, 9
McIver, John, 117
Medford, Oregon, 19
Medical groups, 18–19
Meese, Edwin, 48
Meridian, Idaho, 56, 58
Methodists, 52
Meyer v. Grant, 3
Minority rights, 41–42, 107–25
Moral Majority, 8
Mormons. *See* Church of Jesus Christ
    of Latter Day Saints
Moscow, Idaho, 85

Nampa, Idaho, 54
Narrative Paradigm, 23–32, 99

National Gay Rights March, 53, 58
Nazarenes, 128
No-On-Nine, 65
No-On-One Coalition, 59, 60, 73, 74,
    81–90
No Special Rights (video), 22, 27–28

O'Connor, Sandra Day, 139
Official English Ballot Initiative, 119,
    120–21
Oregon Citizen's Alliance, 17–32, 36,
    51, 63, 65, 81, 116, 139
Oregon State Legislature, 20
Oregon Supreme Court, 25
Oregon YES Campaign, 65
Otter, Butch, 85

Peters, Barry, 46
Plessy v. Ferguson, 137
Pluralism, 103, 106 n.11
Pocatello, Idaho, 82, 85
Political elites, 43, 109, 113
Political symbols, defined, 112
Portland, Oregon, 20
Presbyterians, 52, 59, 128
Proctor, Bill, 59, 79
Progressive Reform Era, 2 3
Public opinion polls: in California, 4,
    114, 117–21, 123 n.2; in Colorado,
    117–21, 136; in Idaho, 43, 55, 57, 60,
    61, 73, 85, 86, 91; Idaho Public Pol-
    icy Survey, 73; National, 35, 45, 109,
    111, 146, 157, 158

Quinn, John, 114

Rational World Paradigm, 21–23, 64
Reagan, Ronald, 114
Reed, Ralph, 10, 12, 13, 14, 15
Referendum, defined, 6 n.1
Regents of the U. of California v. Bakke,
    49 n.3
Rehnquist, William, 139
Religious groups, attitudes towards ho-
    mosexuals, 128–31; 133, 134; in
    Idaho, 52, 53, 58, 59, 82, 83, 88, 92;
    in Missouri, 96; in Oregon, 18, 31
Republican Party Platform, 128

Rhetorical perspective, 64
Robison, James, 10
Roe v. Wade, 5, 10
Rohlfing, Mary, 60, 61
Romer, Roy, 134
Romer v. Evans, 5, 133–39, 139 nn.1, 2

Same-sex marriages, 58, 127, 139; in
   anti-gay ballot initiatives, 36, 37, 38,
   40, 53, 124 n.13
Scalia, Antonin, 138, 139
Schacter, Jane, 41
Secular argument, defined, 95
Self interest, 112
Sheldon, Lou, 13, 96, 99
Slack, John, 59, 88
Smith, Greg, 85
Smith, Randy, 54
Sodomy laws, 46–47, 58
Souter, David, 139
Southern Baptists, 128
Special rights v. civil rights issue, 52,
   54, 55, 61, 69, 70, 72, 78, 99
Springfield, Missouri, City Council, 96;
   debates in, 99, 101, 102, 104; Human
   Rights Commission, 96; referendum,
   96
Springfield, Oregon, 19
Standing opinions, defined, 110
Stefancic, Jean, 43
Steven, John Paul, 139

Stoicheff, Jim, 57
Stop Special Rights PAC, 52
Sun Valley, Idaho, 51, 60, 83
Sunday, Billy, 9

Tarbox, J., 65
Tax-exempt status, 10
Tedin, Kent, 35
Thomas, Clarence, 139
Tourism, 54, 60
Traditional Values Coalition, 97
Twin Falls, Idaho, 85, 87

Ucon, Idaho, 56
University of Idaho, 54
U.S. Citizen's Alliance, 52, 92

Van Valkenburgh, Jack, 47–48
Voices for Human Dignity, 53, 81

Wald, Kenneth, 8
Walton, Kelley, 6, 38, 39, 42, 46, 48,
   52, 53, 54, 59, 61, 116; interview
   with, 77–81, 90–93
White, Mel, 60
Wills, Gary, 8

Younger, Evelle, 114

Zaller, John, 121, 123 n.6
Zschau, Ed, 115

About the Editors and Contributors

LESLIE R. ALM is an Associate Professor of Political Science and Public Affairs at Boise State University.

SHAUN BOWLER is an Associate Professor of Political Science at the University of California, Riverside.

LAURA K. LEE DELLINGER is Director of Communications for the Metropolitan Group, a full-service public relations agency in Portland, Oregon.

TODD DONOVAN is an Associate Professor of Political Science at Western Washington University.

DAVID DOUGLASS is a Professor of Communication at Willamette University.

DANIEL LEVIN is an Assistant Professor of Political Science at Boise State University.

SUZANNE McCORKLE is Professor of Communication and Associate Dean for the College of Social Science and Public Affairs at Boise State University.

MARSHALL G. MOST is an Assistant Professor and Director of Forensics at Boise State University.

SEAN PATRICK O'ROURKE is an Assistant Professor of Communication and Theater at Vanderbilt University.

HARVEY PITMAN is an Associate Professor Emeritus of Communication at Boise State University.

STEVEN SHAW is a Professor and Chair of Political Science at Northwest Nazarene College.

RALPH R. SMITH is a Professor of Communication at Southwest Missouri State University.

STEPHANIE L. WITT is an Associate Professor and Chair of the Political Science Department at Boise State University.

ISBN 0-275-95461-7

90000>

EAN

9 780275 954611

HARDCOVER BAR CODE